CAMBRIDGE LIBRARY COLLECTION

Books of enduring scholarly value

Religion

For centuries, scripture and theology were the focus of prodigious amounts of scholarship and publishing, dominated in the English-speaking world by the work of Protestant Christians. Enlightenment philosophy and science, anthropology, ethnology and the colonial experience all brought new perspectives, lively debates and heated controversies to the study of religion and its role in the world, many of which continue to this day. This series explores the editing and interpretation of religious texts, the history of religious ideas and institutions, and not least the encounter between religion and science.

The Mythological Acts of the Apostles

The twin sisters Agnes Lewis (1843–1926) and Margaret Gibson (1843–1920) were pioneering biblical scholars who became experts in a number of ancient languages. Travelling widely in the Middle East, they made several significant discoveries, including one of the earliest manuscripts of the four gospels in Syriac, a dialect of Aramaic, the language probably spoken by Jesus himself. Originally published in the Horae Semitica series, this fascicule contains an English translation of the apocryphal acts of the apostles. Originally published in 1904 by Agnes Lewis, the text chronicles the lives, adventures and deaths of important figures like Paul, Thaddeus and James, the brother of Jesus. This fascinating volume features extraordinary tales of peril and persecution – one town's sinful population places a naked prostitute at the town gate to deter the apostles, but the archangel Michael levitates her out of their way – and is of great historical and theological interest.

T0371450

Cambridge University Press has long been a pioneer in the reissuing of out-of-print titles from its own backlist, producing digital reprints of books that are still sought after by scholars and students but could not be reprinted economically using traditional technology. The Cambridge Library Collection extends this activity to a wider range of books which are still of importance to researchers and professionals, either for the source material they contain, or as landmarks in the history of their academic discipline.

Drawing from the world-renowned collections in the Cambridge University Library, and guided by the advice of experts in each subject area, Cambridge University Press is using state-of-the-art scanning machines in its own Printing House to capture the content of each book selected for inclusion. The files are processed to give a consistently clear, crisp image, and the books finished to the high quality standard for which the Press is recognised around the world. The latest print-on-demand technology ensures that the books will remain available indefinitely, and that orders for single or multiple copies can quickly be supplied.

The Cambridge Library Collection will bring back to life books of enduring scholarly value (including out-of-copyright works originally issued by other publishers) across a wide range of disciplines in the humanities and social sciences and in science and technology.

The Mythological Acts of the Apostles

*Translated From an Arabic MS
in the Convent of Deyr-Es-Suriani, Egypt,
and from MSS in the Convent of St Catherine
on Mount Sinai and in the Vatican Library*

AGNES SMITH LEWIS

CAMBRIDGE UNIVERSITY PRESS

Cambridge, New York, Melbourne, Madrid, Cape Town,
Singapore, São Paolo, Delhi, Tokyo, Mexico City

Published in the United States of America by Cambridge University Press, New York

www.cambridge.org
Information on this title: www.cambridge.org/9781108018999

© in this compilation Cambridge University Press 2011

This edition first published 1904
This digitally printed version 2011

ISBN 978-1-108-01899-9 Paperback

THE MYTHOLOGICAL ACTS
OF THE APOSTLES

HORAE SEMITICAE No. IV

THE MYTHOLOGICAL ACTS
OF THE APOSTLES

TRANSLATED FROM AN ARABIC MS. IN THE CONVENT OF
DEYR-ES-SURIANI, EGYPT, AND FROM MSS. IN THE CONVENT
OF ST CATHERINE ON MOUNT SINAI AND IN THE VATICAN LIBRARY

WITH A TRANSLATION OF THE PALIMPSEST FRAGMENTS
OF THE ACTS OF JUDAS THOMAS FROM COD. SIN. SYR. 30

BY

AGNES SMITH LEWIS, M.R.A.S.

HON. D.D. (HEIDELBERG); LL.D. (ST ANDREWS);
PH.D. (HALLE-WITTENBERG)

LONDON
C. J. CLAY AND SONS
CAMBRIDGE UNIVERSITY PRESS WAREHOUSE
AVE MARIA LANE

1904

𝖈𝖆𝖒𝖇𝖗𝖎𝖉𝖌𝖊:
PRINTED BY J. AND C. F. CLAY,
AT THE UNIVERSITY PRESS.

CONTENTS.

CONTENTS.

ERRATUM.

Page 181, margin, *for* Ex. xvi. 23 *read* Ex. xvi. 33

INTRODUCTION.

THE manuscript from which I have taken most of these stories was found by Mrs Gibson and myself in the Coptic Convent of Deyr-es-Suriani, or St Mary Deipara, in the Wady Natrôn, Egypt, the monastery from which, fifty years ago, a great treasure of Syriac MSS. was conveyed to the British Museum by Messrs Tattam and Pacho. We photographed it almost completely during our first visit to the Convent in 1901, but as some of our films came to grief in the process of development, we returned in the spring of 1902, and by accepting the kind hospitality of the Egyptian Salt and Natron Company at Bîr Hooker, we were enabled once more to pitch our tent outside the gate of the Convent, and by making use of a dark room kindly lent to us by the monks, to change our film-cells several times, and fill up most of the gaps of our series in the space of a single day.

From Egypt, in 1902, we proceeded for the fifth time to Mount Sinai, and there, in the Convent of St Catherine, I copied, and we together photographed, four of the stories in Cod. Sin. Arab. 539, from which Mrs Gibson had already drawn some of the texts edited by her in Studia Sinaitica, No. V.

When these photographs had been developed by us in Cambridge, I was disappointed to find that there were still several pages more which I had not secured. Four of these, ff. 41^b, 43^b, 49^b and 103^b, and some few lines elsewhere, I filled up very easily from two MSS. in the Bibliothèque Nationale, Paris, Fonds Arabe 75 and 81. But I found, to my great chagrin, that owing to a mistake I had totally neglected to take the last seven extant pages of the Deyr-es-Suriani MS. Without their text my list of apocryphal stories would have been incomplete ; and I therefore applied to the distinguished Arabist, Professor Ignazio Guidi of Rome, to ascertain for me if an Arabic text of the Martyrdom of St James the Just exists in the Vatican Library. He replied by sending me a copy of the legend from the Roman Codex 694, and at the same time he offered to furnish me with the Martyrdom of St Paul, from the same MS. These will be found on pp. ١٢٢—١٢٥ and ١٨٤—١٨٩ of No. III.

I then thought of searching in several parcels of unused photographs, taken by my sister Mrs Gibson during our second visit to Sinai in 1893, and laid aside because she deemed their texts, or rather the photographs of them, imperfect. A little re-arrangement, in one case with the help of Tischendorf's Greek text, in another through a careful study of the little strips of neighbouring pages which so often intrude into the results of amateur photography—an eye-sore to the professional, but a joy to the puzzled editor—I found myself in possession of the Martyrdoms of SS. Peter and Paul from Cod. Sin. Arab. 405; and of a story which Mrs Gibson had already entitled a خبر of the same Apostles, without indicating from which manuscript she had taken it. The fact of there being only twelve lines in each page negatives the idea that it belongs to Codd. Sin. Arab. 405, 475, or 553, and in these, moreover, Mrs Gibson has called the story either a قصة or a سيرة, I presume from their respective titles. The only other books mentioned in her "Catalogue of the Arabic MSS. in the Convent of St Catherine[1]," which contain a خبر of Peter and Paul are those numbered 441 and O respectively. O is described on pp. 130, 131 at the end of the book, and is apparently a manuscript which had lost its label before the catalogue was made. We shall run but a slight risk of mistake if we attribute the tale on pp. ١٥٠—١١٤ to that source. Two of its pages are unfortunately missing; and the efforts which I have made to obtain these from the Sinai Convent have been unsuccessful.

Description of the several Manuscripts.

I. The Deyr-es-Suriani MS. is a paper one, imperfect at the end. It has therefore no visible date; but the script has been pronounced by Professors Guidi, E. G. Browne, and Seybold to be undoubtedly of the 14th century, and therefore within a hundred years of the period when the Coptic legends of the Apostles were translated into Arabic. The facsimiles given in No. III. will enable my readers to perceive the resemblance between its script and that of the Vatican Codex 694. Its likeness to that of the Paris Codex 75 is equally strong.

It contains 148 leaves, divided into 14 quires of 10 leaves each, with the exception of the first quire, which has only 8 leaves, and is of a much later period as regards both paper and script. Another restoration has been made in the middle of the volume which embraces ff. 59—68, and therefore

---

[1] Studia Sinaitica, No. III.

the greater part of the story of St John. The leaves measure $23\frac{1}{2}$ by 16 centimetres, and contain each about 17 lines. Their edges have been carefully mended with strips of paper pasted over the margins. These prevented us from ascertaining whether there are any quire-marks; and they also occasionally hide half a line of the text. In such cases the lacunae have been supplied from the Paris MSS. 75 and 81. On f. 1^b there is a table of contents written in a sprawling hand of a much later period. Ff. 2^a—19^b contain a legend of St Peter so nearly similar to the one already published by Mrs Gibson in Studia Sinaitica, No. V. that I have not thought proper to include it in my volume. F. 148^b, where the Martyrdom of St James ends, contains also the beginning of the story of St Mark. I have followed the sequence, taking that story from the Sinai Codex 539.

The legends of James, son of Alphæus, and of Simon have also been published by Mrs Gibson in Studia Sinaitica, No. V. from Cod. Sin. Arab. 539. But as I was unwilling to make my own series imperfect through their omission, I have given a collation of Mrs Gibson's text along with that of the Suriani MS. I have done the same with a text of the story of Thaddeus, which I found in both MSS. All we know about the history of this manuscript is contained in the colophon at the foot of f. 44^b. This tells us that it was written in Deyr-es-Suriani in the Monastery of Our Lady.

The rubrics which occur in the unpublished part are:

f. 2 a

بعون الهه ابتدى اكتب سير الحواريون الاطهار

ونداهم وشهادتهم ندا القديس بطرس راس

التلاميذ صلاته تكون معنا امين

f. 13 a

❖ هذه شهادة بطرس السليح رييس ❖

❖ تلاميذ سيدنا يسوع المسيح بمدينة ❖

❖ رومية كان تمامها فى خمسة ايام من ❖

❖ ابيب صلاته تكون معنا امين ❖

f. 143 b

شهادة يعقوب الصديق اخى الرب التلميذ المبارك

الذى تمها فى ثمانية عشر يوما من ابيب بسلام الرب امين

f. 147 a

شهادة مرقس الانجيلى بالاسكندرية فى

ثلثين سنة لالام الرب المخلص بسلام الرب امين

II.   Cod. Sin. Arab. 539, from which I have taken the stories of Saint
Mark and Saint Luke, with a version of the legend of Saint John, similar
to that published in Syriac by Dr Wright[1], has been already described by
Mrs Gibson in her "Catalogue of the Arabic MSS. in the Convent of
St Catherine." It is a paper manuscript of the sixteenth century, containing
277 leaves, each having 17 lines and measuring 20 centimetres by 13.
Many of its pages bear Syriac numerals; and I observe that these differ
from those which we have given them by one figure only.   Mrs Gibson has
quite recently ascertained the date of the manuscript to be A.D. 1579.   The
writing is cramped and difficult to read.

III.   Cod. Vat. Arab. 694, from which Dr Guidi has supplied me with
the Martyrdoms of St James the Just and of St Paul, is a paper manuscript
of the fourteenth century, containing 161 leaves.   It measures 16 centimetres
by 12, each page having 15 lines of writing.   The original numeration of
the leaves is in Coptic-Arabic cyphers.   The script of ff. 1—30, which
include the Martyrdom of Paul, is larger than that of the rest of the
manuscript.   A description of it will be found in Mai, *Script. Vet. Nova
Collectio*, Vol. IV. p. 598.

IV.   Cod. Sin. Arab. 405, from which I have taken the Martyrdom
of St Paul and St Peter, has also been described in Mrs Gibson's catalogue.
It is an undated paper MS. probably of a late period, containing 236 leaves,
each measuring 33 centimetres by 21, with 21 lines to the page.   The
script is very clear, but as the texts which I have given from it were found
by me amongst my sister's photographs only after our last visit to Sinai,
I am unable to give any further details about the manuscript.

V.   The same may be said of the Sinai manuscript marked O, from
which I have taken the ‚   It is paper, is imperfect at the beginning,
and contains 224 leaves.   From the script, if Mrs Gibson's photographs
indeed belong to O, we judge that it belongs to some period between the
twelfth and the fifteenth century.

VI.   Cod. Paris. Fonds Arabe 81 is a paper MS. of 241 leaves,
measuring 22 cm. by 15.   It has 11, 12 or 13 lines on each page.   Its
script, which is that of the sixteenth century, is punctuated by red stops.
I have used it to make good the loss of my Suriani photographs, ff. 41^b,
43^b, 49^b.

VII.   Cod. Paris. Fonds Arabe 75, from which I have filled in the
lacuna of f. 103^b, is a paper MS. of 125 leaves, measuring each 22 cm.
by 15.   It has 15 lines on the page.   It is assigned to the fourteenth

---

[1] *Apocryphal Acts of the Apostles*, pp. 4—72.

century, and its script bears a strong resemblance to that of the Suriani MS.

VIII. Cod. Sin. Syr. 30, from which I have copied thirty-seven pages of the Acts of Judas Thomas in Syriac, is too well known to need any further description than that which I have already published[1]. I need only recapitulate. John the Stylite of Beth Mari Qanôn, [in] Ma'arrath Meṣrîn the city Kûrab [or Kaukab] of Antioch, in the year A.D. 778, turned a fourth century Syriac manuscript of the Four Gospels into a palimpsest by writing above its sacred text a collection of biographies of Holy Women. As the Gospel manuscript did not suffice for his purpose, he made use of portions torn from other MSS. one of these being the Acts of Judas Thomas. which furnished him with twenty leaves—forty pages. Eight of these pages, viz. ff. 146ᵃ, 146ᵇ, 159ᵃ, 166ᵇ, 167ᵃ, 168ᵇ, 169ᵃ, 170ᵃ, have been already partly deciphered from my photographs by Mr Burkitt, and published in Studia Sinaitica, No. IX. The text of these will be found almost complete in my Appendix. Three pages only, out of the forty extant, have wholly baffled my efforts. It must be well understood that wherever Mr Burkitt says (Studia Sinaitica, No. IX. pp. 35—39): S illegible, he is referring only to my photographs, and not to the manuscript.

The interest of these fragments lies, as Mr Burkitt has already pointed out, in the fact that they furnish us with a text at least four hundred years earlier than any hitherto known : and I trust that by placing the variants in Dr Wright's text, which is from a MS. of the tenth century, on the same page as the Sinai one, I shall enable scholars to see at a glance on what principles the process of amplification and of would-be improvement proceeded.

As a just tribute to the memory of a great scholar and an esteemed friend, I have indicated by a star those words in which the ancient text agrees with a conjecture of Dr Wright's, whilst he was editing the later one. These have come to light without the slightest design on my part, for I made no use of his marginal notes while I was copying from the palimpsest.

It is worth noticing that the reading ܪ̈ܚܡܝܢ in f. 164 a, col. a, l. 12 was originally in Dr Wright's MS.; and so were ܐܝܠܝܢ l. 3 ; ܐܡܝܪ in f. 157 a, col. b, l. 6 ; ܘܡܣܬܠܐ in f. 141 b, col. a, l. 14 ; and ܡܬܚܫܒ in f. 169 a, col. b, l. 1.

---

[1] See *The Four Gospels in Syriac*, transcribed from the Sinaitic Palimpsest. By Robert L. Bensly, J. Rendel Harris and F. Crawford Burkitt. Introduction, p. xvi.

Value of the Apocryphal Acts of the Apostles.

The Apocryphal Acts of the Apostles in their original Greek form have been edited and examined by many competent scholars, such as Lipsius, Thilo, Tischendorf, Zahn, etc., in their Syriac version by Dr William Wright, and in their Ethiopic version by Malan and Budge, but in Coptic and Arabic we have had until now only a few fragments due to the zeal and diligence of Zoëga, Mingarelli, Guidi, von Lemm, and Carl Schmidt. The subject is a fascinating one, where the legends do not attempt to cover the same ground as that already occupied by the canonical narrative of St Luke; partly because we are not without the hope that some grains of historical fact may be detected amongst a mass of fanciful adventures; and partly because we have here specimens of the kind of history that might have appeared in the New Testament, if that priceless little library of books had come to us from a purely human source.

The great labour of investigation being thus for the most part spared to me, I cannot do better than prefix to my own remarks a few quotations from the writings of some of the great scholars whom I have already named.

Dr Guidi says: "Probably in the fifth or sixth century some Greek texts containing apocryphal Acts of the Apostles were translated into Coptic. Afterwards imitations and local legends, of Egyptian origin, were added to them. More texts of these Acts were gradually formed, not in the Sahidic dialect alone, but one also in the sub-Sahidic or Middle Egyptian dialect. When the Coptic language had died, a translation was made into the language which was then generally understood in Egypt, that is, into the Arabic; and this was occasioned by that ecclesiastical and literary movement which may be observed in the thirteenth century, in the Patriarchate of Alexandria. The Ethiopic translation was made from the Arabic in its turn. The book now forms a systematically arranged whole; it comprehends the Apostles and the Evangelists, and of each it relates separately the Preaching and the Martyrdom. It has served also as a source for later works, like the Synaxaria, etc. We have therefore a special group of Apocryphal Acts belonging exclusively to the Alexandrian Patriarchate, in its own three languages, Coptic, Arabic, and Ethiopic, a group whose Coptic têxts, being the most ancient, are incomparably the most important and most deserving of being generally known[1]."

Of those legends which have been imitated from the Greek rather than translated by Coptic authors Dr Guidi mentions specially the Acts of St Philip, those of St Andrew and St Bartholomew, and those of Judas Thaddeus.

---

[1] *Gli Atti apocrifi degli Apostoli*, page 14.

Lipsius says: "As early as the second century numerous legendary reports concerning the fates of the Apostles were in circulation, in part, at least, of a very romantic character....Not a few of such narratives owe their origin simply to an endeavour to satisfy the pious curiosity or taste for the marvellous in members of the primitive church; while others subserved the local interests of particular towns or districts which claimed to have derived their Christianity from the missionary activity of one of the Apostles, or their line of bishops from one immediately ordained by him. It likewise not infrequently happened that party spirit, theological or ecclesiastical, would take advantage of a pious credulity to further its own ends by manipulating the older legends, or inventing others entirely new, after a carefully preconceived form and pattern. And so almost every fresh editor of such narratives, using that freedom which all antiquity was wont to allow itself in dealing with literary monuments, would recast the materials which lay before him, excluding whatever might not suit his theological point of view—dogmatic statements, for example, speeches, prayers, etc., for which he would substitute other formulæ of his own composition; and further expanding or abridging after his own pleasure, as the immediate object which he had in view might dictate. Only with the simply miraculous parts of the narrative was the case different. These passed unaltered and unquestioned from one hand to another.....

"Although therefore these fables originated for the most part in heretical quarters, we find them at a later period among the cherished possessions of ordinary Catholics; acquaintance with them being perpetually renewed, or their memory preserved in Catholic Christendom, partly by the festal homilies of eminent fathers, and partly by religious poetry and works of sacred art......

"From all this it is clear that any comprehensive critical examination of the apocryphal Acts of the Apostles will have great difficulties to contend with[1]."

We find the titles of some of these legends, together with those of the *Protevangelium Jacobi* and *Transitus Mariæ* included in the Roman *Index Librorum Prohibitorum*, sometimes ascribed to Pope Gelasius (A.D. 494) or to Hormisdas (514) but more probably of the 8th century, and especially

Actus nomine Andreæ apostoli;

Actus nomine Thomæ apostoli libri decem;

Actus nomine Philippi apostoli, apocryphi;

and

Libri omnes quos fecit Leucius discipulus diaboli[2].

"In the second century" (I quote from Lipsius), "there were not only numerous apocryphal legends of the Apostles in circulation, but also many written statements, which are still preserved in a more or less revised condition; Ebionistic κηρύγματα and περίοδοι are to be found in the extensive Pseudo-Clementine literature....But the histories of the Apostles which arose in Gnostic circles have a much greater importance for Church History. Gnostic Acts of Peter and Paul were certainly,

[1] Smith and Wace's *Dictionary of Christian Biography*, vol. I. pp. 18, 19.

[2] See Rev. W. E. Scudamore in Smith and Wace's *Dictionary of Christian Antiquities*, vol. II. pp. 1721, 1722.

Gnostic Acts of John were probably, read in the second century. From the fourth century we meet with distinct traces of a collection of περίοδοι τῶν ἀποστόλων widely diffused in Gnostic and Manichæan circles, which probably had the same compass from the beginning, as Photius (bibl. cod. 114) expressly testifies to us. According to him, it comprehended the Acts of Peter, John, Andrew, Thomas, and Paul. This collection, which is attributed to Leucius Charinus, is considered to be a heretical fabrication, by the unanimous decree of the Church teachers....

But "the use, which Church writers like Clement of Alexandria, and the author of the so-called second letter of the Roman Clement, make of some Apocryphal Gospels, as, for example, of the εὐαγγέλιον κατ' Αἰγυπτίους, establishes a fact important for the history of the second century, viz., that there was a time when the Gnostic Docetism and Modalism were not yet excluded from the Church, and in which also the products of Gnostic literature were used in Church circles.

"Therefore these Apocryphal Acts of the Apostles claim a place as noteworthy documents of Christian antiquity. But not only are they of importance for the history of dogmas and sects, but also for the history of the Canon, for that of ritual and of ecclesiastical use[1].

"Recent investigations have shown, that some genuine recollections have been preserved in a great portion of these Apocryphal histories of the Apostles. These refer, with a few exceptions, not to the Apostolic legends themselves, but to their setting, to the pre-supposed secular historical background, to the geographical and ethnographical scenery, sometimes also to local forms of heathen worship...."

"Attempts to derive profit in any comprehensive way from these legends for the history of the Apostles and of the Apostolic age, have until now almost always proved futile[2]."

But heretical fancies are not the only forces which have influenced the composition of these Acts. Paganism has been as hard to kill as the Lernean Hydra; and its re-appearance in a baptized world may frequently be detected. The Stoic philosophy, taking advantage of some of our Lord's sayings which are recorded in the Gospel, and isolating them from the rest of New Testament teaching, perpetuated itself in those ultra-ascetic practices which we find emphasized on ff. 81 a, 95 a, 106 b of our manuscript. It is not the Ephesian Artemis alone who has lent her virgin attendants, her perpetual maidenhood, her power of bestowing fertility upon the fields of her worshippers, and of healing their diseases, her candles, her gilded crown and brocaded mantle[3] to the humble Galilean maiden whose real and immortal glory no such tinsel can adorn; but as Dr Rendel Harris has lately shewn us, the Heavenly Twins, Castor and Pollux, have been made to transfer their power and their attributes to Judas Thomas, and to his Divine Master[4]. The parallels which Dr Harris has shewn to exist

[1] *Die apocryphen Apostelgeschichten und Apostellegenden*, vol. I. pp. 2—5.
[2] *Ibid.* pp. 10, 11.   [3] See Cod. Sin. Arab. 539 f. 98 a.
[4] *The Dioscuri in Christian Literature*, pp. 20—41.

between the legend of the heathen Twins and that of Judas Thomas, such as that of both practising the craft of carpentry and architecture, their being drivers or tamers of wild asses, and having India assigned to them as their sphere of operations, will apply equally well to the legend which has come to us from the Greek through a Coptic version and to that which is supposed to have a Syriac origin. The hypothesis of a Pagan source for this story will account more readily than any other for the monstrous figment that Judas Thomas was the "Twin of the Christ." And quite possibly Dr Harris may be right in thinking that all endeavours to verify the names of localities and of persons which are found in some of these legends will only lead to disappointment: their true origin being in the unhistorical regions of myth and romance.

These stories have long borne the title of Apocryphal Acts. But the adjective "mythological" surely gives us a more correct idea of their character. For the Apocrypha of the Old Testament bear some sort of relation both to the Hebrew canonical books and to historic fact, whereas in these legends the Apostles of Him Who never wrought a miracle merely for effect are degraded to the level of the heathen wizards for whom we are so frequently told that they were mistaken. And there is a family likeness in the doings of them all. They are represented as adepts in the art of causing people to be suspended in the air, of making the earth swallow up their enemies, and of restoring the dead to life. Some of these ideas are borrowed from Old Testament History, and some from the Gospels; but only one legend, the Preaching of Matthew, has the faintest touch of that convincing simplicity and congruity with the conditions of actual human life which we find in the Lucan "Acts of the Apostles."

NOTES ON THE ARABIC TEXT.

We may safely assume that all the tales contained in the Deyr-es-Suriani MS. are translated from the Coptic. We judge this from the occurrence of the Coptic names of the months, and of the Egyptian word for temple برپا, pl. برابى, which, as Dr Guidi has pointed out, is a corruption of the Sahidic π'ερπε. The letter ﭺ in the MS. and the ﺓ distinctive of feminine words, are written without their diacritical points, but I have generally supplied these in the printed text, as the reader might otherwise have found it perplexing to distinguish the one from ﺩ and the other from the pronominal suffix ﻪ. I have also supplied dots to final ﻯ when it is a possessive pronoun. The vowel points are for the most part clearly and

L. A. _c_

correctly written; but considerations of economy have prevented me from reproducing them in print.

Owing to the loss of three photographic negatives, I have had to fill in the text of f. 41 b in the شهادة اندراوس, f. 43 b in the اعمال اندراوس وبرتلموس, and f. 49 b in the شهادة يعقوب ابن زبدى from the Paris Codex, Fonds Arabe 81, and of f. 103 b in the شهادة تماس from Fonds Arabe 75.

In f. 45 b and elsewhere the final Alif in the 3rd person plural masculine of the preterite verb is frequently omitted.

In f. 54 a I am indebted to Mr A. Cowley of the Bodleian Library, Oxford, for restoring a line at the foot of the page which my camera had failed to include. The words supplied by him are taken from f. 31^b of Cod. Bodl. Or. 541, a very late manuscript.

The word which I have printed مدبر on p. ٣٤, l. 24, is from Fonds Arabe 81. It is مدنة in the Suriani text, and does not exist in the Bodleian one. I could not have edited مدينة without making nonsense, as any one will perceive who attempts to translate the passage. Dr Budge renders the word "Fort" in his translation from the Ethiopic. It had evidently given trouble to more than one Arab scribe, seeing that some have made it quite unintelligible.

The name which I have translated Domna in the story of John is in the Suriani MS. sometimes written زمنه, sometimes دمنه. I have adopted the latter, because it is the form used in the Roman Codex 694. This will be seen from the fragment edited by Professor Guidi in *Gli Atti apocrifi degli Apostoli*, p. 10, l. 1.

The later quire which has been inserted in the story of John, ff. 59^a—68^b, presents many difficulties to an editor, owing to inaccuracies of spelling, which I have corrected without drawing attention separately to them. It will suffice to say that ت is generally written ة and *vice versâ*, that words and sentences are frequently repeated, and that there is no punctuation except what I have introduced.

In f. 66 a (l. 6 of p. ٤٦) a word has been omitted by the scribe. In Cod. Arab. Vat. 694 this word is كامادبى and in Fonds Arabe 81 it is كمادبآ. In Dr Budge's translation from the Ethiopic it is "Kâmâdagî."

The name اردميس is so frequently treated as that of a male divinity in these legends that in f. 67 a, l. 1, we are pleased to find it furnished with a feminine adjective. The mistake of making this goddess masculine is very difficult to account for on the theory of the stories being originally Greek. We suspect that the passages where it occurs have been manipulated by ignorant Egyptians.

In f. 68 a (p. ٤٨, ll. 3, 4) I have ventured to treat the phrase beginning ولا تكون ظاهرة فى العيون والاذان الحاسية not as a direct negative, but as an example of the Semitic idiom to which attention has been drawn in the *Expository Times*, vol. XI. pp. 429, 439 etc., by Dr F. Hommel in connection with Jeremiah vii. 22 and Luke xiv. 12; also, I may add, John vi. 27. Here the introduction of the word "only" after "not" materially alters the sense; but I think that it gives the meaning of the supposed speaker.

In f. 72 b (page ٥٢, l. 1) there is the uncommon word تستصيرون which I have failed to find elsewhere. It is very distinct in my photograph.

In f. 74 a (p. ٥٣, l. 6) we have نحن نعبد تمثال بشر, "we worship the statue of a man." Here the Arabic which lies behind Dr Budge's Ethiopic text must have had تمثال نسر, "the statue of an eagle."

In f. 101 a (p. ٧٧, l. 19) the phrase انه قام is twice repeated. This points to the conclusion that the scribe of the manuscript was copying an earlier one and was not translating from another language. There is a similar repetition at the foot of f. 115 b and the top of f. 116 a of وقال له تقوا يا متاوس المبارك وتشدد امانتك. The word سمع having been dropped in f. 111 b (p. ٨٧, l. 10) is additional evidence of the fact.

In ff. 119 b, 120 a, مارتمريم and لعنهم الله in Cod. Sin. Arab. 539 are in a later hand.

In f. 120 a the scribe of Cod. Sin. Arab. 539 has not understood the Ccptic month امشير (ⲙⲉⲭⲓⲣ) and therefore he has turned it into شهر تشير الاول.

In f. 122 a the name of the bishop appointed by Simon is given in the Suriani text as مرسلس and in the Sinai one as قرنيليوس.

In f. 122 b it is stated that Simon's martyrdom took place فى تسعة من ابيب, while the Sinai MS. has فى عشرة ايام من شهر ايار.

In f. 126 b the readings of the Suriani text are not so good as those of the later Sinai ones marked v, w, and z.

In f. 127 a (p. ١٠٦, l. 6) the word علمنا is written above the line. This is an indication that the text of the Suriani MS. was copied from an older one.

In f. 133 a the name باعل زبول for بعلزبوب is quaint and appropriate.

At the beginning of f. 140 a two lines which I have failed to include in my photograph of the Suriani MS. have been kindly supplied to me by my friend M. Léon Dorez, of the Bibliothèque Nationale, Paris, from Fonds Arabe 81. From the same source I copied a missing line at the end of 140 b.

The Sinai Arabic MS. 539 has a script which is very difficult to Sin. Arb. 539.

decipher, being cramped and too often devoid of diacritical points. I copied the stories of St Mark and St Luke and the variants in that of Thaddeus from the manuscript itself. But for the story of St John I have had to depend on photographs, some of which were very far from being successful, and it is not too much to say that the text of this tale has cost me more labour than that of all the other tales together. I regret that a few lines are at present beyond my power to recall.

This legend of St John has certainly come to us through the Syriac. It is only what we should expect, from the fact of our already possessing the Syriac version edited by Dr Wright. But we also find in it Syriac words for which the translator has not given us an Arabic equivalent. Such are ملوا on f. 99 a and تسعية on f. 106 b.

In f. 99 a الاحزان is evidently a mistake for الاحرار, because the Syriac version has ܚܢܪ̈ܐ.

In f. 99 a (p. ١٣٦, l. 15) several words have evidently been dropped by the scribe; the Syriac equivalent for them being ܘܗܠ ܐܝܟ ܚܕܐ (Wright, p. ܣܘ, l. 8).

The blanks and defects in ff. 101 a, 102 a, 103 a, 104 a and 105 a are due to imperfections in my photographs.

خبر   The خبر of Peter and Paul is, as I have already said, very imperfect. I have been unable to find another MS. which contains it.

In the last line of f. 10ᵇ we find the Syriac word ܩܣܛܠܐ, قسط which I have ventured to translate "cup."

Another Syriacism occurs in the last word of f. 15ᵃ, the last line of f. 19ᵇ, and elsewhere. I have found a difficulty in deciding whether to translate رومي and الروم as "Romans" or as the Palestinian Syriac word ܪܗܘܡܝ, which is used in Matthew viii. 9, xxvi. 57 and other passages (see Schwally's *Idioticon*, p. 88).

Sin. Arab. 405.
    In Cod. Sin. Arab. 405, p. 19, the Vizier of Agrippa is called انارخوس. I can only conjecture that this is a corruption of the Greek word ναύαρχος. Marcus Vipsanius Agrippa was appointed to the command of the Roman fleet in 32 B.C.[1] He was one of the most distinguished and important men of the age of Augustus; and quite possibly one of his sons or nephews may have held a similar position.

In Cod. Vat. Arab. 694, ذ, ة, and ظ are always written without dots; and Dr Guidi has preferred to leave them so, excepting in the case of الذى and of words نظر and other words where the meaning might have been misunderstood.

---

[1] Smith's *Dictionary of Greek and Roman Biography*, vol. I. p. 79.

NOTES ON THE ENGLISH TRANSLATION.

The Preaching of Andrew.

It is satisfactory that the Arabic text agrees with the Ethiopic one in placing Andrew's missionary activity among the Kurds[1]. But it differs from it in sending both Andrew and Philemon to لد, which a reference in f. 19 a to Peter's activity plainly shows to be Lydda in the plain of Sharon, as against the Ledya or Lydia of the Ethiopic version[2].

We meet with Rufus and Alexander again in the story of Saint Matthias f. 134 a. Tintarān is Ṭîṭṭârân in Dr Budge's Ethiopic text.

Rufus the Governor is Rôkôs or Raukas in the Ethiopic.

The name of the negro in f. 26 a is Māgānā. In the Ethiopic it is Makâr.

Both Eusebius (*H. E.* III. 25) and Epiphanius (*Haer.* lib. II. tom. I, xlviii. 1; lxi. 1; lxiii. 2) inform us that the Acta Andreae is the work of heretics. As such it was condemned in the Decretum Gelasii.

This legend is not the same as the Acta Andreae edited by Tischendorf (*Acta Apost. Apoc.* pp. 105—131).

The Acts of Andrew and Bartholomew.

The city in which these two disciples together preached bears in the Ethiopic version the name of Bârtôs. This is evidently a corruption of Parthos, which is found in Coptic manuscripts[3]. I have resisted the temptation to assimilate the Arabic name, which is always either Barbaros, or El-Barbar, to this.

We again meet with the name El-Barbar, as the city where Andrew preached, in the Acts of Matthew, f. 107 b, and in the Preaching of Saint Matthias, ff. 130 a, 139 b, of the Suriani MS. Here the Ethiopic version has "the country of the Greeks[4]," and Tischendorf's Greek text has in the first place ἐν τῇ χώρᾳ, ᾗ ἦν διδάσκων ὁ Ἀνδρέας, and in the second εἰς τὴν χώραν τῶν βαρβάρων. Dr Guidi tells us that the cities of El-Barbar are mentioned by Abû-l-Barakât ibn Kabar (MS. Vat. Arab. 106) as one of the places in which Andrew preached[5].

---

[1] Malan's text has *Acradis*, p. 99. [2] Budge, *Contendings of the Apostles*, vol. II. p. 163.
[3] Lipsius, *Apostelgeschichten*, vol. II. part 2, p. 76.
[4] Budge, *Contendings of the Apostles*, vol. II. pp. 269, 287.
[5] *Atti apocrifi*, p. 7.

The country of the Oases is rendered in the Ethiopic version by "the city (or country) of Sewâ which is called 'Alwâh." This is identified by Dr Budge with the Oasis of Sîwah, or of Jupiter Ammon, in the Libyan desert not far from Asyût[1]. Mâctarân is evidently the same as the Ethiopic Makâtrân and Ghâryanûs as 'Azrĕyânos.

It is difficult to explain how the city of El-Betas has become Mêkôs.

We find the name of Macedonia in both Arabic and Ethiopic, and if the name Bârtôs be a corruption of Parthos, we can only wonder at the wide range of Bartholomew's travels—from the Libyan desert to Parthia, and thence to Macedonia. But if El-Barbar be the true name, it may possibly apply to Thrace, whose inhabitants were still at that period notorious for their ferocity.

Either Parthia or Thrace would be in harmony with the statement at the beginning of the Ethiopic version of St Andrew's martyrdom, that he continued to travel about in the country of 'Askâtyâ (Scythia).

In the Martyrdom of St Andrew the name Aknîs bears a very distant resemblance to 'Askâtyâ[2]. Behind Argânqûs or Argyânôs we are told by Lipsius to find Achaia[3]. The Safras of the Arabic version and the Sûkes or Sakos of the Ethiopic one mean the same place, but we cannot identify it.

The Story of James the Son of Zebedee.

In the story of James, son of Zebedee, we have a gleam of historical truth in the statement that the lot of John his brother was Asia, although the dense cloud of human ignorance through which it comes to us has distorted the province into a city. After preaching and founding a Church in the "city of India" James is evidently confounded with his namesake, the Lord's brother, and author of the canonical Epistle, for he goes out to the scattered Twelve Tribes, who all still remain under the dominion of Herod. He is put to death by that potentate, in accordance with the narrative in Acts xii. 2. Herod Agrippa I died in A.D. 44, and Nero did not succeed to the imperial throne till A.D. 54, so the linking of their names together in this legend is a glaring anachronism. The Arabic version says that the Apostle was buried in Niqta, which is called Ravîna; the Ethiopic in Kôṭ, of Mâmrĕkê = Marmorica. Niqta and Kôt may have something in common, but no successful attempt has been made to identify any of these places. We should have thought that James's burial-place was to be looked for near Jerusalem.

[1] *Ibid.* p. 183.   [2] Malan, *Asacatia*, p. 113.   [3] *Apostelgeschichten*, vol. I. pp. 621, 622.

It is worthy of remark that this legend contains no mention of the beautiful story told by Clement of Alexandria in a lost book, the 7th of his Hypotyposes, and recorded by Eusebius (*H. E.* II. 9); according to which the accuser of James was so moved by witnessing his confession that he declared his belief in Christianity, and after receiving the Apostle's kiss was beheaded along with him. In this case verily truth is more romantic than fiction.

Malan's translation from the Ethiopic gives Antioch as the scene of James's preaching, Bagte and Marke as the place of his burial. In Bagte we recognize our Arabic Niqta, in Marke Dr Budge's Mâmrĕkê.

The Travels of John the Son of Zebedee

The Greek of this story will be found in Zahn's *Acta Joannis*, pp. 3—44. It is said to have been written by Prochorus, one of the seven deacons whose election by the multitude of the disciples and ordination by the Apostles is recorded in Acts vi. 5. Dr Budge's Ethiopic version says that he was of the family of St Stephen, the Arabic versions that he wrote it "because of St Stephen[1]." As Stephen died before St John was established in Ephesus, this may mean that Prochorus had become aware, through the early death of his colleague, that all the disciples were not to remain until the second coming of our Lord; and so for the benefit of posterity he recorded in a written document the narrative of his experiences with St John. The discrepancy betwixt the Arabic and the Ethiopic in this passage shows the kind of alteration to which these legends have been subjected in the process of translation from one language into another.

We learn from Lipsius[2] that the Greek text of these πράξεις Ἰωάννου was first published by Michael Neander in an Appendix to Martin Luther's small Catechism, with a Latin translation by Sebastian Castalio (Basel, 1567, pp. 526—663). Two fragments in the Coptic version were published by Mingarelli in 1785. Thilo, Tischendorf, and Usener have all worked at the Greek text, and critical editions of it have been published by the Archimandrite Amphilochius, Zahn, and Bonnet.

The text of the Ethiopic version has been published by Dr Budge (1901), the translation of it into English by Malan (1871) and Budge (1901)

This legend is fundamentally different from the Leucian " History of

---

[1] Malan, "Companion of St Stephen."
[2] *Apostelgeschichten*, vol. I. pp. 355 ff.

St John at Ephesus," whose Syriac version was published by Dr Wright in 1871, the corresponding Arabic and English of which will be found on pp. ١٣٤—١٤٦ of No. III. and pp. 157—171. Yet they have several features in common. Both begin with an address of Peter to the assembled Apostles; both narrate the arrival of Saint John at Ephesus, and how he became a servant to the keeper of a bath-house. But in one story this keeper is a man, in the other a redoubtable woman. In both a young man is slain and then restored to life. But here the resemblance ends. The tale of the youth Damîs has nothing in common with that of the youth Menelaus, nor is the story of the blazing oil in the least like that of the weeping devil. The Decease of Saint John which follows is substantially the same in both texts, and this makes us hope that underneath both there may be a substratum of truth. In the narrative attributed to Prochorus, Lipsius points out that the dislike of John to go to Asia (f. 51 b) when commanded by the Lord to do so was a stereotyped Gnostic idea, appearing also in the Acts of Thomas (f. 89 a), in those of Andrew and Matthias (f. 130 a), and in the Syriac version of the Acts of Philip (Wright, vol. II. p. 69).

This story contains some of those incidental allusions to heathen customs which give to these legends their abiding value. The story of the living girl in f. 57 a, who had been buried beneath the foundation-stone of Dioscorides' bath-house, has lately received a remarkable confirmation from the exploration at Ta'annek in Palestine conducted by Professor Sellîn. Here not only under temples and public buildings, but under the foundations of ten private houses, human skeletons were discovered; silent witnesses to the iniquity of their own Canaanite and perhaps early Israelite countrymen. And at Gezer, Mr Stewart Macalister has found unmistakeable relics of foundation-sacrifices in the skeletons of five adults and of at least ten children—all Amorite.

That this horrible practice was once widely prevalent amongst heathen nations we have abundant proof through the researches of scholars and missionaries. In a treatise by P. Sartori in the *Zeitschrift für Ethnologie* (XXX. 1898, pp. 5—19), we learn that the name "Dahomey" springs from the story of Tacudonu, King of Foy, in the 17th century, having buried his benefactor, King Da, of Canna, alive under a new palace, whose name was extended over the surrounding district, and that there the custom still prevails.

In Siam, quite lately, human victims were buried under the new gates of cities. At Tavoy in Tenasserim about the middle of the nineteenth century a criminal was placed under every post of a gate and his spirit was expected to become a protecting demon. In Mandalay, in Rangoon, in Cambodia, in Shanghai[1], in Alaska[1], and in Japan, the unholy rite has been recently observed. At Sialkot in the Punjab and Suram in Georgia the only son of a widow had to be sacrificed for the stability of a fortress. Even in Calcutta, so late as 1800, a report was spread that the Government intended to slay a number of human beings during the construction of a new harbour. Persian tradition speaks of a town-wall in which a layer of bricks was made to alternate with a layer of corpses. And the petrified body of the Blessed slave Geronimo, built into the concrete of the city-walls in the sixteenth century, may still be seen at Algiers.

Crossing the Atlantic, we find that the temple of Chibchos in Sagamozo (Colombia) stood upon people who had been buried alive, and a palace in Bogota upon the corpses of girls.

The custom was, and perhaps is still, widely prevalent in New Zealand and the islands of the Pacific. Mr John Jackson saw at Rewa in the Fiji group, when a house was being built for the chief's son, slaves who were made to jump into the holes prepared for the foundation-posts. Earth was then heaped over them, and the posts fixed above. Sometimes these posts were held in the arms of these buried men.

Traces of the custom have been observed in the history of ancient Rome and of Carthage. When Seleucus Nicator founded the city of Antioch on the Orontes, a maiden was slain in the centre of the river by the high-priest, and was supposed to become the Fortune of the city. Alexander the Great offered another when he founded Alexandria. A virgin named Gregoria was sacrificed by Augustus for Ancyra; another named Antigone by Tiberius for the theatre at Antioch; and another named Calliope for the restored city itself after the great earthquake[2].

Traces of the same rite have been observed at Copenhagen, at the cloister of Maulbronn in Würtemberg, the Castle of Liebenstein in Thuringia[1], Scutari in Asia Minor[1], the Bridge Gate of Bremen[1], the Cathedral of Strassburg, a castle at Novgorod, a bridge at Visegrad in Bosnia, and one over the Struma in Bulgaria, at Mostar in Herzegovina, at Arta in Epirus, the Monastery of Curtea de Argis, in Wallachia[1], and in the tower of Cettinje in Montenegro. At Winneburg, on the Moselle,

---

[1] See H. Clay Trumbull, *The Threshold Covenant*, pp. 45—52.
[2] See Lasaulx, *The Sacrifices of the Greeks and Romans*, p. 247.

the ancient seat of the Metternichs, the architect's daughter lies beneath the foundation-stone.

The classical example in Scotland is the burial of the living Oran, by St Columba, while the monastery at Iona was being built[1].

In 1841 the people of Halle believed that a child would be immured in the new Elizabeth bridge, and those of Göltschthal near Reichenbach thought that this had really been done in the case of a railway bridge. For a curious recent illustration from Asia Minor, I am informed by Dr Rendel Harris that, after the laying of the foundation-stone of a new Protestant Church near Harpoot by the American missionaries, the native workmen sacrificed a lamb in the trench, and placed its head in the foundation-stone. We have there the first stage of the abandonment of the human sacrifice by the substitution of an animal; a later stage will be the placing of ransom money in the stone, a custom which prevails at the present time.

Lipsius considers that the prayer of John whilst breaking the bread reported on f. 69 b is unmistakeably Docetic. "Who permitteth Himself to be called by that name," points to the doctrine that the union of the Godhead with the manhood of Jesus was only a temporary arrangement for the benefit of man[2]. And there is a Gnostic idea in the disappearance of John's body f. 71 b (Cod. Sin. Arab. 539, ff. 109 a, 109 b).

Zahn places the first written form of this story quite 400 years after the death of John[3], but considers that it arose certainly before A.D. 160, and probably before A.D. 140[4], and that a material gain for our historical knowledge may be won by a rigid separation of what can be proved in it and what is only imaginary. "Romance," he says, "has laid hold of the forms of the Apostles at a time when reliable information about them was still abundant; at a time also when romance would find acceptance with their contemporaries only by a close alliance with unforgotten historical facts[5]."

He considers the Liturgy of the Lord's Supper in f. 69 b as of equal antiquity with the oldest prayer of the Church and the oldest sermon[6].

---

[1] *This is a most curious tale. The devil threw down the walls of the chapel as fast as they were being built. Columba, having been told in a vision that the only way to prevent this was to bury a human victim, accepted the voluntary offer of his disciple Oran to be the sacrifice. Oran was accordingly buried, but Columba's conscience would not let him sleep. Oran was resuscitated, and forthwith proceeded to describe his experiences in such a manner that it was evident he had been in the wrong place. The monks were therefore glad to silence him by putting him again beneath the sod.*

[2] *Apostelgeschichten*, vol. I. p. 535.

[3] *Acta Joannis, Einleitung*, p. ii.

[4] *Ibid*. p. cxlviii.   [5] *Ibid*. p. ii.   [6] *Ibid*. p. cl.

The Preaching and Martyrdom of Philip.

This story has no resemblance to that in Tischendorf's Greek text (*Acta Apost. Apoc.* p. 75 sqq.), nor to the *Acta Philippi* published by Bonnet, nor to the Syriac text of Dr Wright. It contains no local names, neither in the Arabic nor in the Ethiopic version, except those of Africa, the scene of his labours[1], and Martagena or Cartagena as the place of his burial.

If these localities point to a correct tradition, the legends which place his ministry in Hierapolis of Phrygia probably refer to Philip the Deacon-evangelist, father of the four virgins which did prophesy (cf. Acts vi. 5; xxi. 8, 9).

But we must not overlook the one noteworthy coincidence with which Dr Wright's Syriac text furnishes us. There we are told that Philip went and preached in the city of Carthagena, which is in Azotus. Dr Wright says that though the name is written ܪܝܼܟܠܝܘ, yet *Carthage* is intended, and not *Cartagena* in Spain. Azotus is evidently an echo of Acts viii. 40, and the geographical muddle has arisen from the Apostle Philip and the Deacon-evangelist being treated as one and the same person.

The Preaching and Martyrdom of Saint Bartholomew.

Several nations and several localities, Phrygia, Lycaonia, Parthia, Media, Persia, Armenia, India, claim the honour of having been evangelized by St Bartholomew. Some legends connect his missionary activity with that of Matthew, and some with that of Andrew. This one, which has come to us through the Coptic, assigns to Peter the credit of having been Bartholomew's guide, and leads him in the very opposite direction, to the West instead of to the East, to the Oases of the African desert, till at last he is martyred by being put into a hair sack and thrown into the sea. Our Arabic text gives no name to the place where this occurred; Dr Budge's Ethiopic text gives Nîêndôs or Naidas.

Tischendorf's Greek text of the Martyrdom agrees with our Arabic one in a very few particulars. The name of the king Ἀστρήγης is not very like Agrippus. The unbelieving Greeks do the work attributed to the wicked man in f. 88 a. In both texts the saint is thrown into the sea: and the Greek gives the island of Lipari as the place to which the sea bore his remains. This surely harmonizes better geographically with our legend than with any other.

---

[1] The Ethiopic text translated by Malan gives the city of Assakia as the scene of Philip's labours, but Afrikia as the place of his martyrdom.

It is also worthy of note that these Acts of Bartholomew fall into line with the preceding Acts of Philip, by making the two friends wander forth in the same direction. The *Passio Bartholomaei* published by Bonnet is quite a different legend.

The Preaching and Martyrdom of Saint Thomas.

The story of Thomas in this cycle of legends has many points of resemblance to that of Bartholomew. Both are sold into slavery, the one by Saint Peter, the other by our Lord Himself. Both are skilled workmen, the one as a vine-dresser, the other as an architect and carpenter. One story has evidently borrowed something from the other, but it would be difficult to apportion their mutual indebtedness.

The appearance of our Lord and His speech to Thomas in f. 97 b contains the remarkable allusion which is more fully developed in the Syriac Acts of Judas Thomas, as edited by Dr Wright: "For thou art called the Twin." This points to the strange tradition that Thomas, the doubting disciple, bore that cognomen (Tauma—the Twin) because he was a twin-brother of the Christ, Judas being his proper name. By far the most satisfactory way of accounting for the origin of this idea is the theory put forth by Dr Rendel Harris in *The Dioscuri in Christian Literature*, that we have here a recrudescence of Paganism ; that wherever the cult of the heavenly Twins, Castor and Pollux, had prevailed, a pair of Christian saints came to take their place in a system of baptized Paganism : and so at Edessa, in Macedonia, in Parthia, in Media, in India, and wherever the feet of the Apostle Judas Thomas are supposed to have gone, one need not try to verify either statements or personal names in the light of true history, for the whole legend is a myth and nothing else.

The Syriac form of the story, the full text of which has been edited by Dr Wright, and of which fragments from the Sinai Syriac MS. No. 30 will be found in the appendix to No. III., contains many points of resemblance to our Arabic text, but also many differences of detail. Both narratives begin with the division of the world amongst the Apostles; both make Thomas travel to India and recount how he was sold as a slave ; both make him a mason and a carpenter (a strong point of resemblance to the Dioscuri); both make him build a spiritual instead of a material palace.

But there is nothing in the Egyptian story about the ass that spake, nor about the black snake, nor about the demon which dwelt in the woman, nor about the team of wild asses.

The Syriac story, on the other hand, makes no mention of Thomas's flayed-off skin.

Towards the close of the Martyrdom we find a few further resemblances. Mastâus or Matthâûs, the king in our text, is evidently identical with Mazdai of the Syriac one; Tertia and Tartanâi, Sîfûr and Sirfûr must have a common origin. In both the saint is taken up to a high mountain and stabbed by several soldiers at once, his last words to them being nearly the same. And he was buried by the brethren in the grave of the ancient kings. Judas reappears after his death in both stories with the same message, and casts a devil out of the king's son. The king is in consequence converted, and so both stories end.

Why they should begin and finish in the same manner, and yet be so unlike in the main course of their narrative, is a question which I shall not attempt to solve.

The Indian legend identifies Thomas with Judas the brother of our Lord[1] (Matt. xiii. 55). For my own theory that he may have been the twin-brother of James the Just see *The Expository Times* for June, 1903.

The legend translated by Malan is the same as this one, but in the passage which corresponds to f. 91 a our Lord directs the purchaser of Thomas, whose name is not given, to dress him as a guardsman of Cantacoros, king of India[2]. Lucius becomes Vecius, and Arsânûni Arsenia, and the city of Cantôria Quantaria. Zabadka becomes Actabodi in Macedonia; Margita Marna; Masâsawi Maiturnos; Matthâûs, Mastius; Hersânûs Ziriaos; Tartanâi Tartabania; Atbaniâ Athona. To Malan's legend a portion from the Syriac Acts of Judas Thomas is appended, pp. 206—214.

In f. 102 a, "Mary, the Lord's Mother," becomes "Mary who gave birth to God," in one form of the Ethiopic version—a natural progression in her cult[3].

The Greek text published by Thilo does not correspond with this text, but with Dr Wright's Syriac one to the end of the Sixth Act.

The Acts of Matthew.

The Arabic text of this story corresponds to the Ethiopic version published by Budge in the *Contendings of the Apostles*, and to Malan's translation. But while both place the Apostle's activity in the country of

---

[1] Lipsius, *Apostelgeschichten*, vol. I. p. 227.
[2] Malan's *Conflicts of the Holy Apostles*, p. 190.
[3] Budge, vol. II. p. 345; Malan, "Mary who gave birth to our Lord," p. 205.

the Kahenat, or priests, the Ethiopic states that Peter and Andrew met
with him on their return from Greece[1], and the Arabic "from the country
of El-Barbar." The text of the Suriani manuscript is thus in harmony
with itself (see ff. 28 a, 130a). The name of the city from which Matthew
came is in the Ethiopic Pĕrâkômnôs, *i.e.* Prokumenos. In the Arabic it is
"the country of the Blessed."

There is a confusion in the manuscripts between the names of Matthew
and Matthias, but the task of separating them is not a difficult one.
This legend of Matthew, so far as I can judge, has more beauty both
of a moral and a literary kind than any of the other mythological Acts.

The Martyrdom of Saint Matthew.

Lipsius considers that thêre is no connection between the story of the
Acts and the story of the Martyrdom, because in the latter the scene
is transferred from the city of Kahenat to Parthia[2].

He also thinks that the Egyptian tale of this Martyrdom strengthens
a tradition that the Apostle preached in Parthia. That his body was
given for food to the fowls of heaven, f. 118 b, was quite according to the
custom of the country of Zoroaster. In f. 116b (as in ff. 48 b, 77 a) we
have an indication that both the Arabic and the Ethiopic version were
made after the council of Chalcedon (A.D. 451), for the translator could
not refrain from explaining that the two natures in the God-man were not
confounded[3].

An epitome of this legend of the Acts and Martyrdom of Matthew will
be found in the Synaxarium of the Coptic Church (ed. Wüstenfeld, p. 65),
for the 12th of Bābeh (Phaōphi).

The Martyrdom of James the Son of Halfai.

This James is in all the legends confounded with James the Lord's
brother, so that it is impossible to know whether any trustworthy
tradition concerning him exists. The Egyptian story presents us with
another element of confusion by stating that he was brought before the
Emperor Claudius, though he was immediately afterwards buried beside
the temple in Jerusalem[4].

In this story, and in that of Simon, which follows it, I have adopted
Mrs Gibson's translation so far as the variants will allow me.

---

[1] Malan, "Syria."
[2] *Apostelgeschichten*, vol. II. part ii. p. 117.   [3] *Ibid.* p. 129.
[4] Malan, "within the Church at Jerusalem."

The Preaching and Martyrdom of Simon the Son of Cleophas.

There is a still greater confusion in the traditions relating to Simon. He is said by some to be identical with Simon Zelotes, by others to be a nephew of Joseph, but not an Apostle. Our text, like the Ethiopic one, calls him also Jude, and Nathanael the Zealot.

By some he is said to have preached on the shores of the Black Sea, by some in Babylonia and Persia, by some in Egypt and North Africa, and by some in Britain[1]. Our text makes him succeed James the Just as Bishop of Jerusalem. He is put to death in Jerusalem by the express order of the Emperor Trajan, ff. 123 a, 123 b. The Suriani MS. states that the martyrdom of Simon took place "on the ninth of Abîb" (July), the Sinai MS. on "the tenth day of the month of Ayyâr" (May). The Bishop appointed by Simon is Marcellus in the Suriani MS. f. 122 a, Cornelius in the Sinai one. We cannot attempt to unravel so many tangled threads. This story is the same as that of St Simeon, translated from the Ethiopic by Malan.

The Preaching of Thaddeus.

Tradition links Simon and Thaddeus together in their missionary activity, and these legends in particular give to both the additional name of Judas, identifying them with Jude, one of our Lord's brothers. They assign to Thaddeus the regions of Syria and Mesopotamia; and though they say nothing about Abgar, king of Edessa, they are not in any discrepancy with the Syriac tradition concerning him. There is a local tradition which would place the death of Thaddeus at Ararat in Armenia. The *Acta Thaddaei* edited by Lipsius and by Tischendorf are a totally different legend, but the Conflict of St Judas (Thaddeus) translated by Malan is the same (pp. 221—229).

The incidents of Peter making the old man's field to sprout, of the woman being suspended in the air, and of the camel passing through the needle's eye, will be found in the *Acta Petri et Andreae* published by Bonnet[2]. There the deeds of Thaddeus are attributed to Andrew.

The saying of our Lord reported in ff. 125 a, 127 b, which gives the negative form of Matt. vii. 12, is a Western reading found in Codex Bezae, Acts xv. 29. It is attributed to Hillel in the Talmud of Babylonia, tractate Sabbath f. 31 a; and will be found in Tobit iv. 15.

[1] Lipsius, *Apostelgeschichten*, vol. II. part ii. p. 143.
[2] Lipsius, *Acta Apost. Apoc.* vol. II. part i. pp. 117—127.

The Preaching and Martyrdom of Saint Matthias.

This is the same story as that of the Greek text published by Tischendorf, pp. 132—166, and the Syriac one by Dr Wright in *Apocryphal Acts of the Apostles*, pp. ‏ܩܡܗ—ܩܡܗ‎. Dr Wright calls the Apostle Mār Matthew, and Lipsius is of opinion that all the legends whose texts we have printed ff. 107 b—119 a and ff. 129 a—139 b sqq. refer to Matthew the publican, and that no special tradition about Matthias has ever existed in the Greek Church[1]. He may be right ; but the remark at the beginning of the Martyrdom, f. 140 a, which was probably unknown to Dr Wright, has led me in this story to prefer the name Matthias. The references to Andrew in both stories, ff. 107 b, 130 a—139 b, certainly lead to the inference that both relate to the same person ; and if I am mistaken in considering 'Matthias' as the evangelist of the City of the Cannibals I can only plead that the evidence about him is very conflicting, and that both Tischendorf and Malan have adopted the name of Matthias in this legend.

The Greek text edited by Tischendorf and by Lipsius is substantially the same as the Egyptian one, though it differs in some of its details. It does not mention the name of the city in which Andrew was preaching when he was summoned to help Matthias. Malan's translation from the Ethiopic gives to this the name of "Syria," and Budge's gives "Greece."

The Ethiopic version has "He placed a few loaves of bread upon the grass and the grass became bread[2]," an amplification of the simple statement in f. 132 a.

Tischendorf's Greek text has Ἀμαήλ for the name of the devil whom Andrew rebuked (f. 136 a). If this be a truncated form of Samil, and be derived from a Semitic word (Syriac ‏ܣܡܝܠ‎), it would seem as if the Greek text were not the earliest form of this legend.

Dr Rendel Harris suggests that it may be Sammael, the well-known evil angel of the Jews.

In the same text and also in Bonnet's we find Μύρνη as the name of the cannibal city[3], and Malan's translation has Ba'alatsaby (pp. 147, 149).

The scene of Matthias's martyrdom is Damascus in the Ethiopic text, and the place of his death is Pelwôn[4] in the Ethiopic and Malâwân in the Arabic. Both are very difficult to identify.

---

[1] *Apostelgeschichten*, vol. II. part ii. pp. 136, 259.
[2] Budge, *Translation*, p. 274.
[3] Tisch., p. 169. Lipsius, *Acta Apost. Apoc.* vol. II. part i. p. 220.
[4] Malan, "Phalaon."

The Preaching and Martyrdom of James the Just.

All these legends agree with the Canonical Acts in placing the scene of James's ministry in Jerusalem. The most interesting feature in this story is the account of his relation to the Lady Mary in f. 150 a. There he is described as the youngest of the four sons of Joseph by a first wife. We should have imagined from Matthew xiii. 55 that he was the eldest.

These legends are the same as those translated from the Ethiopic by Malan. There Theopiste, wife of the Prefect, becomes Piobsata, wife of the Judge Aumanius (f. 149 a).

The Martyrdom of Saint Mark.

This legend appears to have more historical fact behind it than any of the others. We are disposed to believe that the lot of St Mark did come out unto Egypt, but we find it strange that the story makes no mention of the saint's travels in Cyprus with Paul and Barnabas (Acts xiii. 5—13) nor of his sojourn in Rome (Col. iv. 10). Nor does it explain from which of the three cities which have been identified with Babylon, Peter sent his salutations to the strangers scattered about in Asia Minor (1 Peter v. 13). We are thankful for the crumbs of confirmation offered to us by Eusebius (*H. E.* II. 15, 16). Anianus, who is mentioned in f. 202 b, is the traditional successor of Mark as Bishop of Alexandria (*H. E.* II. 24).

Dr Chase thinks that the description of Mark's person in f. 204 a is partly borrowed from that of Paul in the *History of Thecla*[1]. The Arabic coincides with this less than the Greek does.

Malan's translation says that Mark was the first to preach the Gospel in the cities of the land of Egypt, Zalonia, Markia, Tamurcke and Barke[2]. The men of Barke send him in a boat to Alexandria, where the incident of the cobbler occurred.

As Mark is said to have been martyred under Tiberius (f. 204 b), who died in March A.D. 37, the period of this wonderful activity cannot have exceeded four years, and this would include his visits to Cyprus and to Rome.

The quotation from 1 Cor. iii. 19 in f. 202 b is much more correct in the Arabic version than in the Ethiopic. There we read : " The wisdom of the world is that which is with the word of God[3]."

---

[1] Hastings' *Dictionary of the Bible*, vol. III. p. 248.
[2] Malan, p. 181.
[3] Budge, *Translation*, p. 312.

The Martyrdom of Saint Luke.

Lipsius tells us that this legend of St Luke is quite peculiar to the
Arabic Synaxarium of the Coptic Church, and to the Ethiopic "Conflicts
of the Apostles," which, as we have already seen, were translated from the
original Greek, not directly, but through the Coptic and Arabic. According
to that text, Luke, in prospect of death, gave his writings for safe custody
to an old fisherman named Silas[1]. It might be possible to read the word
Silâûs into the Arabic text of f. 206 a, but my own conviction is that it is
Theophilâûs. The fac-simile of the page, which I have given on p. ١٣١ of
No. III. will enable scholars to judge of this point for themselves. The
Theophilus of the canonical Gospel and Acts was evidently not a fisherman,
but a man of distinction, who was entitled to be addressed as κρατιστε.
If the word Thabilâûs were written in Arabic without its diacritical points,
the Ethiopic translator might easily read Silâûs, and then drop the last long
vowel.

Lipsius thinks that the passage where, in the Ethiopic version, Titus is
said to be of the city of Galilâ, and Luke of the country of Dalmatia[2],
is simply an amazing misreading of 2 Tim. iv. 10. But this remark cannot
apply to the Arabic text, for in f. 204 b of our MS. Luke is said to be from
the city of Antioch, and this agrees with the statement of Eusebius (*H. E.*
III. 4), Λουκᾶς δὲ τὸ μὲν γένος ὢν τῶν ἀπ' Ἀντιοχείας, and brings a ray of
historical truth into the legend.

The reading of Codex Bezae in Acts xi. 28 συνεστραμμένων δὲ ἡμῶν,
revertentibus autem nobis, is supposed to confirm indirectly the statement
of Eusebius. The *Praefatio Lucae* given in Wordsworth-White's *Vulgate*,
p. 269, and ascribed by Harnack to the 3rd century, says : "*Lucas Syrus
natione Antiochensis arte medicus discipulus apostolorum,*" etc. The same
authority states that Luke died in Bithynia, not in Rome, as our legend
has it.

The Story of John the Son of Zebedee.

Our Arabic text is probably a translation of the Syriac version of this
story, which has been edited by Dr Wright[3], and is attributed to Leucius
Charinus. Lipsius considers it less valuable than some of the other legends
concerning John. Tradition says that Eusebius of Caesarea was the
translator of it from Greek into Syriac, and it claims for itself that he
found it in the archives of the godless Emperor Nero (f. 98 a).

---

[1] See Budge, vol. II. p. 141. Malan, pp. 60, 63.   [2] Budge, p. 137.
[3] Wright's *Translation*, pp. 2—60.

Lipsius places the date of its composition between the first half of the fifth century and the beginning of the sixth. The Syriac version contains traces of the Nicene Creed which are less distinct in the Arabic, such as "Light of light"; "the Son of God, Who was eternally with His Father"; "the Spirit of holiness, Who proceeded from the Father." The baptism of children, described in the Syriac[1] but wanting in the Arabic, was not yet customary in the East at the close of the fourth century. The anointing with oil before baptism (ff. 104 a, 104 b) is in accordance with a Catholic form of the rite used since the fourth century[2]. The Lord's Supper is not called the "Body of God[3]" in the Arabic version, as it is in Dr Wright's text. These things, together with the greater conciseness of the Arabic, suggest that our text is translated from a Syriac MS. older than Add. MS. 17,192 of the British Museum, or even than the sixth century St Petersburg MS. used by Dr Wright.

Lipsius considers that the tale must have been composed before the hut of St John (or the little church on its site), which stood on a hill to the east of the city above the temple of Artemis at Ephesus[4], was replaced by the magnificent church of Justinian (A.D. 527—565).

The use of the dung of animals for the stove of the bath-house (f. 98 b) corresponds with the habits of the peasants in Thessaly and Macedonia, as we have ourselves observed them. In inland districts where neither coal nor wood can be procured bread is still baked over a very insanitary kind of fuel.

The incident of the fire which flashed from the four limbs of John's cross (f. 101 b) and the description of John's means of living are considered by Lipsius to be quite in accordance with Gnostic ideas[5].

Lipsius thinks that the story of John writing his Gospel in a single night, f. 106 a (the Syriac version says "in one hour"), cannot be ascribed to Gnostic influence, but must have sprung from a desire to emphasize the opinion that the Gospel of John is an amplification of the first three Gospels[6]. He also considers that the tradition of John living to the age of 120 years is merely an imitation of the story of Moses (Deut. xxxiv. 7).

In f. 104 b the number of those whom John baptized in one day is given as 39,005 souls: less by 200 than that in the Syriac version[7].

---

[1] Wright's *Translation*, p. 42.

[2] Lipsius, *Apostelgeschichten*, vol. I. p. 434.   [3] Wright's *Translation*, pp. 37, 44.

[4] This was the μαρτύριον of St John, mentioned in the Acts of the Councils of Ephesus, A.D. 431, 449.

[5] *Apostelgeschichten*, vol. I. p. 437.

[6] *Ibid.* p. 440.   [7] Wright, p. ܩܒ, l. 12.

been advanced to the dignity of presbyter. The difficulty will disappear if we recollect that the diaconate was not originally instituted as a step to the presbyterate, but for a totally different and distinct service (cf. Acts vi. 1—6). It is easy to create these difficulties by reading into the New Testament narrative the ideas of a period subsequent to that in which it was written[1].

Zahn considers that these Ephesian legends of the Apostle John, originating as they did before A.D. 160, may perhaps have given a mortal blow to the "Eusebian myth" of a presbyter John, who is supposed to have shared in the authorship of the Fourth Gospel. If such an one had existed, side by side with the great Apostle, Leucius, the author of this legend, who probably lived in the second century, could not have failed to mention him[2].

The Greek of this story from f. 106 b almost to the end of f. 108 b will be found in Zahn (*Acta Joannis*, pp. 238—249) and in Bonnet (Lipsius, *Acta Apost. Apoc.* vol. II. part i. pp. 203—215).

In f. 108 b the reference to John having been blind for two years is clearly an imitation of the story of St Paul (Acts ix. 9—18).

The Story of Peter and Paul.

This legend has so little resemblance to the others that I have hesitated about the propriety of printing it along with them. It seems to belong to the series of the Thousand and One Nights rather than to that of the Acts of the Apostles, even when mythological. We search in vain for any Emperor of Rome who was named Barʿamûs, but the prefect of the Praetorians, Burrhus Afranius, who with Seneca had charge of the education of Nero, is no doubt the person indicated. Perhaps Gnostic doctrine appears on f. 3 b. There we are told that our Lord, after His resurrection, told the divine secrets to His Apostles, before sending them to preach about His kingdom. This seems to correspond with the "esoteric theology of which the popular creed of multitudes of deities, with its whole ritual of sacrifice and worship, was but the exoteric form[3]." The idea was further developed by the Jewish Kabbalists in the tenth century, being by them applied to a secret "system of theosophy which claims to have been transmitted unin-

---

[1] See *Life of Bishop Westcott*, vol. I. p. 139.　　　[2] Zahn, *Acta Joannis*, p. CLIV.
[3] King, *The Gnostics and their Remains*, p. 5.

terruptedly by the mouths of patriarchs and prophets ever since the creation of man[1]."

Possibly the phrase does not refer to Gnostic teaching, but rather to the doctrine embodied in a decree of the Council of Trent (Sess. IV. *De Canon. Script.*). "It teaches that the truth of Christ is contained partly in the Bible, partly in unwritten tradition received by the Apostles from Christ or from the Holy Ghost, and entrusted by them to the Church; and that Scripture and tradition (the latter of course only when proved Apostolic) are to be reverenced alike[2]."

If the number of bishops said on f. 24 a to have been ordained by the Apostles in Rome were intended to rule the Church in that city the statement would be in the highest degree remarkable, as shewing the antiquity of the legend. But we suspect that the statement refers to the Catholic Church of the world.

The Martyrdom of Peter and Paul.

This story is virtually the same as the *Passio sanctorum Petri et Pauli* attributed to Linus and published by Lipsius and Bonnet. From the beginning of p. 8 almost to the end it is like the *Acta Petri et Pauli* published by Thilo.

The first mention of Simon Magus will be found in Acts viii. 9, 10, where we are told that the people of Samaria believed him to be "the great power of God." There seems to be some historical truth in the legend that he preached also in Rome, though Justin Martyr[3] was mistaken when he told of a statue which was erected to him there, on an island in the river, between the two bridges, bearing a Latin inscription, "*Simōni Deo Sancto.*" The statue was discovered in A.D. 1574 and it is to a Sabine deity.

Justin tells us that a woman named Helena was his companion, that she at first stood upon a roof (in Tyre of Phoenicia), and that she was called the "first Thought" ($\tau\grave{\eta}\nu$ $\pi\rho\acute{\omega}\tau\eta\nu$ $\overset{\text{"}}{E}\nu\nu o\iota a\nu$).

Irenaeus tells us that both Simon and Helena were honoured with incense, sacrifices, and libations.

The rites of their worship were too impure to be described, and are perhaps alluded to in 2 Tim. iii. 6, 7, 13[4].

---

[1] Ginsburg, *Encyclopædia Britannica*, vol. XIII. p. 811.

[2] *Catholic Dictionary*, p. 885.

[3] Justin, *Apologia* I. 59, 77, *Dialogus cum Tryphone* 214, *Apologia* II. 98; Irenaeus, *Dissertatio* I. 96—104.

[4] Eusebius, *H. E.* II. 13; Epiphanius, *Haer.* lib. I. tom. 2, xxi.

Lipsius[1] says:

"The statements that Simon was honoured as the πρῶτος θεός, and his companion Helena as the πρώτη ἔννοια, are easily understood to be characteristic features of a Gnostic system, whose agent Simon was considered to be in the time of Justin. In this system Simon appears as the representative of the Gnostic idea of salvation, certainly not as the Eternal God enthroned in hidden silence, but as His highest Power, or most perfect Revelation, as the "Existing" (ὁ ἑστώς), who shall exist, that is, as the Imperishable, remaining changeless in a perishing world (Clem. *Hom.* II. 24; *Recogn.* II. 11). At his side stands the Universal Mother, whom he has allowed to proceed from him as his highest thought, who is also called Wisdom (Σοφία), Lady Ruler, Holy Spirit and Prunikos, but who usually receives the name of Ἔννοια. She plays the same part in this system as the Σοφία or Ἀχαμώθ does in the Ophitic or Valentinian Gnosis. She sinks from the highest heaven to the lower regions, where she gives birth to angels and powers, the most remarkable amongst them being the Demiurgus and the Lawgiver of the Jews. Being detained by the might of these world-ruling angels, she is prevented from returning to her father's kingdom, but after many sufferings and vicissitudes of fortune she is delivered by the ἑστώς. He descends from the highest heaven for her salvation, becomes apparently man, allows himself to be apparently crucified, and redeems the souls who had been imprisoned with ἔννοια, those whose origin was in heaven, by the communication of the true Gnosis."

The legend of Simon Magus's teaching in Rome, of his conflict with Peter, and of his pretending that he would rise again on the third day, is to be found in the *Philosophumena* of Hippolytus, VI. 20 (Miller's edition).

Lipsius considers that the martyrdom of Peter and Paul which has come down to us under the name of Linus shows many remains of Gnostic teaching, although it has been revised in a Catholic sense. Chief of these is a long speech made by Peter as he is approaching the cross on which he was to suffer, but this does not occur at all in our Arabic version[2].

The existing text of these Acts cannot be traced to a period earlier than the fifth century. But Cyril of Jerusalem, who died A.D. 386, Sulpicius Severus, who died A.D. 425, in his *Chronica* (II. 28), and Asterios of Amaseia, who preached a sermon about A.D. 400, all relate incidents, such as that of Simon's fall, which can have been taken from no other source[3].

Lipsius considers that the following passages are interpolations: the conversion of Livia and Agrippina, p. 4; Agrippa's suggestion that Paul

---

[1] *Apostelgeschichten*, vol. II. part i. p. 35.

[2] *Ibid.* p. 258.

[3] *Ibid.* pp. 331, 332.

The Death of St John.

Lipsius considers that this story is a Gnostic one, but that it has been revised by the hand of more than one orthodox Catholic[1]. Perhaps it is from this latter source that we have the description of a Eucharist celebrated in one kind only (D. S. f. 69 b).

Zahn thinks that the περίοδοι, which form the basis of this legend, must be ascribed to the second century, before A.D. 160, perhaps about A.D. 130. The common possession and use of these Acts among Catholics and Gnostics shew that these writings (*i.e.* the Leucian Acts of John, Andrew, and Thomas) are an heirloom from the time when both these parties were still existing in the bosom of the mother Church.

Lipsius remarks that notwithstanding the fall of the temple of Artemis, reported in ff. 64 b, 110 b, it remained standing long after the time of John, and was finally destroyed by the Goths in A.D. 262[2].

The litany or hymn in f. 104 a, which was sung or said on the occasion of the Governor's baptism, is especially interesting as a record of some early form of that service.

Lipsius finds Gnostic doctrine in the idea expressed distinctly in the Greek[3] and in the Syriac version, that our Lord is said to have revealed Himself even among the beasts. But in our Arabic text of f. 108 a this may be taken metaphorically, as about men who had the nature of brutes.

Zahn and Fabricius[4] call attention to the fact that the name Byrrhus (Berus or Verus in Greek), f. 107 b, is identical with the name of an Ephesian deacon mentioned in the Epistles of Ignatius[5], who accompanied the writer on a journey through Asia Minor. "No sensible person," says Zahn, "would take this man and the deacon who helped to dig the grave of the Apostle John in the year A.D. 100 for two separate persons." He thinks it impossible that Leucius Charinus, the presumed author of the legend of Prochorus, should have borrowed from Ignatius, or *vice versâ*. We have therefore here an undesigned coincidence. Zahn finds a difficulty in believing that Byrrhus should have been a young deacon in A.D. 100, and in A.D. 138, when perhaps about seventy years old, should not have

[1] *Apostelgeschichten*, vol. I. p. 355.   [2] *Ibid.* p. 519.
[3] Zahn, *Acta Joannis*, p. 246. Bonnet, vol. II. part i. p. 211.
[4] Zahn, *Acta Joannis*, p. CLII; Fabricius, II. 584.
[5] Ignatius, *Ephes.* II.; *Philad.* XI.; *Smyrn.* XII.

should die a less cruel death than Peter, p. 19; and the embassy from Jerusalem, p. 21[1].

The reversed crucifixion of Peter is mentioned by Origen *in Genes.* vol. III. It belongs equally to the Catholic and the Gnostic tradition.

Lipsius thinks that the emphasis laid upon the fraternal unity and complete harmony between the two Apostles, together with the quarrels and discussions between the Jewish Christians and the Gentile ones, place us in the atmosphere of the second century[2]

The account which Paul gives of his own teaching on pp. 12, 13, is certainly quite Apostolic. Peter's explanation on p. 16 strongly resembles the beginning of the Nicene Creed, or rather of an earlier one reported by Irenaeus (*Haer.* I. 10. 1).

Lipsius[3] considers it a mark of high antiquity that the name "Christians" occurs only once in this story; the terms "believers," "those who believed," "the pious" or "devout people" being used to designate them.

He also calls attention[4] to the fact that the name Claudius is given as that of the Emperor to whom the report of Pilate about the crucifixion of our Lord was sent (p. 7). It ought of course to be Tiberius. This story is first mentioned by Tertullian (*Apolog.* 21).

The Church of San Paolo fuori le mura stands near the second milestone on the Via Ostiensis, and the Liber Pontificalis of the year A.D. 530 says that the body of Paul was buried near the place where he was decapitated[5]. But tradition points likewise to the Church and Abbey delle Tre Fontane (ad aquas Salvias), which are two kilometres further out on the same road.

The Church of San Pietro in Montorio on the Janiculum disputes with the great Basilica on the Vatican the honour of standing upon the site of Peter's martyrdom. St Jerome mentions that Peter was buried on the Vatican; no place named Naumachia has been found there. The traditional spot where Simon fell is on the Via Sacra, near the Church of SS. Cosma e Damiano[6].

The Martyrdom of Peter.

This legend is the same as that published in Arabic by Mrs Gibson, in Studia Sinaitica, No. V. pp. ٥٦—٦١, 52—59, under the title of *The*

---

[1] *Apostelgeschichten*, vol. II. part i. pp. 334, 335.
[3] *Ibid.* p. 356.
[5] *Ibid.* p. 399.
[2] *Ibid.* p. 352.
[4] *Ibid.* p. 365.
[6] *Ibid.* p. 417.

Preaching of Peter. The difference between the two texts is too great
to make a collation of one with the other either possible or desirable.
Mrs Gibson's text is from the Sinai Arabic MS. 445, which is dated
A.D. 799, and is therefore probably much older than that from Sin. Arab.
405. The conversation between the Christ and Peter is considerably
shorter in the more ancient text; the father of the leprous girl who finds
Peter is a rich man, not a gate keeper; Peter's meeting with his fellow-
disciples, Thomas, Andrew and John, is not mentioned; the address of
the Emperor's son to Peter is given more fully; and the youth reports
that he has seen the aged Apostle standing before the Throne in Heaven.

The Martyrdom of Paul.

This story, as Lipsius remarks[1], contains traces of Gnostic doctrine.
The Apostle's last prayer being in the Hebrew language, the milk that
issued from his neck, the wonderful light and the sweet scent which were
diffused around it (in the Latin text), and his reappearances before Nero
after death, point in this direction.

It is also attributed to Linus. The Latin text published by Lipsius
and-Bonnet[2] is the same, with considerable differences.

The story of Patricius falling from a window is evidently an imitation
of that of Eutychus as told in Acts xx. 9—12. The statement that Titus
was from Dalmatia is a mere echo of 2 Tim. iv. 10. Lipsius thinks that
the alarm expressed by the citizens lest the armies of Rome should be
weakened by the Emperor's wholesale executions, with the frequent
references to Roman law, and to military habits, point to the author of
this legend being a Roman[3].

Patricius is called Patroclus in the Latin version.

The lacuna at the end of f. 14 b is evidently only that of a few lines.

The Syriac Acts of Judas Thomas.

In reading the text of a palimpsest, it is often impossible to see the
seyyame points on a plural word, or the dot over the pronominal suffix ܗ
which marks the feminine. I have not ventured to insert these where
I did not see them, but in translating I have always assumed that they
exist where they are required by the context.

[1] *Apostelgeschichten*, vol. II. part i. p. 270.   [2] *Acta Apost. Apoc.* vol. I. pp. 23—44.
[3] *Apostelgeschichten*, vol. II. part i. p. 283.

On f. 158 b, col. a, l. 22, p. ١٩٥, Dr Rendel Harris proposes the following reconstruction :

col. *b* col. *a*

[Syriac text, two columns]

In f. 161 b, col. a, l. 18, p. ١٩٧, the last word ought probably to be [Syriac]. But [Syriac] is distinctly the reading of the manuscript. In a transcript from a Berlin MS. of the Sachau collection now in the Cambridge University Library the reading of this passage is :

[Syriac text]

In f. 167 b, col. b, l. 2, p. ٢٠٠, the words [Syriac] have evidently been dropped through *homœoteleuton*, and this points to our MS. being the copy of an older one.

On f. 167 a, col. a, l. 20, p. ٢٠١, [Syriac] is probably a misspelling of [Syriac].

In f. 164 b, col. a, l. 5, p. ٢٠٢, the word [Syriac] was guessed by Dr Wright, for he translates "(we are commanded to do)" Vol. II. p. 219, l. 25. In line 6 of the same column I am somewhat doubtful about [Syriac]. The three final letters may be seen in my photograph, but there is a possibility that the word ought to be [Syriac]. Dr Nestle suggests [Syriac] and this would make excellent sense, but the last letters are distinctly [Syriac], no room being left for a [Syriac]. [Syriac] in col. b, l. 5, is also his conjecture, [Syriac], "mother," in the preceding line, referring to Eve. But my photograph is here, like the sense of the passage, very obscure.

In f. 157 b, col. a, ll. 5, 6, p. ٢٠٤, I read [Syriac], although it is unusual to find a word thus divided between two lines.

On f. 169 a, col. b, l. 11, p. ٢١١, Dr Wright says (Vol. II. p. 270) that perhaps something has been omitted. The "something" is probably ܐܣܟܝܡܐ, which is supplied by our text.

We observe that an adverb such as ܕܟܐܢܐܝܬ in the later text sometimes takes the place of an adjective (ܕܟܐܢܐ) in the earlier one (see f. 157 b, col. b, l. 13, p. ٢٠٤ and f. 154 a, col. a, l. 23, p. ٢١٢). We notice also that the later text is better furnished with those connecting particles which make a sentence dependent on its predecessor. Several instances of this will be found in f. 146 b, col. a and in the first lines of col. b, p. ٢٢٠. The earlier style seems to me to be more in accordance with Semitic usage.

In f. 146 a, p. ٢٢١, my translation differs somewhat from Mr Burkitt's. But I have to thank him for reading ܘܡܕܒܪܘܬܐ, col. b, l. 3, from my photograph.

On f. 159 b, col. a, ll. 7, 8, p. ٢١٦, we find a form which has caused some difficulty to the transcribers of the Old Syriac Gospels from the same manuscript. Here it is ܡܪܐ ܐܠܦܐ. On f. 146 b, col. a, ll. 18, 19, p. ٢٢٠, we have ܒܫܗܪܐ ܠܠܝܐ. And in Mark xiv. 14 ܘܐܡܪܘ ܠܡܪܐ ܒܝܬܐ, Luke xiv. 21 ܗܝܕܝܢ ܪܓܙ ܗܘ ܡܪܐ ܒܝܬܐ. We ought therefore probably to regard it rather as an archaism, than as a mistake in grammar. The correct form ܡܪܗ ܕܒܝܬܐ appears in Luke xiii. 25.

On f. 159 a, col. a, l. 3, p. ٢١٧, Mr Burkitt translates ܗܢܐ ܡܬܚܪܪ "this, (who) is freed." This is certainly better grammar than Dr Wright's "this, who setteth free." But it is not better sense; so I have adhered to the latter rendering.

The variants between our text and Dr Wright's have been caused chiefly by a process of amplification in the case of the latter. But in f. 141 b, col. a, l. 5, p. ٢٠٨, I think that the word ܗܪܟܐ makes ܐܚܪܢܝܬܐ refer to the possessions which the forsaker of earthly things shall find now, in this life, and not to other sayings of Judas. Also on f. 150 a, at the foot of col. b, p. ٢٠٩, the absence of the word ܘܚܡܪܐ points to a communion in one kind, such as we find also described in the Death of John (Cod. Deyr-es-Suriani f. 69 b). ܘܚܡܪܐ is omitted also at this place in the Cambridge transcript, though found in Dr Wright's text. The cup, however, is restored to the laity on fol. 168 b, col. a, l. 10, p. ٢٢٨.

We notice also the addition of the words ܟܕ ܡܙܝܓ "mingled" to Dr Wright's text in the same passage (Wright, p. ܫܟܕ, l. 6). We can hardly argue from the omission of this detail in the older manuscript that the custom of mixing water with the wine is not an ancient one, for it is mentioned by Justin (*Apol.* I. 65, 67) as customary in his day.

It will be interesting to compare these fragments with Dr Bonnet's new edition of the Greek Acts of Thomas.

Are the Acts Gnostic?

In an important and interesting work lately published, *Die alten Petrusakten*, Dr Carl Schmidt, in agreement with Dr Harnack, contests the opinion of Lipsius, Zahn, and James, that these Apocryphal Acts sprang from a Gnostic source. There is, he says, absolutely no trace in them of any teaching about a dual God, or that the God of the Old Testament is not also the God of the New. No Gnostic would have represented Simon Magus, the founder of his sect, as a magician, a cheat and a malefactor (cf. Sin. Arab. 405, p. 18). Dr Schmidt considers that the legends arose in the bosom of the Catholic Church, probably in the reign of Septimius Severus[1], about the beginning of the third century, at a time when Gnostic views, in a hazy form, were widely held, and had not yet taken a shape definite enough to provoke the hostility and condemnation of orthodox Church councils. The proof of this lies in the fact that events related in the legends, especially those connected with the martyrdoms, have now a secure place in the Roman calendar. The name of Leúcius Charinus is a fictitious one; perhaps adopted because a disciple of the Apostle John really bore it; perhaps for the sake of its resemblance to Lucas, the author of the Canonical Acts. The Acts of John is the only one of these legends which can certainly be traced to his pen; the Acts of Peter is a more or less conscious imitation of it; but as the Acts of Andrew, Thomas and Paul (the last of which Dr Zahn has proved to be free from any taint of heresy) came to be included with these two in one volume, the name of Leucius was transferred, through successive transcriptions, to the whole book. The legends arose to satisfy a perfectly legitimate craving of third century Christians, and their condemnation in the eighth century became necessary because of the frequent appeals to their authority which were made by various schools of heretics. The only really Gnostic portion of them is the Hymn which has been inserted in the Syriac Acts of Thomas and is not extant in the fragments from Syr. Sin. 30. Dr Schmidt gives to these legends the very suitable title of "Wahrheit und Dichtung."

---

[1] *Die alten Petrusakten*, p. 102.

Conclusion.

I have endeavoured to give in Index II. a list of those passages which shew how far the authors of these legends were acquainted with the canonical books of Scripture, and this surely bears witness to the wide diffusion of the sacred writings at the time when they came into existence. The list is, I fear, not an exhaustive one, but a glance at the number of passages cited intensifies our wonder that they should be mingled with incidents so grotesque as those narrated on ff. 36—39 of the Deyr-es-Suriani MS. and f. 25^b of Sin. Arab. O. This Index does not include the Syriac fragments of the Acts of Thomas.

We are also surprised to find very little allusion to the mother of our Lord, and none at all to any intercession having been addressed to her, except a manifest interpolation in the Sinai Arabic Codex 539.

I have, in conclusion, to express my gratitude to Professor Seybold of Tübingen, and to my sister, Mrs Margaret Dunlop Gibson, who have both revised my Arabic proofs; to Dr Nestle, of Maulbronn, who has read my Syriac ones; to Dr Rendel Harris, for several valuable suggestions; to Professor Ignazio Guidi, of Rome, for supplying me with two excerpts from the Vatican Arabic Codex 694; also to M. Léon Dorez, of the Bibliothèque Nationale, Paris, and to Mr Cowley of the Bodleian Library, Oxford, for helping me to fill up lacunae.

AGNES SMITH LEWIS.

CASTLE-BRAE,
    CAMBRIDGE.
      February, 1904.

BIBLIOGRAPHY.

MOMBRITIUS, Boninus. Legendarium. *Milan*, 1474.

{ NAUSEA, Friedrich.
{ LAZIUS, Wolfgang. *Cologne*, 1531, *Basle*, 1551. Abdiae Babyloniae primi episcopi
      de historia certaminis apostolici. *Paris*, 1560.

LIPOMANNUS, Aloys. Vitae Sanctorum, 8 vols. *Rome*, 1551–1560.

NEANDER, Michael. Catechesis Martini Lutheri parva graeco-latina. *Basle*, 1567.

SURIUS, Laurentius. Vitae Sanctorum, 6 vols. *Cologne*, 1569 sqq.

BIGNE. Bibliotheca Patrum. *Paris*, 1575.

BARONIUS, Caesar, Cardinal. Annales Ecclesiastici, 12 vols. 1609–1613, 1617–
      1670.

BOLLANDISTS, Acta Sanctorum, 60 vols. 1643 sqq.

FLORENTINI Martyrologium Hieronymianum. *Lucca*, 1688.

TILLEMONT. Mémoires de l'histoire ecclésiastique des six premiers siècles, 16 vols.
      Paris, 1693–1712, and *Brussels*, 10 vols., 1694–1730, *Paris*, 10 vols.,
      1701–1730.

PERIONIUS, Joachim. De rebus gestis et vitis apostolorum.

ITTIG, Thomas. Dissertatio de Pseudepigraphis Christi, Virginis Mariae et
      Apostolorum. *Leipzig*, 1696.

CHUEDENIUS. Pseudo-Novum Testamentum exhibens Pseudo-Evangelia, Acta,
      Epistolas, Apocalypses. *Helmstädt*, 1699.

GRABE, Johann Ernst. Spicilegium Patrum, 2 vols. *Oxford*, 1700.

WEDDERCAMP. Historia saeculi primi fabulis variorum maculata. *Helmstädt*, 1700.

FABRICIUS. Codex Apocryphus Novi Testamenti. *Hamburg*, 1703, 1719.

BEAUSOBRE. Histoire critique de Manichée et du Manichéisme. *Amsterdam*, 1734.

WOOG, Karl Christian. Epistola presbyterorum et diaconorum Achaiae de martyrio
      S. Andreae Apostoli. *Leipzig*, 1747.

MINGARELLI. Aegyptiorum Codicum Reliquiae Venetiis in bibliotheca Naniana
      asservatae. *Bologna*, 1785.

JONES, Jeremiah. A new and full method of settling the canonical authority of the
      New Testament. *London*, 1722, 1798.

KLEUKER. Die Apokryphen des Neuen Testamentes. *Münster*, 1798.

BIRCH, Andreas. Auctarium codicis Apocryphi Fabriciani. *Copenhagen*, 1804.

ZOEGA, George. Catalogus codicum Copticorum in Museo Borgiano, III. 229 sqq.
      Rome, 1810.

THILO, Johann Karl. Acta Thomae. *Leipzig,* 1823. Acta Petri et Pauli. *Halle,* 1837–38.

GRIMM, Jacob. Andreas und Elene. *Cassel,* 1840.

BORBERG. Die apokryphischen Evangelien und Apostelgeschichten. *Stuttgart,* 1841.

TISCHENDORF, Constantin. Acta Apostolorum Apocrypha. *Leipzig,* 1851.

STICHART, Franz Otto. Die kirchliche Legende über die heiligen Apostel. *Leipzig,* 1861.

WRIGHT, William. Apocryphal Acts of the Apostles, 2 vols. *London,* 1871.

MALAN, S. C. The Conflicts of the Holy Apostles. *London,* 1871.

LIPSIUS. Die Quellen der römischen Petrussage. *Kiel,* 1872. Die Simon-Sage. *Leipzig,* 1874.

MÖSINGER. Vita et Martyrium S. Bartholomaei. *Innsbruck,* 1877.

CATARGIAN, Joseph. Ecclesiae Ephesinae de obitu Ioannis apostoli narratio. *Vienna,* 1877.

USENER. Acta Timothei. *Bonn,* 1877.

Apocryphal Acts of the Apostles in Smith and Wace's Dictionary of Christian Biography. *London,* 1877.

HOFMANN, Rudolf. Apocryphen des Neuen Testaments in Herzog's Real-Encyclopädie.

AMPHILOCHIUS, Archimandrite. (Acta Ioannis.) *Moscow,* 1879.

ZAHN, Theodore. Acta Ioannis. *Erlangen,* 1880.

TICHONRAWOW. Denkmäler der apokryphischen Literatur. Old Slavonic.

BONWETSCH. Zeitschrift für Kirchengeschichte, 1882, p. 506 sqq.

LIPSIUS, Richard Adelbert. Die apokryphen Apostelgeschichten, 3 vols. *Brunswick,* 1883–90.

GUTSCHMID, Alfred von. Die Königsnamen in den apokryphen Apostelgeschichten. Rheinisches Museum für Philologie, N. F. XIX. pp. 161–183; 380–401.

GUIDI, Ignazio. Gli Atti Apocrifi degli apostoli nei testi Copti, Arabi ed Etiopici. (Giornale della Società Asiatica Italiana, II. 1888.) Frammenti Copti. *Rome,* 1888.

LEMM, O. von. Mélanges Asiatiques, x. 110 ff. and 148 ff. in the Bulletin de l'Académie Impériale des Sciences, XXXIII. 354 ff. and XXXV. 294 ff. *Petersburg,* 1890–92.

SCHMIDT, Carl. Koptische Apocryphe Apostelacten, I. and II. in the Bulletin de l'Académie Impériale des Sciences, vol. XXXIII. pp. 509–581 (1890) and vol. XXXV. pp. 233–326, 1892. *Ibid.* Apokryphe Koptische Apostelgeschichten und Legenden in Harnack's Geschichte der altchristlichen Litteratur, Part I. pp. 919–922. *Leipzig,* 1893.

JAMES, Dr Montague Rhodes. Apocrypha Anecdota. (Texts and Studies, II. v.) *Cambridge,* 1893, 1897.

{LIPSIUS, Richard Adelbert and
{BONNET, Maximilian. Acta Apostolorum Apocrypha, 2 vols. *Leipzig,* 1891–1903.

GIBSON, Margaret Dunlop. Studia Sinaitica, No. V. *London,* 1896. No. VIII. 1901.

BELL, A. Lives and Legends of the Evangelists, Apostles and other early Saints. *London,* 1901.

BUDGE, E. Wallis. The Contendings of the Apostles. Ethiopic text with an English Translation, 2 vols. *London*, 1901.

EBERSOLT, Jean. Les Actes de S. Jacques et les Actes d'Aquilas. *Paris*, 1902.

BAUMSTARK, Anton. Die Petrus- und Paulusacten in der litterarischen Ueber-lieferung der syrischen Kirche. *Leipzig*, 1902.

HEADLAM, A. C. Simon Magus, in Hastings' Bible Dictionary, vol. IV. pp. 519–527. *Edinburgh*, 1902.

HARRIS, J. Rendel. The Dioscuri in Christian Literature. *London*, 1903.

SCHMIDT, Carl. Die alten Petrusakten im Zusammenhang der apokryphen Apostelliteratur. (Texte und Untersuchungen, vol. XXIV.) *Leipzig*, 1903. Acta Pauli, aus der Heidelberger Koptischen Papyrus-Hand-schrift Nr 1. *Leipzig*, 1904.

FICKER, G. Die Petrusakten. *Leipzig*, 1903.

HOFFMANN, G. Zwei Hymnen der Thomasakten. (Zeitschrift für die Neutesta-mentliche Wissenschaft, *Giessen*, 1903, vol. II.)

THE PREACHING OF ANDREW THE BLESSED DISCIPLE AMONGST THE CITIES OF THE KURDS.

In the name of God, the Creator, the Living, the Speaking. The Preaching
of Andrew the Blessed Disciple—disciple of Jesus the Christ, which took place
in the cities of the Kurds, and at Lydda. In the peace of the Lord. Amen!

And when the disciples went out into the world to preach the Gospel
of the Kingdom of Heaven, the Lord appeared unto them, and spake unto
them, saying thus: " Peace be unto you, O my brethren, and my beloved!
heirs of the Kingdom. Know that I will never separate myself from you,
I will strengthen you." And He turned to Matthias and commanded him
to go to the city of the Cannibals; and Andrew his brother was to pass
to Lydda to preach in it, he and his disciple Philemon, the son of Philip;
" for I have many people in it whom I have chosen."

And the disciples replied, saying, " Be Thou with us, O Lord! in
every place whither Thou hast commanded us to go."

And the Lord gave them [the salutation of] peace, and ascended
to Heaven whilst they were looking at Him. Thereafter Peter went
to the place which the Lord had commanded him [to go to]. And
Matthias asked Andrew if he would allow his disciple Rufus and
Alexander to go with him to Tintarān. But Andrew and Philemon went
to Lydda. Now Philemon had a melodious voice, there was none like it,
and he had learned wisdom by the strength of the Holy Spirit which
rested upon him; and there was not one among the disciples superior
to him in wisdom, except Peter and John.

And when the disciples were gathered together, they chose these
two men to stand and recite the praises [of God] that [men] might hear
the sweetness of their voices. And Andrew went to Lydda, he and
Philemon; for one half of the city had believed through the instrumen-
tality of Peter[1], and the other half remained unbelievers. And Andrew

---

[1] Cf. Acts ix. 35.

came to the church of the Nazarenes which was in Lydda; and they went out to meet him with branches of trees in their hands, rejoicing; and he went into the church and sat down on the Bishop's chair; and he commanded, Philemon to mount into the pulpit, and recite the hymn Alleluia, and the congregation repeated it after him.

And when the priests of the heathen heard the voice of the multitude, they said one to the other, "What is going on in the city to-day?" [The people] answered them, "A disciple of Jesus the Christ is in the church of the Nazarenes, teaching them and commanding them to reject the gods, and not to appear in the temple." And they took their swords and appeared in the church that they might listen, [so that] if they [the Christians] should insult their gods they might kill them. And they heard the sweetness of Philemon's voice reading and saying thus: "The gods of the nations are gold and silver, the work of men's hands. Having eyes, they see not; and ears, they hear not; and noses, they smell not; and feet, they walk not. They have mouths, and they speak not; and like unto them are they who worship them."

And when the priests heard things like this in the speech of Philemon, and the sweetness of his voice, they wept and went into the church: and they embraced Philemon's feet. And when the congregation saw them, they said unto Andrew, "O our father! these are some of the temple-priests." And Andrew made a sign to the congregation to be silent until they had finished the praises, for they were greatly afraid of them, when they saw that they had swords; and they were silent till the song of praise was finished.

And Andrew rose first and prayed for them. And when he had concluded his prayer he said to the temple-priests, "Sit down." And when they were seated, he said: "O my children! whom I would embrace, whom I would have begotten [again], how have ye come to-day into this church? Every day, when the Nazarenes pass you, ye draw away your garments lest ye should touch theirs." The company of the priests answered him, saying, "O our father Andrew! we will tell thee the truth. When we heard that thou wert come into this city to teach, and we listened to the voices of the multitude, we asked what was going on in the church of the Nazarenes to-day. And they told us that thou wert come to it; and we agreed one with the other, fifty thousand men of us: and we went as thou hast seen us to hear if they would insult our gods; that we might kill every man in the church. And now we have been present as thou seest us. And when we heard the sweetness of this youth's voice, our hearts

f. 19b

Ps. cxv.
4—8

Gal. iv. 19

f. 20a

were turned towards him, and we came unto thee. We ask thee, O disciple! that thou wouldst give us to-day what thou hast given to this congregation: that we may be worthy to approach thy God; and we shall be glad if we are not separated from this youth."

And when Andrew knew this he kissed the head of Philemon, saying, "Truly thou art he about whom the Holy Spirit spake aforetime, that a sweet voice shall gather the multitude to it[self]. Truly it is meet that thou shouldest be called a saviour of souls. As the Lord hath changed our names and made others for us, so is it with thee also." f. 20 b

And when Andrew saw the congregation, they thronged him, [and] he commanded them to go to a wide place, and they went to the sea-shore. Andrew answered and said to the believers, "Whoso amongst you desireth [to please] God, let him come and be bathed by my hand." And the multitude came, and he baptized them all in the name of the Father, and of the Son, and of the Holy Ghost, the One God. And the number of those who were baptized was four thousand and four hundred souls. And he baptized the fifty priests also.

After this Satan came to the town [and] found two young men playing. One of them was the son of John, sheikh of the city, and the other was the son of a nobleman of the city. And whilst they were playing, the young man, the son of John, struck the other a blow, [and] he straightway fell down dead. And his father laid hold of John and said unto him, "Deliver to me thy child that I may slay him as he slew my child. And if not, I will deliver thee up to Rufus the Governor, that he may kill thee in the stead of my son whom thy son hath slain."

And John wept with a great weeping in the presence of the crowd, and the crowd said unto him: "If money is desired of thee, we would pay it for thee, but it is thy life that is required." John said unto them: "I desire not gold, from you, nor silver, but that one of you should give a pledge for f. 21 a my presence until I go to Andrew in Lydda, that he may appear and raise him from the dead."

And the multitude gave a pledge to the father of the young man until John should go to Lydda to Andrew the Apostle of Jesus the Christ, so that he might come and make his son alive for him. And he replied to their speech, and sat down and mourned for his son. And John went to Andrew and found him baptizing the multitude. And he fell down and did obeisance unto him and said, "Have pity on my great age, and let me not die." And Andrew raised him up and said unto him: "Fear God, and be not afraid, tell me all that hath befallen thee." And he told him his misfortune. And Andrew replied to him: "I cannot go with thee at this time, because of this multitude which I am baptizing; but take Philemon with thee, and he will raise the dead man." And he sent Philemon with him that he might raise him from amongst the dead. And the two went out towards the city. And as they were journeying, Satan took the likeness of an old man, and went to the Governor of the city, and cried unto him, saying: "O Rufus! art thou sitting, and murdered people are thrown down in the streets of the city? Rise, and seek the murderer; and if not, lo! I appeal and go to the king, and will tell him of it."

And when Rufus heard this speech, he arose in great wrath and commanded them to saddle his horse, and he rode, being very angry.

f. 21 b   And when the people of the city heard this, not one of them remained in it, save the dead man. Then John and Philemon approached, [coming] from Andrew, and they found the multitude outside of the city. And they said unto John, "Thou hast been long in coming, and we were afraid, and lo! the Governor has made captive the city."

And John wept, saying, "Alas! what shall I do? the dead one is not buried." Philemon replied: "Weep not, I will go and raise him." The multitude said unto him: "Do not go into the city, that the Governor slay thee not." Philemon said unto them: "I am not able to oppose my master; nay, I will go and I will raise him up; as my teacher commanded. Sit ye down in your places, and if ye hear that I have been killed, send to my master, that he may appear and raise me up, me and the dead man."

And Philemon entered the city, and went to [the place] where the Governor was, and cried, saying, "O Rufus! thou dost rule this city to lay it waste. Where are the people of the city? they did not meet thee at thy entrance into it." And the Governor heard his speech, and [he commanded] his soldiers to lay hold of him and hang him in the place of punishment. And he said unto them, "Perhaps this is he who hath slain the dead man, and therefore his blood will not leave him alone." And the soldiers laid hold of him, and set him up in the place of punishment. And Philemon replied: "O Rufus the Governor!

f. 22 a do not torture me, for I am an infant, I have not sinned, and I do not deserve a condemnation. I am like our father Adam, when he was in Paradise, before Eve came out of his side. Where is my master Andrew? that he may see what is being done to his disciple. Is there no pity in thy heart, O thou Governor! when thou seest that I am an infant? Hast thou no child? that ye may have mercy on me? and as thou lovest thy son, so doth my father love me."

And he turned his face towards the soldiers, and said unto them: "Is there no merciful man amongst you, to have pity on me, and to go to Lydda, to my master Andrew, and tell him that his disciple has been set up for torture?"

And when the soldiers heard this, they wept because of the sweetness of his speech. He said also: "Is there no bird in this city which I could send to Lydda to my master Andrew? that he may come and that I may see him before I die." And when he had said this, many birds assembled about him and they talked to him as they did to Noah of old. And they said unto him: "Here we are, which of us dost thou wish to send?" And a little sparrow came near him and said, "I am lighter in body than these, I will go, and will bring thy master to thee." Philemon said unto him: "Thou art a fornicator, thou wilt not hasten [thy] return, for if thou meet a hen of thy kind thou wilt stop with her, and wilt not hasten [thy] return." And the raven arose and said unto him: "I will go." Philemon f. 22 b said unto him: "The first time that thou wast sent thou didst not return with thy report to Noah who had sent thee, and I shall not send thee."

And he called the dove, and said unto her, "O [thou of] honourable race! whom God hath called gentle beyond all other birds, who didst come with the news to Noah when he was in the ship, at the time of the Flood, and the Just One blessed her, go to Lydda, to my master Andrew and say unto him: 'Come and see thy disciple Philemon, for he is set up for torture.'" And the dove answered him, saying, "Be strong, lo! Andrew will come; he is here, and he will hear thy speech."

And when Rufus heard it, he arose in haste and loosed Philemon with his own hands from the torture and said unto him: "Truly if there were ten murdered men in this city I would leave off enquiring about them for thy sake." And when Satan knew that Rufus had believed, he summoned his hosts, and said unto them: "Rufus has believed, and he is our friend and all the city disbelieve in us. And I command you that one of you shall go to the house of Rufus, and shall lay hold of his wife that she may become like a mad woman, with no sense in her: and incite her to attack her children, and kill them." And straightway Satan did what Iblîs had commanded, and went to the house of the Governor, and made his wife mad and incited her to kill her children." f. 23 a

And when her servants knew what she had done, they came together and laid hold of her, and put her into a strong place, and they sent to their master and told him of her state, and of the murder of her children. And the Governor said unto those who were about him: "If the house had fallen upon them and all who were in the court were dead, I would not forsake this boy." And Rufus the Governor returned to Philemon, and said unto him: "O my lord! hast thou not heard what this messenger saith? I ask thee to go with me to my abode, and if thou wilt not go I will not go." Philemon replied to him: "Let us finish what we are doing here, and after that we will go to the house."

And Philemon called the dove, and said unto her: "Go to the house of Rufus, and say to those in his abode: 'Do nothing in my house, till I am present.'" And the dove went, and brought the message. And when the crowd heard the dove speaking, they wondered greatly.

And Philemon asked the Governor to send and bring the people of the city, that he might raise the dead man. And the Governor sent his soldiers to bring the multitude. And when they had approached, they went together to the place of the dead man. And they found Andrew within the city. Philemon said unto him: "Come, O my master! that thou mayest raise the dead." Andrew said unto him: "Truly it is thou who shalt raise him."

f. 23 b   And Philemon went to where the dead man was, and knelt upon his knees, and entreated the Lord thus:

"Hearken unto me, O Lord our God! the Good Shepherd, who will not leave us as a pledge in the hand of the Enemy, but has delivered us by His pure blood. Hearken unto me, I am thy servant, I ask from the abundance of Thy mercy that my prayer may be heard; and that this dead man may arise in the power of Thy name." Then he lifted up his head, and stood, and cried with a loud voice: "In the name of Jesus the Christ, the Nazarene, arise, O dead man!" And straightway the dead man arose.

And when the crowd saw the dead man standing alive their faith in the Lord Jesus the Christ increased greatly. And Philemon told Andrew the state of the Governor's wife and her deed to his children. And everyone who was present went with Andrew and Philemon to the dwelling of Rufus: and the widows and the orphans followed them, hoping that they would receive alms. And when Andrew went to the Governor's house, he found his son, and round him a great company weeping for him; and the dove standing at his head. And Andrew said unto the dove, "What age art thou?" She said unto him, "Sixty years." Andrew said unto her, "Since thou hast hearkened to the voice of Philemon my disciple,

go out into the desert, and thou shalt be allowed to go free from the f. 24 a
service of the people of the world; no man amongst men shall have
power over thee." And she went out into the desert as he had commanded her.

And Andrew called the dead man, saying: ".In the name of Jesus
the Christ who has sent us into the world to preach in His holy name;
arise, live." And straightway the dead man arose, and did obeisance
before Andrew. And he raised him up, and said unto him: "Believe in
God, O my son!" And he replied, "I have believed: and I ask thee,
O my father Andrew! if thou wilt allow me to tell what I have seen?"

He said unto him, "Speak." And the boy said unto his father, "O my
father! if thou wouldest give the half of what thou possessest to the orphans
and to the widows and the poor. Wilt thou not repay something of
what is fitting for the gift of God which abides with thee? For what
thou hast given to the needy, thou hast given it for thyself. Know,
O father! in the hour when my mother rose up against me and slew
me there was a great good in it for us. For people came to me who had
wings like the eagles; and they took my soul to a place which is called
Gehenna. And I looked at a large house being built with sulphur and
pitch. And the number of the builders was thirty; and they had great f. 24 b
burning lamps. And [some people] called out commanding them about
the building. 'How long shall we build this house? We are commanded to
set it on fire with these lamps.' He said unto them: 'Will ye burn it
before its building is finished? for by the time that its owner dies
then you shall burn it.' Said the angel who had charge of my soul,
'Hast thou seen these things?' I said unto him, Yea,' and I asked him
for whom this house was built, and why it was built with sulphur and
pitch. And he said unto me, 'These are the sins of thy father which he
hath committed; and it will be built until the time when he shall die.
They will toss him into it.'

"And when I heard these things about thee, I wept sore and I said:
'Woe is me! how shall I let my father know the like of this?' And
while I was weeping, he who was walking with me said unto me,
'Weep not.' And when he had spoken, he approached with an aged
man, and a hundred men followed him, and a young man[1] whose
age was twelve years, very beautiful in appearance, and he conversed
with the master of the builders in a speech which I did not understand.
And thereafter he commanded that the house should be pulled down;

---

[1] Cod. + followed him.

and he commanded the angel who was walking with me to bring me out to a very wide place. And another man came with a golden reed in his hand of three colours, and he laid the foundations of a large house in thy name, the height of each of its walls was a hundred reeds at the further end; and its breadth and its length the same.

f. 25 a

"And the angel said unto him: 'Are the hundred reeds finished?' The master of the building replied: 'It is not yet finished; for the wheat has not come into the storehouse, and when it arrives we will finish it.'"

Said Andrew to Rufus, "Hear what thy child says; for if a stranger had spoken like this, thou wouldst not have believed it; but he is thy son." Rufus replied: "Andrew, I ask thee, O thou true man, that thou wouldest take all that belongs to me, and divide it amongst the poor and the needy." And Andrew said unto him: "Arise, take this my disciple to thy house, that he may cure thy wife."

And Philemon did as Andrew had commanded, and he [Rufus] went to his dwelling, he and Philemon. And he found his wife standing, passive as a statue, her hand holding a black man by the hair; and he was running away from her hands, and she would not let him go. And he took hold of her right hand, and came with her to where Andrew was; she holding the black man with her left hand. And when the multitude saw the black man they were greatly agitated, and they cried out and became like a flock of sheep when the wolf has come into their midst.

f. 25 b

And Andrew said unto them: "Fear not, come near to me and let your hearts be strong until we learn who he is." And Andrew commanded [her] to let him go, and made the sign of the cross in her face. And he laid his hand upon her head, and said: "In the name of Jesus the Nazarene, Whose name I preach, let thy senses be silent, and let thy reason return." And she became quiet and sat down before the disciple. And the disciple turned to the negro, and said unto him: "What is thy name? and [what] is the reason that this woman hath clung to thee?" The negro said unto him: "I will be true with thee. When a strong youth dwelleth with a weak king and he maketh war with him, and the strong youth is victorious in the war, the victory belongeth not to him, but to the king. Thus I have great power amongst the devils, and behold, I sojourn in thy house."

And Andrew said unto him: "What shall I say about thee, O thou unclean one? and thy wicked character? for the time of prayer is come. But thou shalt be hung up outside the city to-morrow." And Andrew began his prayer, and finished it; and gave of the holy mysteries to the believers. And he sent them away in peace.

And when the morrow was come, the multitude were assembled. And Andrew was present, and called to the negro, saying: "I will expose thee, O thou foul unclean negro! thou unjust spirit, I will reveal thy state to this f. 26 a multitude that they may all see thee." The negro answered him: "Thou art not he who shall judge me, or do this thing to me. Yet my deeds are evil, for I have lost my glory, and have ruined my honour." Andrew said unto him: "O unclean one! unjust one! hadst thou any honour?" He said unto him: "Thou sayest that I am black, unjust. Dost thou not know my nature, whence it is? and if it be thy will to show this multitude who I am, woe is me! what will save me from this [plight] in which I am?" And he began to call on the names of the powers in the height. Andrew said unto him: "Be quiet, and refrain from speaking, except thou sayest to this multitude who thou art." He replied saying: "I am one of the two hundred angels who were sent to see the earth. And when we had seen it, we disturbed it, we rebelled; and we did not return to Him who had sent us. And my name is Māgānā." He answered him: "Thy wound is great, and thy grief, and thy shame shall return upon thee. And thine arrogance shall be thy ruin. In the name of the Lord Jesus the Christ, flee to Gehenna, and do not show thyself again for ever." And from that hour no person has ever seen him.

And Rufus the Governor said unto Andrew: "Dost thou command f. 26 b me to distribute all my property to the poor and needy?" And he brought all his goods to Andrew and he distributed it as he had said. And the news reached the king that Rufus the Governor had distributed his property amongst the poor, and had resigned his office, and he doth not oversee any of the citizens nor judge between them, but saith "Would that I could judge mine own self! for what I have done ignorantly." And when Seleucus, the vizier of the king, saw that the king desired his ruin and to kill him, he entreated him to desist from it. And he said unto him: "If he hath gone with the good man who is one of the servants of God, who worketh miracles, [who is] from the cities of the Hebrews, thou canst do nothing against him. But write to him that if he be a devotee of this faith, he shall deliver up all his goods that they may be in the king's treasury." And he wrote letters and they were sent to Rufus the Governor; and he was not found in his dwelling; and messengers were sent to where he was with Andrew, who was teaching a new learning, not the learning of the Romans. And they appeared in the street of the city; and they found

Andrew and Rufus; and he was casting a devil out of a man who had
been possessed by it for seventy years. And when the envoys of the king
saw the wonder, they believed in God and they delivered up the letters to
Rufus, and he read them.

And when he heard that all his goods were taken to the king's
treasury, Andrew laughed and said to Rufus: "Is thy heart sad because
the king is taking all thy property?" Rufus answered him: "Thou
knowest how my heart is, and that I will not separate from thee, to
whatsoever place thou mayest go. What need have I of the things
that perish? From destruction they are gathered; [and] unto it is their
return." Andrew said unto him: "All the waters return unto the sea,
and it is not filled, and everything [which is put] into the stomach goeth
to the dust."

And while Andrew was conversing with Rufus, a voice called him,
commanding him to dismiss the assembly, and to go into the city
which was before him; knowing that in it there was a great community
for him, and a noble and glorious service. And afterwards he returned
to this city; and it was revealed to him that there would be toil in it for
him, and great persecution from the king; because of the messengers
who had believed: "and let your hearts be strengthened by My name, and
you shall learn that I am with you, and dwell within you."

And Andrew blessed the multitude, saying: "May the Lord make
you firm in the right faith, you and your sons and your daughters to the
uttermost end, Amen." The multitude answered, "Go in peace; but do
not prolong [thine absence] from us; for we have heard the voice calling
thee that great persecution from the king shall come upon this city,
because of the messengers who have believed." And Andrew strengthened
their hearts and said: "Fear not; the Lord, in Whom ye have believed,
is strong, and He hath power to keep it from you." And when he had
said this he went forth away from them in peace.

Praise be to God, always and for ever.

f. 27 a

Eccles. i. 7
Mt. xv. 17
Mk. vii. 19

f. 27 b

THE ACTS OF ANDREW AND BARTHOLOMEW.

The Acts of the Disciples Andrew and Bartholomew, which they did in the city of Barbaros, after their return from the country of the Oases; in the peace of the Lord Jesus the Christ. Amen.

After the Resurrection of our Lord Jesus the Christ from amongst the dead—He not ceasing to be King over the heaven and the earth—He appeared unto Bartholomew in the city of the Gentiles, in the regions of Mâctarân, which is the city of Ghâryanûs. And He said unto him; "Peace be unto thee, O Bartholomew, and love, and victory, in every place where thou shalt dwell. Fear not; for he who worketh is worthy of reward, and layeth up for himself everlasting life. Ye are the trusty reapers who reap the field of their Lord; and when ye go out of this period of time, ye shall f. 28 a receive your wages. Arise, O my chosen Bartholomew! go to the city of El-Barbar. Preach the Gospel in it; and thou shalt teach the way of salvation; that they may leave off their wicked works and the service of idols; and repent, that they may inherit everlasting life. Behold, I will tell thee beforehand what shall come upon thee in this city. Before thou shalt enter it thy body shall be burnt with fire three times. Thou shalt be crucified many times; thy body shall be sawn asunder with saws; thou shalt be thrown to the wild beasts that they may eat thee. Thy feet shall be tied with stones, and thou shalt be thrown into the sea. But take heed lest thou fear; rather be strong; thou art the conqueror; no one can prevail over thee. Be patient, O my chosen one! and remember what the tribe of the Jews did unto Me; these wicked things which they did unto Me, when I was hanging upon the Cross. And I did not recompense them, for I am a merciful Lord. I forgive the sins of those who return unto Me; and I will accept their repentance. Behold, I will direct Andrew towards thee; he shall bring thee to this city; and many mighty deeds and wonders shall be shown by you; and many people shall believe by means of you." And when the Lord had finished His speech to Bartholomew, He gave him [the salutation of] peace, and ascended to Heaven in glory. And f. 28 b Bartholomew turned towards the city unto which the Lord had commanded him to go.

And the Lord appeared unto Andrew at midnight in the town where he was; and commanded him to go to the town of Ghâryanûs to Bartholomew, and they should go to the city of Barbaros and preach in

it the tidings of the Gospel "which I have given them, that they may leave off the evil of their deeds and their worship of idols, and repent, so that they may inherit everlasting life. And beware lest thou be alarmed by them, but increase [thy] patience, and use long-suffering. Remember that I am thy Master and thy Lord—thou knowest all the pains that came upon Me from the Jews; and I did not requite them for what they did unto Me, but I was long-suffering with them, that they might be saved from their sins. And fear not now, O my child, and let not thy spirit be oppressed; be patient, until thou shalt have turned them from error to faith by the greatness of thy patience with them. But I will send you a man fearful in appearance like the face of a dog. And through fear of him they will believe; and through your speech he will follow you, and will become your disciple all the days of your preaching the Gospel. And when the people of Barbaros have believed, take him out with you to the city of El Betas, and they also shall believe through the number of the
f. 29 a wonders and the mighty deeds which shall take place through you." And when the Lord had finished His commandments to Andrew He ascended into Heaven in glory.

And on the morrow Andrew arose, and his two disciples Rufus and Alexander; [and] they went out of the city in which they were, desiring to go to the city of Ghâryanûs, to Bartholomew, that they might go together to the city of Barbaros, and El Betas, that they might preach in them the good tidings of the Holy Gospel, as the Lord had commanded. And when they arrived at the sea, they did not find a boat to convey them. And Andrew was greatly alarmed and anxious; and they stood on the shore of the sea for three hours of the day. And Andrew said unto his disciples, "Arise, O my brethren, let us stretch out our hands unto God, and entreat him to make our way easy. For I believe that He will not forsake us." And they stood together and prayed a prayer in Hebrew; and when they had finished the prayer, they sat down on the shore of the sea beneath a tree, and sleep overcame them, and they slept. And God permitted a large fish to come up out of the sea; and it opened its mouth and swallowed Andrew and his two disciples, whilst they were asleep: and they were not aware of it. And they remained in its inside for three days and three nights, and it journeyed with them by the will of God and threw them out outside the harbour of the city of Ghâryanûs, at a distance of
f. 29 b forty days' journey before it arrived [there] and they awoke and were not aware of it. And Andrew said unto his two disciples, "O my brethren! how long shall we remain, and no boat come towards us to convey us

to the city of Ghâryanûs? and my spirit is oppressed." And he spake thus:
"Was it not thou, O Lord! Who didst appear unto me and didst command
me to journey to the city of Ghâryanûs?" And he said unto his two disciples,
"Return to the city until the Lord permit us to go, and direct a boat
towards us that will carry us." They said unto him: "Let it be as He
willeth." And while he was talking with them, Rufus, one of the two
disciples, looked, and lo! a ship approached in the midst of the sea. And
he told it to Andrew his master. And he rejoiced at it with great joy.
And they all arose to welcome it. And when it reached the shore, they
asked the owner of the ship, "Where dost thou wish [to go?]" But the
Lord had made for them a spiritual ship: and in it there were sailors and
a captain of the boat, before it came unto them. And Andrew arose and
welcomed the boat, and gave a greeting of peace to the captain: "The
Lord be with thee, O thou good captain of the ship!" The Lord Jesus
the Christ, who was like the captain of the boat, replied unto him: "On
thee be the peace of the Lord, O thou beloved brother!"   f. 30 a

Andrew said unto him: "To what town art thou going?" The man,
who was our Lord Jesus the Christ, replied unto him: "By the will of God,
to the city of El-Barbar." Andrew said unto him: "O thou good man, hast
thou not lost thy way in the sea? this is the city of El-Barbar, thou art
in it." He replied unto him: "This is not the city of El-Barbar: this is
the city of Ghâryanûs, and this is the third day since I arrived at it."

And while they were continuing the conversation men came from
Macedonia, seeking [to go to] the city of Ghâryanûs, directed to Bartholomew, that he might go with them and cast out a devil with which
the wife of the King of Macedonia was possessed. And they saw the
Lord and Andrew on the shore of the sea. And he said: "What is this
city?" The men replied unto him: "This is the city of Ghâryanûs." He
replied unto them: "What is the reason of your presence in it?" They
said: "The chief of the city hath sent us to Bartholomew, that he may go
with us to Macedonia [and] cast out a devil by which his wife is possessed."
And the astonishment of Andrew increased; and the men went into the
city, and they remained only for a little, until they came, and Bartholomew
with them. And when Bartholomew and the men arrived at the ship and   f. 30 b
saw the Saviour sitting in it, they thought that it was he who conveyed
people over to Macedonia. He [Jesus] replied unto them, saying: "We want
to go to the district of Barbaros, but go ye to those men who are sitting
under the tree, perhaps they are the ferry-men." And Bartholomew
went to the tree; and he saw Andrew and his two disciples sitting. And

when Andrew saw him, he hastened to meet him; and he kissed him
and said unto him: "Whence comest thou? and what city is this?"
Bartholomew said unto him: "This is the city of Ghâryanûs, which came
out as my lot that I should preach in it." And Andrew was greatly
astonished, and said unto Bartholomew: "What thanks and what praise
shall my tongue pay to the noble Lord, who hath done this great deed
unto me, and hath brought me to this far-off city in one night; and hath
brought me and thee together that I might go to the city of Barbaros and
El Betas, that we may preach in them the good news of the Gospel." Then
the Lord came from the ship, and they asked what would be their fare
to the coast of Macedonia, because the wife of the chief had assembled to
herself the poor and needy of the city to give them alms; and whilst she
f. 31 a   was among them, a wicked spirit took possession of her; and she brought
together and stoned with stones every one who was in her house. "And
the chief laid hold of her and put her into a strong place; and he hath
sent us to this city, to Bartholomew, a disciple of the Lord, that he may
come and cast the devil out of her." The Lord said unto Andrew:
"Every man who forsaketh what is in this world, and followeth the Lord
Jesus and becometh His disciple, he shall cast out devils like you."
Andrew said unto him: "Truly it is so, and if he saith to this mountain
ırk xl. 23   'Be removed,' it shall indeed be removed."

The Lord said: "And if I renounce this world with all that is in it, and
carry my cross, shall I be able to cast out this devil from this woman?"
Andrew said unto him: "The Holy Ghost the Teacher, hath not rested
upon thee; but sell this boat, and distribute its price among the poor, and
the widows, and the orphans, and follow us to any place whither we are
going. Thou shalt do whatsoever we do." The Lord said in answer:
"Arise, and let us entreat in the name of Jesus that each one of us may do
his miracle."

And Andrew stood and stretched out his hands, and prayed thus:
saying, "In the name of our Lord Jesus the Christ, transport me, O thou
f. 31 b   sea, and every one who is with me here, and make us reach the coast of
Macedonia." And straightway the water of the sea overflowed; and it
came to where they were, and it circled round them, they being in the
midst of it like a boat, and it made them reach the shore. And the
multitude said unto Andrew: "Truly thou art servant to a good Lord."
And the envoys did obeisance unto him, and they said: "There is no God
but thy God."

And Bartholomew arose [and] prayed thus, saying in his speech:

"O my Lord and my God, Jesus the Christ! send Thy good angel to the abode of the chief in Macedonia; and may he cast the devil out of the woman and bring her to us before we arrive at the city." And Michael came down from heaven at that moment, and entered the chief's house. And he took the woman and her husband and the people of her household, and came with them to the sea, where the disciples and the Lord were. And when the devil saw the Lord Jesus, he wished to cry out, and let the crowd know; but [the Lord] rebuked him and commanded him not to speak about that, but to come out of the woman.

Bartholomew said unto Andrew, "This woman in whom there is a devil, rise thou, and cure her in the name of the Lord." He replied unto him: "Do thou cure her." He said unto him: "Arise, lay thy hand upon me, and bless me, and I will do according to what thou hast commanded me." f. 32 a Andrew said unto him: "The Lord, that sweet name in which all blessings are completed, bless us all together."

And Bartholomew arose and drew nigh to the woman, and he said unto the bad spirit: "In the name of the Lord Jesus the Christ: come out of this woman, and get thee down into the depths of the sea until the day when the Lord shall pass judgment upon thee and thy father Satan, and do not return to her for ever." And immediately the woman was made whole and she arose and did obeisance to the disciples, she and her husband, and all her household, saying: "There is no God but Thee, O Jesus the Christ, the Son of the Living, the Eternal God, Lord of Heaven and earth." And the disciples blessed them, and the woman asked them: "If I have found grace with you, come with me to the city, and rest in the house of your servant." And she sent on her servants before her to arrange the dwelling.

Then the Lord said: "I also will do a miracle in the name of your God." Then He said: "In the name of Jesus the Christ, let the wind carry me and Andrew, and Bartholomew, and their disciples, and make us reach [the place] whither they desire [to go]" And straightway the disciples received shining wings, and they arrived at the city of Barbaros.

And our Lord Jesus the Christ went before them; and they knew f. 32 b not that it was the Lord. And they halted upon the top of the theatre which belonged to the city where the crowd was assembled. And that day was the festival of the idol which the people of the city worshipped; and they were all together eating and drinking and rejoicing.

And when the crowd saw the disciples standing upon the theatre they were greatly amazed. And Gallion the Governor was not present;

but the people were waiting for him. And Andrew said: "Tell me who thou art, and [what is] thy faith by which thou hast said this." And the Lord smiled and said unto him: "Were not your hearts heavy[1]? Open your eyes, and know that I am He." And He appeared unto them with the countenance which they knew. And He said unto them: "Be strong and brave, O my holy disciples! I will dwell with you wheresoever ye are. I commanded the whale to snatch you away whilst you were asleep; and ye did not know it until it made you arrive at the coast of the city of Barbaros. Be ye patient and long-suffering with the great people which is in this city, for they will not all believe quickly, but by many signs which shall be [done] by you." And He gave them [the greeting of] peace, and revealed Himself, going up to Heaven in great glory.

And lo! the disciples were standing on the top of the theatre, and all the crowd gazing at them and saying:

f. 33 a   "How are these people at such a great height?" And some of them said: "These are the gods of this city; they wish to do wonderful things. Or the priests have neglected them, and they are angry, and wish to go out of the city; but let us tell the Governor speedily about their affair." And behold! whilst they were talking, Gallion, the king, drew nigh, riding, and all his army with him. And he sat down upon his seat; and the crowd appealed to him. And he rebuked them, thinking that the thing had taken place in the temple. And they said unto him: "Lift up thine eyes[2] in the direction of the gods; they wish to go forth from the city. Inquire about this, lest the priests have diminished their service. And if they go out of our city our foes will conquer us, and slay us, and there will be none to help us."

And the Governor commanded the priests to be brought, and that the gods should be present. And they put on their finest raiment. And they carried the four idols, and brought them to the theatre; and their trumpets in their hands, till they had seated them according to their rank. And when the crowd saw them they lifted up their voices, and gave them glory: and it was on the day of their festival. And when the disciples saw that the crowd which was in the city had gone into the theatre they came down on that day from the height.

f. 33 b   And when the multitude saw them they laid hold of them, and brought them into the presence of the Governor. And the Governor asked them, "Who are ye? O ye men!" Andrew answered him: "We are disciples

---

[1] Luke xxiv. 32. This is the reading of the Old Syriac version; and of the Sahidic.
[2] Literally "thy sight."

of a good Lord; his name is Jesus." Some of the multitude said: "These are the twelve wizards who journey among the cities, and separate women from their husbands. Put them away from us, lest they should bewitch us, and separate us from our wives and our children."

The Governor said to the crowd: "Be patient, and I will go up; and do not make a disturbance until I have proved them with questions." And he said unto the disciples: "If your God be God in truth, doing what He will, do a sign or a miracle before me, that I may know the truth of your speech."

And Andrew went near to where the idols were; and he commanded the crowd to be silent. And they held their peace. And he cried with a loud voice to the idols: "Are ye gods? as this multitude thinks about you?"

Loud voices from them replied unto him, saying: "We are no gods, but false things, the work of men's hands, they deceive by means of us." He replied to them: "Thus saith the Lord Jesus the Christ, the Son of the Living God, King of all kings, Go up to the top of this theatre until I command you to come down to Gehenna." And immediately they went up.

And Andrew said unto the multitude: "If they were gods and if they f. 34 a had power, and hearkened to their priests, they would return and remain in their places." And when the multitude saw that, they were greatly ashamed; and the Governor said unto the priests: "Call on your gods, that they may return and remain in their places." And the priests multiplied their entreaties to their gods that they should come down; but they moved not from their places. And the devils who dwelt in them spake by their mouths: "O people of the city! if ye lay not hold of these men and burn their bodies with fire, we will go out from this city. Hearken not unto the speech of these seditious men, who have turned the world upside down. And if we go forth from amongst you, the city will be laid waste. And do not receive their words."

And when the multitude had heard that from the devils, they were very angry, and they took stones and stoned the disciples. And the Governor commanded that they should bind the disciples with chains of iron, and they hung them upon the gallows[1] to burn them in the fire in the presence of their idols. And straightway an angel of the Lord came down and rescued them from their hands, and loosed them from the chains. And the devils returned the speech: "Not thus is it fitting

---

[1] Literally "wood."

f. 34 b that they should be burnt; but cast them into the furnace until they
be consumed." And they did unto them as the devils had commanded.
The angel of the Lord came down to the furnace and rescued them from
the burning. And the multitude cried out with a mighty cry, and they
were standing opposite him, [and] the angel of the Lord brought out
the disciples and set them in the midst of the multitude, without their
seeing them. And they talked and rebuked them and derided the devils
who were in them. And the Governor said unto the multitude: "What
shall we do with these men? Lo! three times he hath burnt them with
fire; and it hath not consumed them nor hath it hurt them at all.
Behold! they are going far from us; we shall not find them to accomplish
our will with them."

Andrew replied: "Lo! we are standing in your midst; either overcome us, or we shall overcome you, by the power of our Lord."

The Governor answered and said: "It is not meet for us to corrupt
this law of the gods." Then the commandant and all the soldiers laid hold
of them and took them before the tribunal of justice[1] and the multitude
threw many stones at them. And Andrew waxed wroth in spirit, and
would fain have cursed the city and all who were within it that they should
go down to hell for their little faith; but he was patient and remembered
the commandment of the Lord, which He spake: "Do not requite them
for their little faith." And the Governor commanded the multitude to
f. 35 a be silent. And he said unto the disciples: "What hateful deeds are these
with which ye lead the people astray? I will strip off your skins, and
will throw you to the ravening wild beasts, that they may eat you."

Andrew replied unto him: "For what cause wilt thou do this unto
us?" The Governor said unto him: "Because ye have come into our
city, and when our gods saw you, they went forth out of it."

Andrew replied unto him: "Your gods are no gods, as ye suppose, but
are made by men's hands. There is no God but the Father, and the Son,
and the Holy Ghost." And when the multitude heard this speech, they
said unto the Governor: "Either thou shalt slay these men, or if not, we
shall slay thee and all thy household."

And when the Governor saw the chief men and the multitude shouting,
and their voices getting louder, he said unto them: "What do ye wish
me to do with them?" They said unto him: "Thou shalt saw them
with saws, or cast them into a copper furnace till their bodies melt, and
thou shalt throw them into the sea."

<hr>

[1] Or "Court of Session."

And the Governor commanded that the holy ones should return, and they fastened them to a wooden wheel, and turned it round upon them. And they brought the large saw that they might saw them asunder. And while they were busy sawing, their hands were withered and they could not move them: and they screamed, saying: "Woe unto us! we have no strength for it."

The Governor said unto the multitude: "What do ye wish me to do with them? I have no power over them."

Then he commanded the wheels to be set up, and the holy men to f. 35 b be laid upon them and tied with ropes and dragged with them in the streets of the city; and afterwards be thrown into the sea, being bound to the wheels. And when the servants of the king wanted to take hold of the ropes, their bodies were dislocated and their hands were cut off from their elbows, and fell upon the ground. And there was great grief and much sore weeping in the city. And on that day the Governor said unto the multitude: "What do ye wish me to do with these men? Ye have seen what we have done with them; and we can do nothing with them in the way of ill-treatment."

The multitude said unto him: "Arise thou: [and] we will go together and ask them if they will consent to our request and will go forth out of our city."

And the Governor did what the multitude had asked him, he and they [both] drew nigh to the disciples, and he said unto them: "O ye blessed brethren, what money do ye wish that we should pay you, and go ye out of our city; so that our gods may return unto us? And if ye will not do it, all our city will perish."

The disciples replied unto them: "We have no need of gold nor of silver."

And the multitude were wroth, and drove the disciples outside of the city. And they pelted them with stones and left them thrown down like dead men.

Then did the Lord Jesus appear unto them and said: "Arise, O my f. 36 a holy disciples! be patient and fear not, for in this city there is a great tumult because of you; but go ye out to this desert, I am abiding with you, fear ye not, I will direct a man towards you whose face is like the face of a dog, and whose appearance is frightful exceedingly. Take him with you to the city."

And after the Lord had given them this commandment He departed from them, going up to heaven in glory.

And the disciples went out to the desert, grieving because the city did not believe; and they stayed only a little while to rest; and they slept; and the angel of the Lord lifted them up and brought them to the city whose people were cannibals, and left them beneath a rock of the mountain, and departed from them. And when they awoke, they were astonished, and glorified God. And whilst they were talking beneath the mountains, behold! a man had come out of the city whose people were cannibals, seeking a man whom he might eat. And he had remained all that day without finding anything to eat. And the angel of the Lord appeared unto him, saying unto him: "Help, O thou man whose face is like the face of a dog. Lo! thou shalt find two men, and two disciples with them, and they are sitting beneath this rock. And when thou shalt have reached them, let nothing unpleasant from thee come to them; for they are the servants of God; lest their God be wroth with thee and

f. 36 b cut thee in twain." And when the man, who was like a Dog's Head, heard speech like this, he trembled exceedingly, and replied, saying to the angel: "Who art thou? I know thee not; and I know not the Lord; but tell me who is God the Lord, of whom thou speakest unto me."

The angel replied unto him, saying: "He it is Who created the heaven and the earth, He is God of a truth. This heaven is a tabernacle above thy head, and thou treadest on the earth, and He created them, and the sun, and the moon, and the stars, and the sea, and all that is therein; the wild beasts, and the birds, and all the cattle, and the fowls, He created them all. And He hath power to take [away] the breaths of them all." Dog's Head replied to him, saying: "I desire a sign from Him, that I may believe all that I have heard from thee."

And straightway fire came down from heaven and surrounded Dog s Head, and he could not get out of it. And he stood in the midst of it, escape being impossible; and he feared greatly. And he cried with a loud voice, saying: "O thou God whom I have not known! save me from this affliction in which I am, and I will believe in Thee." The angel answered, and said unto him: "If God save thee from this affliction of fire, wilt thou follow His disciples to every place whither they shall journey, and wilt thou hearken unto all that they shall say unto thee?" Dog's Head replied and

f. 37 a said unto him: "O my lord, I am not like most men; for my appearance is not like the appearance of most people; and I know not their talk. And if I were to walk with them, what could they do about my food? And if I were hungry, where shall I find men to eat? I should turn round upon them and eat them. Lo! I have made known my state unto thee, lest I should do them evil, and their God should be angry with me."

The angel said unto him: "God will give unto thee the nature of man, and will strip from thee the nature of the wild beast." And immediately the angel stretched out his hand, and pulled Dog's Head out of the fire, and signed him with the sign of the cross, and called on the name of the Father, and the Son, and the Holy Ghost. And then the nature of the wild beast went out of him, and he became gentle as a lamb. And the angel said: "Arise, go near to this mountain; thou wilt find four men sitting beneath the shadow of a rock, follow them; and let no unpleasant thing from thee come near them. For it is the Lord, Who hath sent thee to work miracles in every place whither they shall go." And the angel departed from him.

And Dog's Head arose, and went to where the disciples were, rejoicing and glad, in the knowledge of the right faith. And his appearance was f. 37 b fearful exceedingly; his height was four cubits; his face was like the face of a large dog, and his eyes like lamps of burning fire, and his back teeth like the tusks of the wild boar; and his [front] teeth like the teeth of a lion; and the nails of his feet like a curved scythe; and the nails of his hands like the claws of a lion, and his whole appearance frightful, terrifying.

And when the disciples awoke from their sleep, with hearts sorrowful because of this city and the little faith of its people, whilst they were sitting, behold! Dog's Head arose upon them. And when Alexander, the disciple of Andrew, perceived him coming nigh to him, he became like a dead man from fear of him. And the disciples thought that he was possessed with a bad spirit, and they made a sign upon him in the name of the Lord, and traced a cross over his face. And after that Andrew looked at Dog's Head, and trembled greatly at his appearance, and he motioned to Bartholomew with his hand. And when Bartholomew saw him they ran away together, and left the two disciples under the cliff[1], Rufus and Alexander.

And Dog's Head came, and found the disciples like dead men from fear of him. And he took hold of the hands of both, and said: "Fear f. 38 a not, O my spiritual fathers!" And God took away the fear of him from their hearts, and sent upon them the power of the Holy Ghost, and they were not afraid of his appearance. And Dog's Head did obeisance to them, and begged them to call their fathers; that they might tell them all that the Lord Jesus the Christ had commanded him. And they sought eagerly for Andrew and Bartholomew. And when they had

---

[1] Or "rock."

found them, they said unto them : " The man whose face hath made you sorrowful is calling you." And the two disciples came [to the place] where Dog's Head was. And they were not able to look at his person, for he was very fearful. And when Dog's Head saw them, he did obeisance to them, down to the ground ; and he said unto them : " Fear not my appearance, O servants of the Most High God ! Your God hath sent me to you, that I may go with you to every place that you desire. And I will obey you in whatsoever ye command me. And the disciples marvelled at Dog's Head. Andrew said unto him : " May the Lord bless thee, O my child ! I believe that we shall have a great consolation in thee ; but tell us thy name."

f. 38 b   Dog's Head said : " My name is ' Bewitched.' " Andrew said unto him : " Truly a secret is hidden in thy name. And it is sweet and it is honourable, but from this day thy name shall be ' Christian.' "

And they prayed and went forth out of that city. And the Lord sent His angel as a guide along with them[1]. And on the third day they arrived at the city of Barbaros. And they sat down outside the city to rest. And Satan got to the city before them, and he was in the likeness of a rich man of the city, and he went into the presence of the Governor, and with him were all the chief men of the tribe. And he said unto him : "The men whom ye have driven out of the city with stones have appeared again, seeking to enter it. And if our gods were to know of their approach they would go forth out of our city. And the nations will hear, and will rise up against us and take us captive, we and our children."

And when the Governor heard this he commanded all the gates of the city to be shut, and he placed guards over them. And when the disciples sought to enter into the city, Dog's Face said unto them : " Cover up my face before I go into the city, lest the people see me and flee from me." And they covered his face.

And Andrew arose and prayed, saying : " O Lord ! hearken unto my
f. 39 a supplication. And he drew nigh unto the gate of the city and said : " In the
xlv. 2 name of the Lord Jesus the Christ, Who hath broken the gates of brass, and cut in pieces the bars of iron, let this city be speedily opened." And when he had said this, the gates of the city fell, and the disciples entered, Dog's Head being with them. And the gate-keepers hastened to tell the Governor and all the people of the city what had happened. And when they heard it they were perturbed exceedingly. And they all hastened, bearing the weapons of war—he who had a sword, and he who had a

---

[1] Literally " between their hands."

spear, each man according to his ability.	And they went out to meet
the disciples that they might slay them.	And the Governor commanded
them to lead the disciples forward into the midst of the crowd, and
to bring wild beasts of prey against them, so that they might let
loose seven lions and three lion-whelps, and a lioness which was bringing
forth young, and two tigers, against them.	And the guards of the king
seized Andrew that the wild beasts might kill him.	And when Dog's
Face saw what they were going to do unto him, he said unto Andrew:
"Command me 'O good servant!' to uncover my face."	Andrew said
unto him : "Whatsoever I command thee, do."	And Dog's Head prayed,
saying thus: "I entreat thee, O my Lord Jesus the Christ! Who didst
turn me from hardness of heart into meekness, and didst make me meet f. 39 b
to be the companion of Thy disciples, I entreat Thee that thou wouldst
restore to me my original nature, so that this crowd may see me: and
strengthen me by Thy power, that they may know that there is no God
beside Thee."	And straightway he returned to his original nature which
was in him ; and he waxed exceeding wroth, and was filled with rage, and
he uncovered his face, and looked upon the crowd with great anger.	And
he sprang upon all the lions [that were] amongst the multitude, and began
to slay them ;	and tore their hides, and ate their flesh.	And when the
people of the city saw this they trembled greatly, and were disturbed
and fled, and sought to get out of the city.	Because of the violent pressure
of the crowd one against the other six hundred men and three noblemen
died.	And of the remainder, he who was safe sought for a place to hide
himself; and they went out of the city.	And the Lord sent a great fire
[which] surrounded the city ; and not one of them could flee from it.

And the Governor and the chiefs assembled, and drew nigh unto the
disciples, weeping in fear and trembling, saying: "We believe and we f. 40 a
know that there is no God in heaven nor on earth, save your God, the Lord
Jesus the Christ.	We entreat you to have compassion on us, and deliver
us from this death which surroundeth us from two sides, from the fire,
and from the dread of Dog's Head."	And the disciples took pity on
them, and besought the Lord Jesus the Christ that He might take the
fire from off them.	And Bartholomew said unto the Governor: "Assemble
the people of the town unto us, men and women.	And let them bring to
us whatsoever idols are in their houses ; that they may know that they
are no gods, but are made by men's hands; stones, there are no souls
in them."	And the Governor commanded the multitude about that,
and they brought them.	And the disciples arose and prayed, and their

feet smote the earth, saying: "O God! Who at that time didst command the earth, [and] it opened and swallowed up Dathan and Abiram and all their host who withstood Thy Name, let the earth open at this hour, and may these idols be swallowed up; and bring them down to Gehenna, whilst this multitude are witnessing it." And that came to pass speedily. And the Governor, and the crowd of women and men lifted up their voices and said: "There is one God, the God of the Nazarenes, Jesus the Christ."

f. 40 b

The disciples said unto them: "Let us go together to the theatre; and ye shall receive the completion of faith therein." And the Governor and the multitude entreated the disciples and said: "O our lords! forgive us, for we cannot reach that place for fear of Dog's Face; lest he should eat us, as he ate the wild beasts." Bartholomew said unto them: "Fear ye not; but follow us; ye shall see the glory of God and great wonders in this city to-day." And a great crowd followed them to the theatre; and the disciples went first, and laid their hands on the man who was like a dog's head, and they said unto him: "In the name of Jesus the Christ, let the nature of wild beasts leave thee, and return to the nature of man. It is enough for thee, O my child! thou hast completed the service in which thou wast sent." And in that hour he returned to be like what he was before, meek as a lamb; and he came and did obeisance to the disciples. And when the multitude and the Governor saw this wonderful thing they took in their hands branches of olive, and did obeisance to the disciples. And they said unto them: "Let your blessing abide on us; and baptize us." The disciples said unto them: "Possess ye your souls in patience; the gift of God hath remained upon you."

f 41 a

And there was a pillar in the midst of the city, beside the theatre. And when they reached it Andrew arose and smote it with his foot. And straightway the pillar was opened and sweet water gushed from it. And the disciples stood in the midst of the water, and baptized the multitude in the name of the Father, and the Son, and the Holy Ghost. And when the multitude had been baptized, Dog's Head entreated Andrew and said unto him: "O thou good father! let thy mercy lighten upon those who have died, that they may live, and be baptized, and may rejoice with their brethren. And that they may know that the Lord hath power to give life unto the dead."

And Andrew arose and made supplication. And another loud voice called from heaven: "At length it shall come unto the beloved Dog's Head: that I shall give unto him the gift of giving them life, for they died through fear of thee; and by thy hands shall their life come." And they were baptized along with the people of the city; and the disciples did many miracles [and] wonders in the name of the Lord. The blind opened their eyes; the lame walked; the deaf heard; the dumb spake; the devils were cast out. And in all the city there remained not one who had a disease who was not cured in the name of the Lord Jesus the Christ. And after these things he built them churches; and ordained for them a bishop, and presbyters and deacons. And he made them all the servants of the temple, and taught them the Holy Gospel and all the rites of the Holy Church. And they offered up the pure Mysteries, and finished the prayers about them; and gave the multitude the offering and the Holy Mysteries. And there was great joy in this city at their being held worthy of the joy of baptism and of receiving the Holy Mysteries, which are the Body of the Lord and His precious Blood. And they confirmed them in the holy faith in the name of the Lord Jesus the Christ. And they went out from amongst them, praising God; to Whom be glory for ever and ever. Amen.

Cod. 81
Fonds
Arabe
f. 26 a

THE MARTYRDOM OF ST ANDREW.

The Martyrdom of Andrew, the Blessed Disciple, on the fourth day of Khoiak, in the peace of the Lord.

And it came to pass that Andrew had journeyed to the city of Aknîs, and the city of Argânyûs, and the city of Safras, the rebellious and wicked cities which were neighbours one to the other; and they were united in his lot wherein he was to preach the good news of the Gospel. And these were the last of the cities to which he journeyed. And his departure from this world drew near. And when he entered these cities he preached to them with a loud voice, thus: "Whoso forsaketh not father or mother, and sons, and daughters, and brothers, and sisters, and wife, and silver, and gold, and raiment, and treasures, and goods, and fields, and everything in this world, and followeth not after Me, is not worthy of Me." And he commanded them about it, that they should believe in the name of the Lord Jesus the Christ with the right faith. And they begged him earnestly for more about it; (because) he had mentioned before that he who did not do it would have no right to the kingdom of heaven, and would not have everlasting life.

And the people of this country were a very wicked folk, and they had little religious faith. And when they heard Andrew speak in this way, they were wroth against him with a great wrath. And (in) many places they heard of the wonders which he did in the name of the Lord Jesus the Christ; and everyone who asked him was cured by him, and he bestowed the cure without price. And many of the people spread his name abroad in that region; and he brought them near unto God, Who receiveth everyone that cometh unto Him with all his heart.

Then it entered into the heart of the people of this city in which Andrew was preaching about the knowledge of God to assemble themselves and take counsel together about the disciple. And the magistrates said unto each other: "Come, let us unite and agree concerning the killing of this deceiver, who hath corrupted our religion and

cf. Luke xiv. 26 xiv. 33

f. 42 b

hath come to us in the name of a new god, whose name we know not, neither we nor our fathers."

One of them said: "Let us go out to him and entreat him to go out of our country that no discord may happen; for many (men) of the city have believed by his speech; and if we do not make haste and do something by our own will, there will be some ruin to the inhabitants of the city." And they sent trusty folk to him of those who f. 43 a were of noble race. And they went to him joyfully. And this was by the will of God, that the envoys also who had gone to him might believe. And when they had entered into (where) the disciple (was), he began and said: "The peace of the Lord be with you." They replied unto him: "May thy peace be with us." And they spoke in words of peace. The disciple said unto them: "Sit ye down, O ye good brethren, whom the good Lord hath called to the Holy City." They replied unto him, saying: "Forgive us, O servant of the good God, in whom we have found the knowledge of God. O thou just one! about whom we took counsel for the evil, which Satan had sown in our heart. O thou innocent man! who art like a lamb playing and submissive to him who is seeking to kill it. Truly we, since we have seen thy person, every thought of evil is put far from us; and thou hast made our hearts new by the fear of God. Have we not commanded evil concerning thee, and brought it upon thee? We have come to entreat thee to go out of our city; and we have said in the ignorance of our minds that thou art he who didst trouble our city. But now we Cod. 81 know certainly that thou art he who shall save us from the enemy, and shalt Fonds Arabe intercede for us with the Lord, that He may forgive our sins. And now, O f. 28 b holy father! we will not separate ourselves from thee, and we desire thee to make us thy disciples. And Andrew blessed them, and sent them to their houses in peace, and exhorted each of them to learn the faith of the Lord Jesus the Christ. And they went away from him praising God; and they went about in all the market-places of the city, and in its streets, reciting the praises of God. And they left the blessed Apostle Andrew.

And when the company of evil men who had sent them on that business heard these things, they were greatly perplexed. And they took counsel about it amongst themselves: and they said, "Let us go together to the place where Andrew is, and let us burn him alive in the fire; so that he may not return to our city, and everyone who hath believed in him may hear of us and be afraid of us. And they went out to the place where he was, and they surrounded him and said unto him, "We will burn thee f. 29 a alive." And when the disciple saw that they were endeavouring to do evil, he looked at them, and spake to them in words of peace; and said unto them: "O ye rebellious men! do not fulfil the evil which ye have determined, which Satan its father hath taught you.   And return unto God.

And if ye will not receive [this] from me, I have entreated God about the fire in which ye have purposed to burn me, and He will send fire from heaven from Himself to burn you and your city; that ye may know that there is no God who is mighty in heaven and earth, save Jesus the Christ my Lord."   And they reviled the Lord Jesus the Christ, and the holy disciple. And when he heard their reviling he was wroth with a fierce wrath, and he lifted up his hand towards heaven and made supplication, saying: "O my Lord and my God, Jesus the Christ! hearken unto my supplication, and send fire from heaven to burn these wicked people who have reviled Thy holy name."   And before he had finished his supplication fire fell from heaven and burnt up this wicked multitude.   And the saint became known in all the town and its district because of the wonder which had come forth from his hands.   And the rest of the wicked never ceased, but they plotted evil again.   And they said: "If this man remains in our city he will ruin us with his sorcery, and there is worse in store for us from his doing, for he will separate us from our wives."   They sent treacherously to him with soft speech until he came into their midst; and they gathered themselves together against him and beat him with heavy blows.   And they went round about the city with him, he being naked, and cast him into prison until they had taken counsel against him how they should kill him.   And the custom of this city was, that whomsoever they wished to slay they hanged him on a piece of wood in the form of a cross, and threw stones at him.

And when they had thrown Andrew into prison he arose and prayed earnestly; and entreated the Lord that He would send fire from heaven and burn these three cities as (He did) the first time, because of the beating and the acts of violence which they had done to him.   Then the Lord appeared unto him in the prison and said unto him: "Peace be unto thee, O Andrew! My beloved disciple; be not anxious, for thou hast finished thy course, and hast attained to thine apostleship.   And this is the place in which thou shalt complete thy testimony, and shalt inherit the kingdom of heaven with the just ones who have pleased Me."

And when Andrew heard it he rejoiced and was glad; and he remained for the rest of the night praising God.   And when it was the morrow he went forth out of the prison; and they hanged him upon the cross, and stoned him till there was an end of him.   And believing folk took him and left his body in a grave. And this was the completion of his testimony on the fourth day of the month of Khoiak ; and praise be to the Father, and the Son, and the Holy Ghost, for ever and ever. Amen.

(*Colophon.*) *And praise be to God ever and always. This blessed book is the enduring perpetual guarded inheritance of the Monastery of Our Lady, the Lady whose lord is Anba Bishai, and is known as the Syrian Fathers. And no man shall have power from the Lord—praise be to Him! to take it out of the Monastery on any pretence or by way of loss. And after he shall have taken it out his lot shall be with Judas, the betrayer of his Lord. And it was written for God's sake by permission of our Father the Metropolitan Abbot of the Monastery above mentioned. And praise be to God always and for ever.*

THE STORY OF ST JAMES.

f. 45 a   *The story of James the son of Zebedee, brother of John the Evangelist,*
and his preaching of the Gospel of the Lord Jesus the Christ in the city
of India.

It came to pass when the disciples divided the cities of the world, and
each of them knew his lot given to him by the Lord, they praised His name
greatly.   And the lot of James was the city of India; and (of) John his
brother the city of Asia.   And James said unto Peter, "O my father
Peter! go forth with me until thou hast brought me to my city."   And
Peter said unto him, "Not thee alone, but all of you will I bring to your
cities, as the Lord hath commanded me."   And Peter and James went
towards this country; reciting on their way the praises of God, and
rejoicing their souls with what the Lord had taught them about the abundance of their reward in the kingdom of heaven.   And they said: "It is
meet that no sloth should overtake us and no laziness, but let us hasten and
be watchful in zeal for proclaiming the Gospel and preaching in the world,
so that we may be worthy of the everlasting promises."   These words did
Peter and James speak strengthening one another in effort; and whilst they
were talking in this way, the Lord appeared unto them like a young man of
fair face, rejoicing in their conversation, smiling in their faces.   And He
said unto them: "Come unto Me, O ye good labourers!   I am your
f. 45 b Master, and Strengthener, and the Payer of your reward.   Know, O My
disciples, that all your toil in this world will not be like a single hour of the
rest which will be in the kingdom of heaven."   And He enlightened the
eyes of their hearts; and shewed them all the just men who have gone
to their rest from Adam to John, and they were shining in glittering
raiment.   And they drew nigh to them and embraced them with a spiritual
kiss, and departed from them in peace.

And when the disciples had seen this spiritual vision their hearts were
strengthened, and they were glad, and fell to the earth and worshipped,
saying: "We thank Thee, O our Lord and our Master, Jesus the Christ!
for the beauty of Thy work to us poor men."   And the Lord made them rise,

and gave them (the greeting of) peace. And He said unto James, "Be strong and finish thy service with a (true[1]) heart, and preach in the world in the name of the Lord, to those who are His image and likeness. And in this thou shalt have a great reward."

And the disciples arose, with faces shining like the sun, and the Lord disappeared from them into heaven with great glory. And Peter said unto James, "It is meet that we should be diligent in our journey so as to bring back all the lost sheep of the race of Israel, for this great reward is certain to be ours." And they journeyed together. And as they drew nigh to the city, behold! there was a blind man on the path eating bread. And when he knew that the disciples were approaching, he went, by the grace of God, and cried with a loud voice and said: "O servants of the Christ! give me light on my eyes." James said unto Peter: "Take pity on him, f. 46 a O my father! that he may not cry behind us." Peter said unto him: "It is thou who shalt give healing in this city." James said: "Bless me, O my father!" Peter said unto him: "The Lord Jesus the Christ will effect his cure by thy hand." And James called the blind man and said unto him: "If thine eyes be opened, and thy sight established, wilt thou believe in the Lord Jesus the Christ, the Crucified?" The blind man said unto him: "I believe in Him with a true faith." James said unto him: "In the name of Jesus the Christ, in whom thou hast believed, the true God, let thine eyes be opened, and do thou see with full sight."

And this happened as he had said. And when the multitude saw it, they cried out and gave glory to God. And a company of them believed. But some of them said: "These are wizards." And they went to the magistrates of the city, and told them what they had witnessed; and the magistrates commanded them (the disciples) to be brought. And when they stood before them, one of them asked them, "From what country are ye? whence are ye? and what do ye want?"

Peter answered him, saying: "We are the servants of a good Lord, whose name is Jesus the Christ." And when the magistrates heard the name of Jesus, they rent their garments, and cried out with loud voices and said: "O ye men! ye inhabitants of this city! beware of these folk, for they are wizards. For many days we have heard no news of them. Twelve men went forth from Jerusalem, disciples of a good man whose name was Jesus; this was the name they called him."

And the magistrates commanded that they should put ropes on their f. 46 b necks, and drag them through all the city. And when the guards were

---

[1] A word seems to have been dropped from the MS.

about to throw the ropes on their necks, their hands withered, and they stood still on their feet. And the magistrates chided them, saying: "Ye have not fulfilled what we commanded you." They said unto them: "We cannot move, and we have become like stones." The magistrates said unto them: "Did we not tell you that they are wizards?" The disciples said: "We are not wizards; but servants of a good Lord." And the men whose hands were withered entreated the disciples, saying: "O servants of God! have compassion on us." They said unto them: "God hath commanded us that we should not requite evil with evil, but good instead of evil." And they drew nigh unto the men, saying: "In the name of Jesus the Christ, Whose disciples we are, and Whose name we preach, we command you by faith that ye return to what ye were, whole." And straightway the guards rose up whole, as they had been, and did obeisance to them, crying out: "There is no God but Jesus the Christ, the Lord of these good men."

And when the multitude saw it they returned the cry like the speech of the guards, "There is one God, Whom these two blessed men proclaim." And the magistrates did not believe; for their hearts were hard. And there was a magistrate among them who had a son, and his feet were withered; he could not walk. The magistrate said: "I will bring my son to them, and if they have power to make his feet whole like (those of) all men, I will believe in their God."

And he commanded one of his servants to bring his son to them. f. 47 a And he hastened and left him in the presence of the disciples. And they both arose, and stretched out their hands, and prayed, saying: "Our Lord Jesus the Christ, Resurrection of souls and of bodies, the Good Shepherd Who restoreth every good soul, we entreat Thee, O Thou Lord Who art near with an answer, that Thou wouldest hearken unto Thy servants, for Thou hast promised that Thou wilt not separate Thyself from us; to shew Thy glory at this hour in this city; that they may know that Thou art God; there is no God beside Thee[1]."

And when the two disciples had finished the prayer, James said unto the lame boy: "In the name of Jesus the Christ, the Nazarene, in Whose name I preach, rise, walk like all men."

Then he sprang up and stood, whole, and walked. And when the multitude saw this wonder which had been (done) by the disciples, they cried out, saying: "God is one, the God of these two men." And the magistrate, the father of the boy, did obeisance at the feet of the

---

[1] Literally "between the hands of."

disciples, saying unto them: "I entreat you to come into my house to eat bread"; and he sent to his wife with the son who had been cured. And when his wife saw her child walking, she cried out, saying: "God is one, the God of these two men who have cured my son." And she cried in her dwelling for the presence of the disciples, and she sent back her child f. 47 b to his father, insisting on his bringing them. And when they were within the magistrate's house, the idols which he had in his house straightway fell down. And when the magistrate and his wife saw this wonder, their faith was strengthened, and they brought much goods unto the disciples. And they said unto them: "Accept these goods from us, and distribute them amongst the poor."

James said unto him: "Distribute it with thine own hand." And he did as James had commanded him. And he laid the table for them, and they ate. And the name of the magistrate was Theophilus. And he entreated them to baptize himself and his wife and his children. And when the disciples saw the strength of their faith, they gave him the commandments of life, and baptized him and his wife and his children in the name of the Father, and the Son, and the Holy Ghost, the one God, and every one in his dwelling. And their number was thirty souls. And after this James said unto Peter: "Arise with us, O my father! let us go hence and journey round about the rest of the cities and warn their inhabitants, and preach amongst them the good news of the gospel; and perhaps they will receive it and repent."

And they went forth into the midst of the city to a famous spot where the magistrates of the district were sitting. And they began to teach the multitude the spiritual commandments. And they testified to them about the sufferings of the Lord, and about His Resurrection, and about His f. 48 a ascension to heaven, and about His second coming to judge the quick and the dead. And the multitude heard their words and marvelled at the sweetness of their speech.

And when the rest of the magistrates of the city saw that their friend had believed, they came forward and did obeisance at the feet of the disciples. And they said unto them: "We entreat you, O good servants of God! to give us the gift of God, which ye have given to our friend." And when the news was spread abroad in the city that all the magistrates had believed in the message of the disciples, they all cried out, saying with a loud' voice: "We entreat you, O disciples of the Christ! that ye would make us meet for the gift of the Christ; and give us the token of faith."

And when they saw the power of their faith, they said unto them:

"Whoso truly believeth, let him follow us." And the multitude went before until they (the disciples) arrived at a mighty river in the midst of the city. And they prayed; and after the prayer they preached unto them and taught them the laws of God. And they baptized them in the name of the Father, and the Son, and the Holy Ghost. And when they had received baptism, they rejoiced with exceeding joy and were very glad. And they commanded them to build a church; and they abode with them until their faith had become strong; and they appointed them priests, and

f. 48 b gave them the holy mysteries. And James read the Law and the Prophets unto them; and Peter interpreted into the language which they knew. And he abode with them many days until their faith had been strengthened. And they appointed them a bishop; and all the servants of the temple; and they went forth from amongst them with the praise of God, the One in substance, the Three in Persons, to Whom belongeth praise and glory and honour and worship for ever and ever. Amen. And praise be to God always and for ever.

THE MARTYRDOM OF JAMES.

The Martyrdom of James the son of Zebedee, the disciple of Jesus the Christ, which took place on the twenty-seventh day of Pharmouthi, in the peace of the Lord. Amen.

And when James the son of Zebedee, the disciple of Jesus the Christ, went out to the scattered Twelve Tribes, and preached the Gospel to them in the name of the Lord Jesus the Christ, the True God, all the tribes did not worship the One God; but each tribe of them had chosen a god, and each of their idols had a false teaching which led them astray. And they were under the dominion of Herod; they paid him service in different ways; and the property which came to him from these sources was very great, until his authority increased and his kingdom became larger. And it came f. 49 a to pass that when James drew nigh and preached to every tribe in its own language, because the Lord inspired them with the knowledge of all languages; not only the tongues of man, but the tongues of the birds and the beasts, and the creeping things, and the wild beasts; when they chattered in their own language, the disciple knew what they were saying by the help of the Holy Ghost. And James preached amongst them and commanded them to leave off their ugly deeds, and believe in God the Father, and His Only Son Jesus the Christ; and in the Holy Ghost, Who giveth life to every creature; in Whose hand are all their spirits; He will judge the quick and the dead. And he said unto them: "Give not all your goods unto earthly kings; but give some of them to the poor, for the salvation of your souls." And immediately the gift of the Holy Spirit dwelt in them, and the fear (of God) was firmly fixed in their hearts. And the news spread in all their borders; and they believed in the word of James the disciple; and were confirmed in the faith of the Lord Jesus the Christ, King of the heaven and the earth; Who doth not refuse those who seek Him and turn to Him with a sincere conscience. And they renounced all they had worshipped; and their wicked deeds Cod. 81 which they had done. And they approached the Lord with a sincere Fonds Arabe mind; and received the word of James which he preached unto them. f. 37 b l. 7 And James taught them much because of the quickness with which they received his preaching and forsook the false doctrine in which they were, and the error. And he made haste and built them churches in all their borders, when he saw the beauty of their faith. And he baptized them in the name of the Holy Trinity. And they were glad and rejoiced. And

f. 38 a   he commanded them the precepts of the Gospel ; and the laws of religion ;
and said unto them : "Hearken, O ye blessed children ! who have returned
from error unto the knowledge of the truth ; whom the Lord hath chosen
and made meet to receive His clean Body, and pure Blood. Behold,
I deliver unto you the truths of God ; which He hath entrusted unto us ;
and hath commanded us to convey to the nations. And they received
them with joy, so that they might be always joyful and triumphant in the
Paradise of the Eternal Lord. Behold, the Lord hath made you meet,
every tribe, that in Him ye may be [ready] and that your fruits, and your
vineyards, and your fields, and your sheep may be the Lord's." The
multitude consented ; and they said : "We will fulfil all that thou hast
commanded us. We believe in God with all our hearts ; the eldest of us
and the youngest." And thus every tribe offered all of what it possessed
f. 50 a   to the Church.

    And when Herod heard all about their faith, and about their offerings
to their churches, his wonder grew, and he learnt from a wicked man that
a disciple of Jesus the Christ had come to them, and had taught them not
to give gifts to the kings of the earth, nor tribute to Nero the Emperor,
nor to Herod the Governor ; but to pay it to Jesus the Christ the Lord,
King of the heaven and of the earth. And when the king heard the like
of this, he commanded them to bring James the disciple to him. And
when he saw him, he said unto him : "Of what nation art thou? and in
whom dost thou believe? O thou man whose deeds are worthy of death !"

    The blessed disciple replied to him, saying : "I believe in the Lord of
the Nazarenes, Jesus the Christ, Son of the Living God, He Who is Lord
of all that is in the heaven and upon the earth ; and their spirits are in His
hand. And thou, O Herod, and Nero the Emperor, your spirits are in
His hand ; and He hath authority over your kingdom."

    And when he heard this he was wroth with a fierce wrath against James,
the holy disciple, and he said unto him : "I cannot suffer thee to return
me another answer" ; for Nero the Emperor and Herod had heard about
f. 50 b   James the disciple, that he scorned their royalty, and reviled their idols.
And he arose in haste and struck the saint with a sword on his shoulders ;
and in that hour he gave up the ghost ; and thus Saint James, the son of
Zebedee, finished his testimony on the twenty-seventh day of Pharmouthi ;
and he was buried in Niqta, which is called Ravîna[1]. May his prayer
preserve us for ever. Amen. And praise be to God always and for ever.

    [1] The Ethiopic says : "in the seventeenth day of the month Miyâzyâ (April 12th) and they
buried him in Kôt of Mâmrîkî." (Cf. BUDGE, p. 308.)

THE TRAVELS OF
JOHN THE SON OF ZEBEDEE.

The travels of Saint John the son of Zebedee, the Evangelist, and his removal from this world to the Lord. Saint Prochorus wrote it, because of Saint Stephen, the chief of the deacons and first of the martyrs, one of the seven ministers whom the disciples appointed for the ministry of the strangers. In the peace of the Lord. Amen.

And it came to pass, after the ascension of Jesus the Christ to heaven, the disciples were gathered together at Gethsemane[1]. Peter said unto them : "Ye know, O ye brethren, when the Lord Jesus the Christ commanded us and ordered us to teach the faith to the nations ; and to baptize them in the name of the Father, and the Son, and the Holy Ghost, One God ; and after He had sent the Holy Ghost upon us, we have not enquired about what it was that our Master commanded us, and our sorrow is the more from the departure of His mother from this world, who is the mother of us all, and mother of all believers."

"Come now, O my beloved brethren ! in the grace of the Trinity, let us f. 51 a communicate the commandments which our Master commanded us to all the nations. Remember the saying which He spake : ' I send you forth as lambs among wolves ; be subtle as serpents, and gentle as doves.' For ye know that when a man desireth to kill a serpent, it exposeth all its body to him, and protecteth its head ; thus we, O my beloved ones ! let us expose our bodies to death, and let us protect the head, which is the Christ, and the right faith in Him. And likewise the dove, when her masters take away her children, doth not become furious against them. Ye know that the Lord hath said : ' If they have persecuted Me, they cf. John will also persecute you ; and, if sorrows beset you in the world, never- xv. 20 theless He for Whose sake they grieve you, He dwelleth with you.' "

James the brother of the Lord replied, saying : "Yea, O our father Peter, thou art careful about this business."

---

[1] Ethiopic "unto the grave of Mary." (BUDGE, p. 222.)

Peter replied unto him, saying: "If thy lot is to abide in this city, leave it not." And they cast lots again. And the lot of John was to go out to Asia, that he should preach in it, and this was very grievous unto him.

f. 51 b   And he prostrated himself three times in succession, and worshipped, and his tears fell upon the ground. And the disciples worshipped with him. And Peter took hold of him, and set him up, and said unto him, "We look on thee at all times as a father, and we imitate thy patience. And thou hast never acted in this way and thou hast disturbed all our hearts."

John replied with tears and said: "O my father Peter, I have sinned in this hour, because as for me, great afflictions must needs befall me on the sea. But pray for me, O my beloved brethren! that God may forgive me." And the company of the disciples arose in that hour and they asked James, the brother of the Lord, to pray for them. And when he had done this, they embraced each other with a spiritual kiss; and they gave (it) to every one of the seventy-two lesser disciples. And it fell to my lot to follow my master John.

And we went forth from Jerusalem; and we reached Joppa. And we remained on the shore for three days, and we sailed in a boat which came from Egypt, laden with a cargo. They brought the cargo to Joppa, and wished to go forth towards the west. And we sailed in the boat, and sat
f. 52 a down in a place. And John began to weep and he said unto me: "O my son Prochorus! in this sea a great tribulation will befall me, and my soul shall be tormented. But death or life shall the Lord reveal unto me. And if I be saved, O my son! from the tribulation of the sea, I will go to Asia, and will repair to the city of Ephesus. And I will abide in it for two months. And I will come to thee after the two months, and we will fulfil our service. But if it pass by, and I come not unto thee, return to Jerusalem, unto James the Lord's brother, and what he saith unto thee, do."

And this speech which John made was at the tenth hour of that day. Then mighty winds disturbed the sea, and the boat was greatly shaken, and they were nearly drowned. And we remained in this condition until the third hour of the night; and the boat was hurt, and every man clung to one of its planks. And we were knocked about with it, and the sea roared with a mighty voice, and the waves grew bigger in it, and the power of the water increased, and the floods gathered themselves together against the boat. And its woodwork and all that was in it were scattered. God, Who seeth all things, and directeth His creatures like the shepherd who guideth his sheep, saved in this way every one in the vessel who was
f. 52 b clinging to it. Like a river which overfloweth with water, and returneth

to its place, at the sixth hour of the day, the waves cast us on Seleucia, about fifteen[1] parasangs from the harbour at the border of Antioch. And the number of those who were saved from the boat was forty-six men.

And when [the boat] stopped with us on the shore of the sea, we could not speak one to the other for the little food, and the terror and the toil. And we remained prostrate on the face of the earth from the sixth hour until the ninth hour. And when our spirits returned to us, those who had sunk with the ship rose up against me saying unto me every ugly word: "that the man who followeth thee is a wizard, and therefore he hath done a work of sorcery. And he hath made the boat to sink, and hath taken all that was in it, and hath fled. But thou must deliver him up to us; and if not, we will deliver thee to the Governor of the city that he may slay thee. For every one who had been in the boat is present except thy master alone."

And the people of the city were wroth against me, and they made good their word, and cast me into prison. And on the third day I was brought out to a great place, where the magistrates of the city were seated, and they f. 53 a received me with all unpleasantness. And they said unto me, "Whence art thou? and of what religion? and what is thy handicraft? and what is thy name by which thou art called? Tell us the truth before we torture thee."

I said unto them: "I am a Nazarene from the land of Judea; and my name is Prochorus, and I sank in the sea like this company, and behold! I am present like all these [men]."

The magistrates said, "And how was every one who was in the boat saved, except thy master? Truly it is like what these people say, that ye are wizards; ye have bewitched the boat; and ye do not allow any one to know. As for thee, thou hast fallen [out] and thy master hath taken all that was in the boat, according to what you two had agreed upon. Truly ye are evil doers, and in your necks there is much blood. But as for thy master, the sea hath swallowed him up. And as for thee, it hath revealed thee and thy work. After thy deliverance from the sea, in this hour thou shalt perish in this city." And they made me afraid and they spake against me, and they said: "Tell us, where is thy master?" Thereupon I wept with a sore weeping, and I said: "I have told you that I am a disciple of the Lord Jesus the Christ. The lot came out for my master, that he should go to the regions of Asia. And when we embarked in the f. 53 b ship everything that hath happened unto us—he told us before it took place. And he told me that I should betake myself to the city of

---

[1] MS. "stadia" deleted.

Ephesus, and should wait for him there a number of days, and if the days should be finished, and he did not come to me, I should return to my country. And my master is not a wizard, nor am I one either; but we are Nazarenes, well known for trustworthiness."

And a messenger came from Antioch, one of the king's privy councillors, whose name was Seleucus, to carry the money of the tribute. And when he heard this from me he commanded the magistrates to let me go my way. And they did as he had commanded them. And I journeyed for the space of forty days until I reached Asia; and I arrived at a wide region on the shore of the sea whose name was Marmarwân. And I sat down on a rock[1] which projected over the sea, to rest myself from fatigue and grief, and I slept a little, and I opened my eyes, and I saw in the sea a huge wave. approaching. And it cast John out from itself. And when I saw it, I rose up quickly to take hold of his hand, and help him to safety; and I knew not that he was John. And when I drew nigh unto him, he got before me in climbing out. And when I saw him, I rejoiced

f. 54 a exceedingly, and embraced him; and we wept together. And we thanked God for what He had given [us] by bringing us together after despairing. And after a little rest, and [when] his reason had returned to him, we told each other what had happened unto us. And he told me that he had stayed forty days and forty nights in the depths of the sea; and I told him what had happened unto me. And we stayed together until we came to the other end of this land, which is called Marmarwân. And we asked for food, and [the people] gave us bread and water. And we ate and our hearts were strengthened, and we journeyed in the way to Ephesus.

And when we entered the city we sat down in a place called the seat of Artemis, near the beginning of the city. And there was in the place a bath [house] belonging to the chief magistrate of the city, whose name was Dioscorides.

And John said unto me: "O my son! let no one in this city know who we are; nor why we have come to it, till God allows us to disclose it, and we shall find a way to reveal [ourselves] and we shall preach in it."

And whilst he was saying this, a woman drew nigh unto us [who was] terrible in strength. She was the caretaker of the bath-house, a barren woman [who] had never borne a child; and she was stout in body like a great mule; and she boasted of her strength and beat the labourers who

f. 54 b served [in] the bath-house, with her hand; and she did not allow them to rest for a single hour. It was said of her that she had gone out to

---

[1] Or, "pillar."

the war, and had fought, and had thrown stones with her hand; and she was boastful about her deed. And she imagined herself to be wise, and she decked herself out to captivate those who beheld her. And when she saw us sitting and our raiment mean, she meditated by herself, and remarked that we were strangers. She tried to make us become servants in the bath-house. And she said unto John: "Whence art thou, O thou man?" He said unto her: "I am from a far country." And she said also: "From what country art thou, and what is thy religion?" And he said unto her: "I am a Nazarene." She said unto him: "Wilt thou be stoker, [and] heat the bath? and I will pay thee thy wages and thy provender." He said unto her: "Yea." And she turned to me, and said: "What wilt thou be?" John said unto her: "He is my brother." She said: "I have need of the other to be a bath-man." And she brought us both together into the bath-house; and John became stoker and I bath-man; and she gave us three pounds of bread every day; and we stayed four days and John did not find fuel; and she laid hold of him and flung him down on the ground, and gave him a terrible beating without mercy; and she said unto him, "O thou wicked servant, thou fugitive from f. 55 a thy country! thou dost not deserve to live. If thou didst know that thou wert not fit for this work, why didst thou come into it? But I will shew thee thy doings. Thou hast come hither [to deceive] Domna, whose fame [hath] reached unto the city of Rome; but thou canst not escape from my hand; for thou art my slave, whilst thou art eating and drinking bravely; but during the time of work thou art idle. Put away from thee this bad nature, and go on with the service of Domna, a good service."

And when I had heard this wicked discourse which she had made unto John, and had seen how she had beaten him, I was grieved exceedingly. John said unto me, when he saw me sorrowful, "O my child Prochorus, why art thou perplexed? Knowest thou not that we were both drowned in the sea; and I remained in the depths of the sea forty days; and by the mercy of God I was saved. And art thou grieved because of a single blow from an ignorant woman, whose wrath is but a trifle? Hie thee to thy work with which thou art entrusted, and work with cheerfulness. Our Lord, Jesus the Christ, was beaten, and they spat in His face; and He was crucified; and we are His creatures who have been bought by His blood; and He was like unto us, but without sin. And He has told us all this f. 55 b beforehand, that it would happen unto us; but let us be patient, and possess our souls." And when the multitude had heard this speech from him, I went to the work which Domna had commanded me to finish.

And on the morrow Domna came to John and said unto him, " If thou hast need of clothing, I will give it thee, but nevertheless do thy work well." John replied unto her, " What thou hast given me is sufficient for me ; and as for the work, I will do it well."

She said unto him, " Why do the multitude reproach thee that thou dost not do thy service well ? "

He said unto her : " This craft upon which I have entered is the beginning of my work ; and therefore I have little knowledge of it ; and when I have made some progress thou wilt find out that I am a good craftsman, for the beginning of everything is difficult."

And when she had heard that, she returned to her dwelling. And Satan, the hater of all good from the beginning, made himself like the person of Domna, and appeared to John and said unto him, " Why dost thou not do thy work well, O fool, [and] weak fellow ? thou hast spoilt the work. And I cannot put up with thee. Make thy work and thy fuel good, or else I will fling thee into it. And thou shalt never again see this light, for thou art not fit to live ; and I do not wish to see thy face again. f. 56 a Get thee out, O deceiver ! and take thy friend, and return unto thy city from which thou hast come out because of the wickedness of thy deeds."

And Satan laid hold of the iron rod, with which he subdued the people, in anger, to strike John. And he said unto him : " I will kill thee ; get out of here, I do not want thee to serve me in anything, get away." And when John knew by the Spirit that it was Satan, he called on the name of the Father, and the Son, and the Holy Ghost, and immediately Satan ran away from his presence, and fled.

And on the morrow Domna met John and said unto him : "A certain man hath spoken much to me about thee, that thou art not earnest in thy work, and that thou dost make excuses that I may let thee off [thy task] ; and thou canst not do that, and if thou hast planned [this] I will not let thee off whilst there is a whole limb in thy body." And to all that she lectured about he returned her no answer. And when she saw his patience and his meekness, she thought that he was a simpleton, and she spoke to him with every offensive word, and threw the dust in his face ; and said unto him : " Thou art my slave, dost thou not confess that ? tell me." John said unto her, " Yea, we are thy slaves, I am the stoker, and Prochorus the bath-man."

And the cursed Domna had a friend amongst the officers of the judge ; f. 56 b and she went and said unto him : " I have two slaves whom my father bequeathed to me. And a long time ago they ran away from me ; and they have just returned to me; and they acknowledge my right to their service. And I desire thee to write me a deed of their servitude to me." He said unto her: "That is justice. If they acknowledge that they are thy slaves, get three just witnesses to testify about them; and do thou write a deed of servitude about their confession."

And John knew by the Spirit all that she was meditating about him; and he said: "O my child Prochorus! this woman wishes us to acknowledge to her that we are her slaves; and O my child! let not thy heart be grieved for that; but let it rejoice greatly, and let us agree to what she wishes. And from an act like this our Lord Jesus the Christ is able to make her know who we are."

And before John had finished his exhortation to me, Domna drew near with great haughtiness, and laid hold of John and said unto him: "O thou bad slave! why, when thy mistress approached, didst thou not hasten to meet her and do obeisance to her down to the ground? Art thou not my servant? O thou fugitive slave!" And she beat him, and she said unto him: "Tell me." John said unto her: "Did I not say unto thee that we are thy slaves, I the fireman, and Prochorus the bath-man?"

And she retorted, saying, "Tell me, of whom are ye the slaves?" He f. 57 a said unto her: "This is the third time that I have acknowledged that we are both thy slaves." And she brought us to the temple of the city, to three witnesses; and wrote a book of servitude about us. And in this bath-house there was a Satanic power, which had dwelt in it from the first, when it was built, because when the makers laid the foundation, they dug in the middle of it and placed a living girl there, and heaped up [the earth] over her; and laid the foundation-stone. And because of this the Satanic power dwelt in it. And every year three times did Satan strangle a soul in this bath-house. And Dioscorides, master of the bath-house, understood the days on which this happened in it. And he had a very handsome boy, beautiful of countenance, whose name was Damîs, and his age was eighteen years. And his father prevented him from entering the bath-house on the day when this deed which Satan did was happening.

And after we had remained three months in this bath-house, the son of Dioscorides went to the bath-house alone, to bathe himself; and I went into it, as was customary for the service, and he got in before me; and that devil laid hold of him and strangled him and killed him. And when f. 57 b his slaves knew it, they went out screaming, saying: "Woe unto us! for our master is dead." And when Domna heard it, she rent her clothes, and tore out the hair of her head, and said: "Woe unto this wretched woman!

what shall I do? and what face can I lift up to the face of Dioscorides; and tell him about the death of his child? But he also, if he should hear that his beloved child is dead, he too will die from the bereavement." And she sought help from the idol which was in the temple: "O Artemis! help me, and bring Damîs, my master, to life; that all we people of Ephesus may know that thou rulest the world." And she did not cease to pull out the hair of her head from the third hour until the ninth hour; and she wept deliriously. And a great crowd assembled because of it, some of whom were grieving for the death of the lad; and some were astonished at Domna, and at her way of weeping and wailing.

And John came out of the fuel-house. He said unto me: "O my son Prochorus! what is that screaming in this city from that woman?" And when Domna saw him speaking unto me, she hastened to lay hold of him, and she said: "O thou man, [thou] corrupting wizard! by thy sorcery my god hath gone far from me, and will not hearken unto me."

f. 58 a   And she smote John, saying: "O thou bad slave! hast thou come to look at me, and hast rejoiced at what hath befallen my master?" And when John heard the voice of Domna he went into the bath-house and stood near the head of the dead boy, wondering at what had befallen him. And he rebuked the bad spirit, and cast him out of the boy. And he made the sign of the cross on his face; and took hold of his hands; and made him stand up; and led him out of the bath-house alive into the presence of the multitude. And he said unto Domna: "Take thy master, he is well, [and] whole, there is nothing wrong with him. Behold! he is alive by the power of my Master, Jesus the Christ."

And when Domna saw what had happened she was bewildered, and her mind was confused, she was struck with terror and fright, she and all the people of the country who were present and had seen the miracle which [John] had done. And Domna could not lift up her head to John's face for shame and fear. And she went on saying: "Woe is me! what shall I do with the man to whom I have done all these ugly deeds? He is not my slave; and what lies I have told about him, and have been very severe in beating and buffeting him." And she was very sad, longing for death rather than life.

f. 58 b   And when John saw her face, and what grief and shame and regret were in it, he took hold of. her hand, and made the sign of the holy and honourable cross on her face, in the name of the Father, and the Son, and the Holy Ghost, the One God. And her senses were soothed at once, and she threw herself down[1] before the saint, and said: "I entreat thee to forgive me and to tell me who thou art. Perchance thou art God, or the Son of God, that thou hast been able to do a deed like this."

John said: "I am not God, nor the Son of God, as thou dost imagine, but a disciple of the Son of God, and if thou wilt believe on Him thou shalt become one of His people."

Domna replied with fear and trembling, and said: "O good servant of God, forgive me all that I have done unto thee of ill and insult and falsehood."

John said unto her: "Believe in the Father, and the Son, and the Holy Ghost, and all that is forgiven unto thee."

She said unto him: "O good servant of God! I believe in all that I have heard from thee."

Now one of the servants of Dioscorides had hastened to tell him of the death of his son, and that John had brought him to life, and that the crowd were surrounding him. And when Dioscorides heard that his son was dead he fell fainting on the ground, and became as one dead; and the lad returned to the bath-house [where] Damîs and John were catechising f. 59 a Domna; and she said unto him: "Woe is me! O my master Damîs! for my master Dioscorides, thy father, is dead."

And when Damîs heard that his father was dead, he went forth, away from John, to the place in which his father was; and he found him prostrate upon the ground dead. And he returned to John, and said unto him: "O servant of the good God, thou art he who hast made me alive after death; and behold, when my father heard about me that I was dead, he died also. And I entreat thee to have compassion upon him also."

John answered and said unto him, "Fear not, thy father's death is not death, but life." And John went with him to the place where he was lying, and Domna followed him with a very great crowd. And when he had come nigh unto him he took hold of his hand and said: "Dioscorides, in the name of the Father, and the Son, and the Spirit, one God, arise, stand upon thy feet." And straightway he arose, whole, and there was nothing wrong with him. And they all marvelled at the miracles and the wonders which John had done. And some of the crowd said that he was a wizard; and some of them said: "A wizard doth not bring a dead man to life." But Dioscorides, when his senses were soothed, threw himself down before the feet of John and said unto him, "Art thou the Son of God, who hast brought my child and me also to life?" John said unto him: "I am not

---

[1] MS. "this."

f. 59 b what thou dost imagine; I am a servant and disciple of God; thou and thy
son—ye would not have come to life save by the power of Jesus the Christ,
the Son of the Living God." Then Dioscorides turned and did obeisance
to him, and said unto him: "Command me what I should do, that I may
live." He said unto him: "Believe in the name of the Father, the Son,
and the Holy Ghost, the One God, and be baptized, and thou shalt receive
eternal life."

Dioscorides said unto him: "Behold! I am in thy hands, and all my
household. Command what thou wilt."

And Dioscorides made John go into his house; and shewed him all
his goods, and said unto him: "Accept all this, and make me and my
household Christians." John answered and said unto him: "I have no
need of thy goods, neither I nor my God, for we have forsaken everything
and have followed our God." And he spoke many words to him from
the sacred books. And Dioscorides did obeisance to the holy John and
said unto him: "O good servant of God, have compassion on us; and
baptize us in the name of the Father, and the Son, and the Holy Ghost."

John said unto him: "Bring all who are in thy dwelling to me, and
I will preach to them, and will teach them the precepts of religion, and
will baptize them in the name of the Father, and the Son, and the Holy
Ghost, one God, that they may receive the pledge of life."

After that came Domna, with the deed about John in her hand which
she had written [to shew] that John was her slave. And she threw herself
down before him at his feet, weeping [and] saying: "I entreat thee,
O good servant of God, to give me the token of the religion of the Christ,
f. 60 a and to accept from me the written deed of my sin."

And John took the deed from her, and cut it in pieces, and baptized
her in the name of the Father, and the Son, and the Holy Ghost. After
that John went out of the house of Dioscorides, and returned to the
bath-house, and drove out of it that unclean spirit which used to strangle
people, and went back to the house of Dioscorides. And many people
were gathered together unto us, [but] when we had come into the house
the crowd dispersed. And Dioscorides laid out a table for us; and we
gave thanks to the Lord, the Christ, and partook of the food. And we
stayed that day in that place, until the morning of the second day.

And the people of the city held a great feast to their god, who was
called Artemis; and John was present at this place, and stood opposite
to the idol which was called Artemis. And all the people of Ephesus
were present, and they were arrayed in most gorgeous raiment for the

day of the feast; and he was clothed as he was serving in the heating of the bath-house. And when the heathen saw him they approached him with stones; and the idol was hit until it was broken in pieces. The holy John, the disciple, replied to them, saying: "O ye men! people of the city of Ephesus, do ye celebrate thus a feast of unclean devils; and forsake [the] God who made all creatures? and God is [greater] than man."   f. 60 b

And wrath against John took hold [of them]. And he said unto them: "This god of yours hath been broken in pieces by the quantity of stones which ye have thrown at me; and if ye had wished and if ye wish to see the power of God, understand, and awake, and hasten to receive [Him] when ye shall see Him."

And John stood and prayed, and made supplication thus, and said: "O my Lord Jesus the Christ! cause Thy fear to be in the hearts of these people that they may know that there is no God but Thee." And immediately they heard a voice calling over the ground. And when the voice ceased two hundred men fell down and became like dead men. And the rest [of them] came back and did obeisance to John, saying unto him: "We entreat thee to raise up these dead men; and we shall be stedfast and believe in thy God."

And John answered and said unto them: "O people of Ephesus! ye are hard of heart; I know that if the dead arise ye will not believe in the Living God, because of the hardness of your hearts; for they are like the heart of Pharaoh."

And John raised his eyes[1] to heaven, and said: "O Thou Who dwellest in the Father at all times! my Lord Jesus the Christ, Son of the Living God! may these dead men arise by Thy power, that they may believe in Thy name."

And immediately there was a great noise in the earth, and an earthquake, and those two hundred dead men arose, and threw themselves down with their faces to the ground, doing obeisance to John [and] saying unto him: "What dost thou command us: O good man?" And f. 61 a he preached unto them the laws of religion, and baptized them in the name of the Father, and the Son, and the Holy Ghost, the One God.

And after that we sat for several days in a famous place in the city, [where] the multitude were assembled. [And] a woman came and did obeisance to John, saying: "O good servant of God! I have an only boy, [and] an unclean devil hath possessed him for eight days. And he is lying in the house tormented by that devil, in great pain. And I entreat

---

[1] Literally "his sight."

thee, and implore thee to take pity on my child and heal him; and we will
believe, I and his father, in thy God." And John arose, with Dioscorides,
and they went into the house of the woman; and he looked at her boy,
and he was lying on the couch speechless. And his mother did homage
at the feet of Saint John, and she said unto him: "I adjure thee by the
Living God, Whom thou servest, to take pity on my boy."

And John took hold of his right hand, and said unto him: "In the
name of my Lord Jesus the Christ, the Blessed One, O thou boy! arise."
[And] straightway the boy arose, quite well, and gave praise to God.

And John preached unto them, and baptized them in the name of the
Father, and the Son, and the Holy Ghost, the One God. And the Jews
sprang upon John like bloodhounds seeking to kill him; and Dioscorides
f. 61 b saved him from their hands. And we went forth from that place; and
we arrived at a place called the Broadway of the City. And in this place
there was a man who had lain for twelve years unable to stand up on his
feet. And when he looked at John he cried with a loud voice, saying:
"Have mercy upon me, O disciple of the Lord Jesus the Christ!" And
John, when he saw the faith of that man, said unto him: "In the name
of Jesus the Christ, arise!" And straightway the man arose quickly, in a
moment, praising God.

And when the devil who dwelt in Artemis saw a sign like this, which
John had done, he took the form of a man, one of the privy councillors
of the king, having written papers with him, [and] he sat in a well-known
place and wept. And while he was weeping two men of the king's suite
passed by him. And when they saw him in that dwelling they drew
nigh unto him and saluted him and said unto him: "O thou friend! what
makes thee weep?" And he shewed them the writings with which he
deceived them; for they were not writings, but fabrications of the devil.
And they said: "What are these? and what is in them? and what is
the reason of thy correspondence? and who hath smitten thee?"

And he wailed and wept the more, and said unto them: "I am in
f. 62 a great straits, and I cannot live any longer. And if ye are able to serve
me, I will tell you of my state."

And they said: "We are able."

And he said unto them: "Swear unto me by the great Artemis, that,
whether it be for death or for life ye will devote yourselves on my behalf,
and I will tell of my state."

And they sware unto him that they would be with him in all his
circumstances; and he made for them the first leaf in the fictitious

writings.   Thus he made a false appearance to them of many purses filled with dinars, and said unto them: "I will give you this property as a reward for your toil on my behalf."

And they said unto him: "Explain unto us thy desire, and we will satisfy thee."

And he said: "I am a poor man from the city of Cæsarea, which is in the country of Palestine, I am a chamberlain in the palace.   Two wizards of Jerusalem were entrusted to me, the name of the one was John and of the other Prochorus.   And I took good care of them, and put them in prison.   And on the fourth day the rulers of the city enquired about them; and I brought them forward; and the evil of their deeds was made certain, and [the case] became very strong against them.   And they [the rulers] commanded me to take them back to the prison until the rulers should assemble to decide concerning them as to what [kind] of death they deserved.   And whilst I was going with them as they had commanded me, that I might leave them in the prison, they escaped out of my hands and fled.   And when I told their condition to the Governor, he was sorry for me and said unto me: 'Go, O wretched man! and seek for them.   And unless thou catch them know that thou shalt die by the worst of deaths.'"   f. 62 b

"And he said unto me: 'If thou find them not, return not to me, [but] make the round of the provinces.'"   And then he presented this money to them and said unto them: "This is the money which I have made as a provision for my way; and I have learnt from a company of people that the two are in this city; and therefore I have been going after them."

And he went on weeping and saying: "I have left my ease, and my child, and my dwelling for their sake, and behold I am wandering about in strange countries, and I desire you, O my beloved ones! to have compassion on my exiled state."

Those friends of the king said unto him: "Grieve not, O friend!" He said: "Are there wizards in this country?"   They said unto him: "Yea, I fear that they have fled to this place by their sorcery.   But I entreat you if ye lay hold of them, put them in a hidden place of which no man knoweth and slay them secretly, and we will take this money."

They said unto him: "Good luck to thee! if we catch them we will take them with thee to thy country."   He said unto them: "Kill them, and I am not sad about my return to my country, and I shall not rejoin my people."   And they made a treaty with him about killing them secretly; and they took the money.

And Saint John knew by the Spirit what Satan wanted to do. He said unto me: "O my child Prochorus! let thy soul be strong and enduring about what is thy duty. For the devil who dwelleth in the temple of Artemis hath raised up a great persecution against us. He hath raised up against us two men of the officers of the army, and he f. 63 a hath talked with them about us in hateful words: and my God Jesus the Christ hath revealed unto me what the devil hath said unto them both. And let thy heart be strong, and fear not."

And while John was saying these words unto me, behold, these two men appeared and laid hold of us. And Dioscorides was not present at that moment. And John said unto them: "Why do ye lay hold of us? and what is our crime?" They said unto him: "Because of sorcery." John said unto them: "And who is he that beareth witness against us about this?" They said unto him: "We know and will put thee into prison till thine accuser shall come." John said unto them: "Ye cannot cf. Corân accuse me until the assessors of the Cadi are present with you." And they Sura II. v. 282. smote John and seized us, and went with us to the prison. And they went far away with us to a waste place in the desert where no man dwelt, that they might kill us as they had agreed with the devil to do.

And Domna hastened to Dioscorides, and told him what had happened to us. And when he heard a thing of this nature he arose speedily and sought us until he found us. And he saved us from their hands; and he spake hard words to them, and said unto them: "What right f. 63 b have ye to write an indictment against two innocent men, whose accuser is not present? Ye laid hold of them and brought them into a desert place, where the Governor was not sitting, that ye might kill them secretly. Behold, these two men [shall be] in my dwelling until their accuser shall appear, and let them be judged as the law ordaineth." And the two men said to each other: "It will be well that their accuser should come and judge concerning them, as the law judgeth; and it will prevail over some of them and will force them to do what is right."

And they went away from us and removed to the place in which the devil was staying; and they did not find him; and they went round about all the city, and they did not find him; and they learnt no news of him; and they feared to return unto Dioscorides, because he was the foremost in the city: and they sat down in poignant grief.

And after that the devil appeared unto them in that form; and said unto them: "O my beloved ones! why are ye in despair?" And they told him what had happened: and that Dioscorides had put them [the disciples] out of their hands : "[but] if thou wilt come with us, we shall have power over each one of them."

And he walked with them, weeping and very sad.   And a great crowd assembled, and he said unto them and he told them the story which he   f. 64 a
had already told the two men and they were very angry with John, because most of them were Jews, and they came to the house of Dioscorides.   And the multitude said unto him : "Thou art one of the first men in the city, and it is not meet that thou shouldest entertain wizards in thy dwelling.   But thou wilt deliver them up to us—or if not, we will burn thy house and plunder all thy goods, and slay thee—thee and thy children ; and we will take them without thy consent."   And the news was spread abroad in the city ; and the people gathered together to the house of Dioscorides, seeking for John and his disciple.   And when John saw the great crowd, and the multitude who were present, he said unto him : "Dioscorides, we do not care about what thou wilt say, do thou make an agreement about thy goods, and as for us, we will not spare our bodies, but we have learnt to bear our cross and to follow Him."   And   Mark viii. 34
Dioscorides said unto John : "Behold ! my house will be burnt, and my goods will be plundered, and we shall be slain, I and my child, for thy sake."

John said unto him : "Neither thou nor thy goods, nor thy child, nor one hair of your heads shall fall.   Deliver us up to the men who are in your dwellings that ye may see the power of God."   f. 64 b

And Dioscorides delivered us up to them, and we went to the temple of Artemis.   And when John drew nigh unto the temple, he said unto the men who had laid hold of us : "O people of Ephesus, what is this temple ?"   They said unto him : "This is the temple of Artemis."   John said unto them : "Let us stand here a little while."   And they stood as John had said.   And he lifted up his eyes[1] unto heaven, and said : "O my Lord Jesus the Christ, make this temple fall by thy power : and let no man of the multitude die."   And straightway his word came to pass, and the temple fell.

And John said unto the devil who dwelt in the temple : "I say unto thee, O thou unclean devil !"   [Satan] replied unto him : "Who is he ? and what is thy will ?"   John said unto him : "How many years hast thou dwelt in this temple ?"   The devil said unto him : "Forty-five years."   John said unto him : "Art thou he who didst set the friends of the king against me ?"   The devil said unto him : "Yea, I am he."   John said

---

[1] Literally "sight."

unto him: "I command thee in the name of my Lord Jesus the Christ,
f. 65 a the Nazarene, get thee out of this city, and do not return to it again."

And the devil went out quickly, and after that the multitude were
ashamed when they beheld [it] and they were all gathered together in
one place. They said one to the other: "Have ye ever seen [anything
like] what these folk do? Come ye all with us; let us seize them, and
hand them over to the ruler of the city, and he will punish them according
to the law." And there was amongst them a man, a Jew named Marawân.
This man said, and all who were with him: "[They are] wizards, and they
know all evil crafts, and it would be well for us to kill them, and not
consult about them."

And they said unto him: "Thou hast spoken well." And Marawân
stirred up the multitude; and they did not reply to what he said; [but]
took us to the rulers of the city, who had the decision, and delivered
us over to them. And the rulers said unto them: "What have they done
of the wizard's craft?" Marawân said unto them: "A man, one of the
king's friends, from their city asked about them; and he it was who told
us of the evil of their deeds." And they said unto Marawân: "Let the
man whom thou hast mentioned appear before us, and tell us about this,
f. 65 b if he be trustworthy in speech. But let these men be thrown into prison
until their accuser shall appear."

And they put us into the prison, and bound us with chains; and the
multitude went forth into all the quarters of the city seeking the king's
friend. And they did not find him; and the town-crier cried within the
whole city and without it for three days, and no man found him. They
answered and said: "Where are the men who were in the prison?"
And the rulers of the city replied, saying: "It is not right for us to
leave these foreigners in the prison, when no trustworthy witnesses appear;
and no accuser reviles them."

And the rulers sent to bring us, and they examined us, and reprimanded
us, and commanded us not to stay in the city; and not to teach anything
of what we were teaching. And they sent us out of the city under a guard,
and chased us from all its borders; and we arrived at a place called Mîrawât
where John had clambered out of the sea; and we stayed for three days;
and the Lord Jesus the Christ spake unto John in a vision. And John
said: "Behold, O Lord!" And the Lord said unto him: "Arise, and
f. 66 a cross to the city of Ephesus. And after three days thou shalt journey
to an island which hath need of thee, and many trials shall happen unto
thee and thou shalt stay in it a long time."

Then we arose quickly and we returned to Ephesus; and when we entered it, the temples which were in it fell down, and nothing remained in them. And all these things John did in Ephesus before he was driven away.

And the reason for what had befallen him through the Jews and the heathen, whom Satan had stirred up against him, and all the wonders which were shewn by him, and the driving away, and the persecution which befell him in the island of Patmos, [all] this is written in very many books which we call....

Therefore praise be to the Father and the Son and the Holy Ghost now and at all times and for ever and ever. Amen, Amen, Amen.

THE DEATH OF SAINT JOHN.

The Death of Saint John, the Son of Zebedee, the Evangelist, the disciple of our Lord Jesus the Christ, who spake about the Divinity : and his removal from this world. And this was in the island of Patmos on the fourth day f. 66 b *of Tûba. Peace be from the Lord ; Amen. May the Lord Jesus the Christ have compassion on us through the accepted prayers of the two, and protect us! Amen.*

It was after the ordinance of the Lord, the Saviour, to all the world, and His Ascension to heaven with glory, and the departure of the pure disciples, each one of them into the region for which his lot came out in the presence of the Lord ; and the lot of John the son of Zebedee the Teacher, was Asia. And when he went into Ephesus, he preached unto them, and evangelized them in the name of our Lord Jesus the Christ, the Son of the Living God, with great zeal and toil, and privation and labour, and wonders untold ; and afterwards with patience in the trials and the temptations which befell him from the people of that place ; for they were worse idolaters than the people of all [other] regions—as the scribe who was from the city of Ephesus sheweth ; whose report is written in the Book of the Acts of the Disciples—where they boasted of a vain thing. And without dispute he who taught the Ephesians said, "They were abundantly devout in the service of the temple which belongeth to Artemis the Great."

f. 67 a   And after John the Evangelist had made that impure temple and its people useless by his Gospel, and had done signs and wonders without number in the name of the Lord Jesus the Christ, the kings cleansed all the provinces from the defilement of idols, and had delivered them from the death which endeth not, and had restored them to the knowledge of the Lord Jesus the Christ, and had appointed many bishops for them, and elders, and deacons. And he made churches in this city, and he built the churches in all this region, in the name of the Lord Jesus the Christ. And righteousness increased in it, and faith grew amongst them in the name of the Lord Jesus the Christ, and their knowledge of Him, after the disciples had finished all their labour, and had departed from this world.

As for Peter, he was crucified in the city of Rome ; and Paul—his neck was smitten in it ; and Mark—his body was dragged through the city of

THE DEATH OF SAINT JOHN.

55

Alexandria, and he was living for two days before he died.   And thus all
the disciples ; each one of them in the region wherein he was teaching.
And they all died by tribulations and hardships and divers kinds of torture.
And as for John, he lived in the world many years, until Domitian reigned. f. 67 b
He remained for seventy years after the Lord's Resurrection, and became a
very old man.   And he did not taste of death by the sword, nor by any
kind of torture ; for the Lord loved him much, for his purity ; as it is
written in his Gospel that he was the beloved of the Lord, who was
counted worthy to lean on the breast of the Christ, the Son of the Only
God, Who sitteth in the bosom of His Father in heaven ; because of the
purity of his soul and of his body.   And after he had written his divine
Gospel, which transcends all understanding ; and the Apocalypse, which
he saw in the island of Patmos, which is full of the mysteries of God ;
God—blessed be His name—wished to deliver him from the toil of this
world, which was upon him for the sake of His name.   And the Blessed
John was rejoicing greatly in the Lord ; and all the brethren were
gathered together with him in Ephesus ; glad and joyful at seeing him ;
as if they were beholding his Lord, Jesus the Christ.   And it happened f. 68 a
that on every first day [of the week] the people were gathered together,
rejoicing in the spirit, reciting songs and spiritual psalms like those in the
church, the church of the virgins, the heavenly Jerusalem.   [And] John
began to speak to the multitude in spiritual words ; and said unto them :
"O my brethren ! and my beloved in the Spirit, partakers of the service
which belongeth to the inheritance, which is the kingdom of our Lord
Jesus the Christ, how many mighty deeds have ye seen which the Lord
Jesus the Christ hath wrought by my hands ? and how many spiritual
gifts ? and how much hath He taught you about the knowledge of Himself ?
[coming] from our Lord Jesus the Christ ? and how much hath He taught
[you] and increased your knowledge of Him[self] ? and how many
precepts, and how many commandments and how much consolation and
virtue from Him by the abundance of His mercy unto you ? in what your
eyes have seen, and ye have heard with your ears : and let it not be manifest
in the eyes and the ears of sense only, but let it be in the hearts.   And be ye
eager to finish the work, so that ye may be counted worthy of the blessing
of which He spake when He said : ' Blessed are ye, when ye labour.   Be
strong in the Lord ' ; and be ye workers of His will at all times, without
slackness.   And ye have known the providence which is the root of the
great mystery, which the Lord Jesus the Christ wrought for your salvation ;
and He it is who entreats you, O ye brethren ! by my tongue, that ye may f. 68 b

be stedfast in obedience, fearing Him. And grieve not His Spirit, and provoke Him not to wrath; and plot not against Him; and do not evil entreat Him; for He knoweth the secrets of the hearts, [and] what proceedeth from you; and all the plots, and all your opposition, and His commandments. And provoke not the merciful, the compassionate Lord, Who is long-suffering, pure and purifying; in Whom there is neither defilement, nor impurity, nor deceit, nor wrath. He alone is to be loved; the sweetness of which God is not weary; the Name which is above every name; not in this time but also at all times. And He is the Name which it is meet that ye should lay hold of, that He may be made glad by your obedience, and in your straight paths; and He rejoiceth in your lives which are [spent] in meekness, and in striving to be obedient, and in uprightness, and in quietness. And He delighteth in the beauty of your works; and your patience in tribulations; and may He be pleased with your purity, and your love for Him, by Jesus, through His mercy; and may He accept your repentance! And be not faint in your following of His commandments;

f. 69 a and even if ye have done ten thousand wicked things, if ye entreat Him with a sincere conscience, He is long-suffering, abundant in mercy, if [any man] return unto Him, and He will receive him in faith, as a virgin. And if he turn again, and repent, and make his path straight, God in the abundance of His mercy will have compassion upon him. And if he persist in the wickedness of his works, and trust in the mercy of God, let him know that God will judge him according to the wickedness in which He findeth him, and will shut him out from His mercy for ever.

"This is my speech unto you, O ye brethren! and I hasten to accomplish that which the Lord hath commanded me."

And whilst the Holy one was exhorting the brethren, he rose up, and stood, and stretched out his hands towards heaven. And he made supplication thus, saying: "O Thou Lord Jesus the Christ, Who hast bound this perishing garland together with the everlasting one; and all these coloured flowers unto the Flower of sweetness; Who hath sown His Life-giving Word in our hearts, He who alone maketh beautiful the sweetness of the souls and the bodies; the Meek and Lowly of heart, the

f. 69 b Compassionate, the Lover of mankind, Who alone is the righteous Judge, the Ever-existing, Whom no place can contain, the Lord Jesus the Christ, do Thou in the abundance of Thy compassion and Thy mercy preserve all those who hope in Thy name. Thou knowest the doings and the temptations of the opponent, which are planted in every place. We entreat Thee to make them of none effect by Thy power."

And when he had finished his prayer, he took bread, and gave thanks, and spake thus: "What blessing, or what acknowledgment, or what word of exaltation, or what thanks, or what name shall we speak over the breaking of this bread, save Thy name? Thou Who alone art Jesus the John vi. 51 Christ, the Saving Name. Thou art the Life-giving Bread which came down from heaven for the salvation of the world. We bless Thee Who hast made us meet for the path of life. We thank Thee; Thou art the Creative Word; Thou art the Guide and the Door into grace; the abundant Salt; the Rich in Jewels; the Ear of Corn; the Life, Righteousness, Strength, Wisdom, the Refuge, the Repose, the Rest, the Vine-stock, the Root, the Fountain of Life; Who permitteth Himself to be called by that name because of man, that he might be saved and renewed from the former open wickedness of his deeds into which he had fallen through sin. For to Thee belongeth glory for ever and ever."

And when the holy John had finished the breaking of the blessed f. 70 a bread, he took some of it, and drew nigh and gave it to the multitude. And he entreated also that they might be worthy of it. And he gave them [the greeting of] peace, and he sent them to their homes.

And after these things, he said unto his disciple Prochorus to take two of the brethren with him, and also baskets and a spade, and to follow him. And he did as [John] had commanded. And he went out of the city with them secretly, outside of it, walking. And he said unto us: "Dig here." And we did according to his commandment. And we made a hole, as he had directed us. And he took off his clothes, and threw them into the hole. And he stood above it, the rest of his dress being a linen garment, and he stretched out his hand upward; and looked toward the east, and made supplication thus, saying: "My Lord Jesus, the Christ, Who didst choose a poor creature like me to be Thy disciple, a herald of Thy holy name, in which Thou didst begin to preach by the tongues of Thy holy prophets. Who alone and always dost save those who long for salvation with their whole hearts. Thou art He Who in His own self gavest His life that all beings might know Him. Who careth for all His creatures, and loseth neither great nor small from amongst them; Who made the wild, waste soul humane and gentle; Who f. 70 b appeared unto her when she was dead; and accepted her when she was stained and polluted with the filth of sin, and made her unto Himself a pure bride, after she had been polluted with the uncleanness of sin, and conquered by Satan. And Thou didst take hold of her hand and set her up from the downfall [caused by] the Enemy, and madest her victorious over her Enemy, and madest him a contemptible thing to be trampled under her feet. He Who alone is pure; and Who dwelleth with the pure, Jesus the Christ, my God, the sweet name, Whose memory never palls; Joy of the heavens; Guardian of those who are upon the earth; Terrible to those who are beneath the earth; Delight of the good, and Protector of the upright in heart; Who accepteth those who are worthy of Him with glory and honour; Accept me, for I am Thy servant, according unto Thy word and commandment at the beginning; which Thou madest necessary for me so that Thou shouldest make me escape from the toil of this fleeting world. I thank Thee, O my Lord! Who hast kept me clean unto this time, pure from the filth of the world. Thou art He Who didst put Thy fear clearly into my heart, so that Thou didst remove far from me all longing for sin, and therefore I have been able to destroy the

f. 71 a motions of the body. Thou art He Who didst cause the currents of sin to cease from my body; and didst make my soul hate the works of manifest evil; which excite in my body the sensations of sin that were too strong for me; He Who hast made my paths straight without stumbling; and hast given to me the right faith in Thee without a doubt. Thou art He Who didst write Thy law within me, and didst give to me no desire for aught but Thyself. And what thing is there that is more glorious, or more honourable, or sweeter, or more to be desired than one like unto Thee? And who is like unto Thee? Receive now, O Lord! him who is Thine own; receive John, Thy servant, unto Thyself, who doth hope in Thee. And now I have finished the service for which Thou didst make me meet, and I have come unto Thee. I am consoled and delighted with Thy power, O Lord! I know that Thou wilt make my path easy before Thee, in peace, unto Thy glorious dwelling."

And when the blessed John had spoken all these words, he fell on his face upon the ground, worshipping. And he said: "I adore Thee, O Thou to Whom every knee shall bow; and all glory belongeth to Thee, the Father, and the Son, and the Holy Ghost, for ever and ever."

Then he said unto us: "O my children! the peace of the Lord be

f. 71 b with you. Go to the city, and say unto the brethren that they should keep all my words which I have commanded them. And we must certainly answer for it; and I have hidden from you nothing of the will of God. Ye are they who shall be tried; and I am innocent of your blood. I have not left any knowledge nor learning, that ye have not heard from me; and that I have not told you, and ye have learned it. Beware lest ye transgress and your debts be double; for to whomsoever much is given, of him will much be required, as the Lord hath said ; and Luke xii. 48 may He, the Lord Jesus the Christ, be with you for ever, strengthen you, and fulfil all your desire in obedience without sin. But from this time John will not be with you in the body."

And when we had heard this from him, we kissed his hands and his feet ; and we wept bitter tears ; and we left him in the hole, and went away to the city. And we told the brethren what had happened ; and they went forth with us in haste to that place ; and we did not find the holy John ; but we found his clothes, and his shoes, and the earth had filled up the place, and the hole which we had dug. We did not recognize it, and we returned to the city, and we give thanks to the Lord who bestoweth gifts worthily on those who are worthy of them ; Who honoured f. 72 a His beloved John by a wonderful death like this beyond [that of] many of the disciples. And for this we glorify the Lord, because He made him worthy, and His Son, and the Holy Ghost to all ages. Amen. And praise be unto God always and for ever.

THE PREACHING OF PHILIP.

The Book of the Preaching of Philip, the Disciple of Jesus the Christ,
which he preached in the city of Africa, in the peace of the Lord.   Amen.

It came to pass, when the disciples were gathered together at the Mount
of Olives, and they were reciting amongst themselves the commandments
of the Lord, then the Saviour Jesus the Christ appeared unto them, and said
unto them : " Peace be unto you, O My beloved ones.   Why are ye seated ?
and why do ye not go out to the world and preach unto them the Gospel
of the Kingdom ?   Behold now, cast lots among yourselves, and make the
world into twelve lots, that ye may go forth and preach in it."   And He
gave unto them the [greeting of] peace, and disappeared from them in
glory to Heaven.   And they cast lots, and the lot of Philip came out
f. 72 b that he should go forth to the country of Africa.   And he made no delay
about going ; but he said : " O my father Peter, the Lord hath commanded
that thou shouldest go forth with each one of us to his country ; and I
would fain have thee go with me to my country."   And he consented.

Then they journeyed together ; and the Lord appeared unto them, and
said unto them : " Peace be to you both, O My chosen disciples !   Go ye
and preach unto all mankind, that ye may draw them away from the hand
of Satan.   Verily I say unto you, that if ye labour at this until ye make
them turn from error to the knowledge of the truth, verily I say unto you,
that your reward shall be great, and ye shall attain unto rest, and shall
forget the toil."

And when He had spoken unto them, He gave them the [greeting of]
peace, and disappeared from them in glory.   And their hearts were
strengthened, and they went on their way.   And when the disciples
drew nigh unto the city, a man who was possessed with an unclean spirit
met them ; and he cried, saying : " O disciples of the Christ ! ye cannot
enter into the city."   And Peter knew that it was the spirit of a devil ; and
in that hour he rebuked it, and the devil went out of him.   And the man
was cured, and followed the disciples to the city.

And there was on the top of the gate of the city a very tall pillar.   And
f. 73 a when they reached the gate, Peter entreated the Lord, saying : " I beseech
Thee, O my Lord Jesus, to throw down this gate and this high pillar which is

above it to the ground, that my hand may reach unto it and lay hold of it."
And straightway the gate became fixed in the earth, and the pillar which
was on the top of it, so that they became level with the surface of the
ground. And Peter commanded him from whom the unclean spirit had
gone out to climb to the top of the pillar and to speak of what was
happening unto him, so that fear might come upon the people of the
city. And the man climbed upon the pillar which was over the gate.
And Peter said : " In the name of my Lord Jesus the Christ, by Whom ye
have become fixed in the earth so that ye have come nigh unto us, return
to where ye were." And immediately the gate was raised up, and the
pillar which was above it till they reached their [former] height. And
the man cried out with a loud voice, saying : " O men ! inhabitants of this
city ! gather yourselves together unto this place wherein are the disciples
of the Lord Jesus the Christ, that they may bless you, and may entreat
that your sins be forgiven." And when the man who was standing upon
the pillar had said this there was thunder and lightning. And the people f. 73 b
of the city trembled and were much afraid ; and they went into the caves
and the holes and the islands; and the lightning followed them whither
they had gone, until many men died and women, from the sounds of the
thunder and the flashings of the lightning. And the man cried : " Come
to where I am." And the multitude gathered themselves together unto
him, and they saw the two disciples with their hands outstretched, making
supplication unto God. And they fell down on the face of the ground,
and did obeisance unto them ; and they were weeping [and] saying : " O
servants of God ! we entreat you to have compassion on us. O ye new
gods ! whom we did not know, have mercy upon us ! and teach us what
is your will; and what is your sacrifice, so that we may bring it unto
you. And we beseech you that this thunder may cease from us, and
this terror."

And the two disciples besought the Lord for their sakes, and they
sought pardon for them. And the thunder stayed, and the lightning ceased,
and the man spoke no more; and the gate and the pillar which was above
it returned as they had been, so the man came down from the top of it.
And when the multitude saw that the man was silent, and that those
frightful things were at an end, they said : " This man is a god." And
they cried out with one voice, saying : " Thou art a god, and we did not f. 74 a
know thee." The man replied, saying : " I am not a god. I am a man
like unto you. The Holy Spirit hath spoken by my mouth, through the
commandment of His pure disciples. But come ye nigh unto the holy

disciples Peter and Philip, and whatsoever they shall say unto you hearken unto it, and know it that ye may be saved." And they arose and came unto the disciples; and they kissed their feet, and said unto them: "Who are ye?" Philip said unto them: "Which of the gods do ye worship?" They said: "We worship the statue of a man." Philip said unto them: "Go, bring him to me." And they did what he had commanded them. And it was of gold. And the priests cried, saying: "Do not destroy the gods who save you at all times. For if war rise up against you, and ye seek safety with them, they will not help you." The citizens said unto them: "It is better for us to accept the sayings of the disciples than your sayings. This god is the work of men's hands; he seeth not; he heareth not; he smelleth not; he walketh not."

And when they brought him to the two disciples, the priests cried, saying unto the disciples: "Ye lead the people astray by your sorcery. f. 74 b Ye say of a man, that he is God. Mary gave birth to Him, and Pilate put Him to death. Hast thou ever seen a god die? But nevertheless these are gold and silver; we worship them, and we call them gods; they see not, and they are of no profit."

And the Holy Spirit descended upon Philip, and the Lord Jesus the Christ helped him by His strength; and he made supplication, and said: "O my Lord Jesus the Christ! let fire come down from Heaven by Thy will, and burn up these wicked, evil priests, that they may know them to be deceivers until this day." And straightway there came down a cloud of fire, circling round them, apart from the multitude. And they remained in the midst of the fire [weeping] from the fierceness of its burning. Philip said unto them: "Why do ye weep and howl? Have ye not said that if war should rise up against you ye would make supplication unto your gods, and they would save you and your city?"

And Peter took up that idol, and flung it into the fire wherein the priests were. The [image of] gold answered: "O disciples of the Christ! do not punish me, but have mercy upon me; and judge between me and these sinful men. I am one of the instruments of the earth; these men have taken me and smelted me, and have made me what you see; and they have set me up in the temple. And they sacrifice beasts and mingle f. 75 a their blood with wine, and deceive the people; and say unto them that it is I who have eaten those sacrifices, and I neither eat nor drink, nor speak to any man. And it is not I who am speaking to you, but the power which rests upon you, it hath made me able to speak these things to the multitude, and to rebuke them for the wickedness of their deeds."

And when the idol had said this it was silent. And the priests be-sought the disciples that they would bring them out of the fire, that it might not consume them. And whatsoever they commanded them they would do it.

Philip said unto them: "If ye will leave off your impure worship and say: 'We believe in the Lord Jesus the Christ,' we will say: In His name let this cloud of fire depart from us." Then they all cried out with a loud voice, saying: "We believe in God; the Lord Jesus the Christ is His Word." And straightway the heat of the fire was lifted up from them: and it became like a lake of sweet water, white as milk, so that the two disciples were astonished. And the multitude asked them what it was their duty to do that they might make sure of their faith. Philip said unto them: "We command you to build a church in this place: and we will teach in it, for this is the place in which ye have believed." And they consented to their commandments.

And he commanded them to bring him plenty of straw; and the quantity f. 75 b of it was to be what would be for the foundation. And he commanded some of the men to dig until they had laid the foundation. And when the command had been fulfilled and the work was completed, he came unto the gate of the city with the pillar standing above it, and he said: "In the name of Jesus the Christ the Nazarene, Who is raised high above heaven, I command you to be removed hence to the site of the church which hath been called by the name of the Lord." And the gate fell, and the pillar which stood above it in the presence of the multitude to the site of the building. And no sound was heard in them; and no dust came out of them. And the multitude said: "There is no God but the God of Peter and Andrew and Philip, the servants of Jesus the Christ."

And Philip said unto the multitude: "We have begun to build the house of the Lord: and I desire you to bring together the girls who are maidens, that they may carry water; and the adult men and the young men, and all the citizens, every one according to his ability, that they may work in the house of the Lord. And let none of the multitude refuse what I have commanded." And the disciples were lodging in the house of Marwân, a governor of the city. And they were rejoicing that the multitude had responded to the faith so promptly.

And the Lord Jesus the Christ took on the likeness of a man of f. 76 a shining countenance; and He appeared unto the disciples and said: "The peace of the Lord be with you, O ye two blessed disciples. Ye have seen the beauty of the faith in the people of this city; and why do ye sit still in the house? go ye out unto them; and teach them the commandments of God, and life. And be not careless about them, and whatsoever ye shall ask Me, I will give it you."

cf. John xiv. 14

And when the Lord Jesus the Christ, in the likeness of a shining man, had spoken unto them, He disappeared into heaven with glory. And their faces shone with the glory of the Lord Jesus the Christ, Who had appeared unto them in the house. And they went out unto the multitude. And when they saw the radiance of their faces they did obeisance to them on the ground. And they blessed them; and raised them up; and taught them, and confirmed them in the faith of the Lord Jesus the Christ. And they commanded them not to return to any of their former sins. And the multitude increased upon them; and were blessed by them; and they were amazed at the glory of God which rested upon them. And a man amongst them who was possessed with a devil cried out with a loud voice, saying: "I entreat you, O servants of the Christ, do not punish me. I will go out of him." And the evil spirit threw the man down upon the ground and came out of him. And Peter and Philip commanded that devil to go out of him, and never to return to him. And the man who had been cured threw himself at their feet and kissed them. Then they gathered the multitude together to that lake which had been a cloud of fire, surrounding the priests at that time, and had become water. And they baptized them in the name of the Father, and the Son, and the Holy Ghost.

f. 76 b

And the disciples said unto the multitude, "God hath forgiven you your sins which ye have committed without knowledge: and begin ye to become worthy of the kingdom of heaven with good works; and of everlasting good things." And they cried with a very loud voice, saying: "We thank Thee, O God! the God of Peter and of Philip, that Thou hast had mercy upon us; and hast been compassionate to us."

And the two disciples consecrated the church, and the multitude gathered themselves together to it with joy and gladness. And they listened to the word of God; and Philip read to them from the Law and the Prophets, and Peter interpreted it to them by the Spirit of the Lord Jesus the Christ. And when they had preached to the multitude with the doctrines of religion and had made them worthy to receive the holy Mysteries; then they stood up in holy prayer, and finished it, and allowed each of the multitude to approach and receive that honoured Body in faith.

f. 77 a

And they gave them [the salutation of] peace. And they stayed with them for six days teaching them the commandments of the Lord until they knew them. And they appointed unto them a bishop and presbyters, and deacons. And they went out from amongst them, bidding them farewell, giving glory to God, and wondering at the miracles which they had wrought in the name of the Lord Jesus the Christ; unto Whom be glory and honour with the Father, and the Son, and the Holy Ghost for ever and ever. Amen.

THE MARTYRDOM OF PHILIP.

The Martyrdom of the blessed disciple Philip on the eighteenth day of Hathôr ; in the peace of the Lord.

And when Philip went into the city of Africa to the people of this country, and preached unto them a new God whose name they did not know, Jesus the Christ, they hastened unto him with all who belonged to them and listened to his speech. And they replied unto him: "Who is Jesus the Christ? we have never heard this name save from thee." For they had been serving the Devil.

Philip replied unto them: "Gather yourselves together unto me, O all ye blessed men! for I see that the grace of the Living God resteth upon you. The God Whom I preach unto you—He is the Living God ; and He giveth life unto all who believe in Him. And the Son, dwelling in the Father, and the Father in the Son ; and the Holy Ghost proceeding from the Father, f. 77 b Who is in the Father and the Son ; One God, One in substance, Three in Persons; before all time ; and unto all ages ; Who is invisible ; Who created all things by His wisdom ; Who hath restrained the sea and the rivers and the springs; and unto Whom all that is within them is subject. He brought into being all that is seen, and all that is unseen, in the beginning. And He took dust from the earth, and made of it a man in the likeness of His own image; and called him Adam. And He it was Who blessed him, and made him the father of all reasoning creatures ; Gen. i. 28 and said unto him : "Grow and multiply and fill the earth with thy seed ; and have dominion over all that is in it."

The multitude said unto him : "Where is that God Who hath created all of which thou speakest?"

The disciple said unto them : "He is in heaven and upon the earth; He dwelleth in every man who doeth His will."

And when the Devil saw that Philip was trying to turn the multitude to the knowledge of God, Jesus the Christ, the Lord, he made haste and sowed wicked thoughts in their hearts, and stirred up the evil within them ; and made them spring upon the disciple Philip ; and they chained him, and were intent on killing him. And the eyes of every one who laid a hand upon Philip became blind.

And when the multitude saw it they cried with a loud voice, saying:

"There is One God, the God of Philip. Why are ye killing this blessed disciple by whom God hath delivered us from error unto faith?" f. 78 a

And thus the crowd saved Philip from the hands of those who wished to kill him. And he went forth preaching in all the country round about and proclaimed the Word of God every day. And he healed every one who had a sickness; until all the people of the city and in its borders gathered themselves together unto him. And he taught them, and preached unto them about the kingdom of Heaven. And the blind drew near unto him and he opened their eyes, and the lame became straight by the word of his mouth. And the deaf heard with their ears; and the dumb spake by the power of the Lord Jesus the Christ Who was dwelling in him. And the lepers were cleansed when he raised his hand and entreated God on their behalf. And those in whom there were devils— he cast them out by the sign of the cross, thanking God for what He had given him in this noble gift until he had healed them all from every disease.

And when the magistrates of the city saw what Philip was doing, the wonders which were made manifest by his hands, and [how] he healed divers sicknesses and other things; for they saw that their brethren, and their friends, and their sons, and their daughters, and their companions had no faith in their worship, and had entered into the faith of the Lord Jesus the Christ; then those who did not believe in what pleased Philip gathered f. 78 b themselves together, and withdrew to a place, and took counsel how they might lay hold of the disciple, and bind and kill him secretly, so that the city might not perish, and they might boast to the king that an alien could not enter their city and destroy their religion. And if they were to tarry until that was accomplished, he would send [men] to slay them and to lay waste their city, and to say unto them: "Are ye waiting for this one man, until he hath chosen [from] this multitude those who will resist my commandment?" And they covenanted together concerning it. And they laid hands upon the saint and bound him, and lectured him to his face with insulting words; and the disciple laughed in their faces, and rejoiced. And they said one to the other: "See how he is laughing: he is mocking us; perhaps he desireth to lead us astray and deceive us like the multitude whom he hath left, [who] rejected the decree of the king; and he hath separated them from their wives."

And when he heard that he said unto them: "Truly this is falsehood if it be completed. And ye ought to return unto God, and He will forgive you your sins; and will make you meet for His kingdom, which never faileth."

Another of them answered and said: "Kill him; if we leave him he will lead us all astray." Then their wrath waxed hot against him, and they

f. 79 a laid hold of him and hanged him upon a cross, and they bound him head downwards, saying: "lest he should move his body." And they tortured him with cruel torments; and they never ceased following him and torturing him with the worst of torments, until he gave up the ghost upon the cross. And they took him down, and took counsel together and said: "Let us kindle a huge fire, and fling his body into it, that it may be burnt up, and may not be found."

And when they had kindled the fire that they might throw his pure body into it, the Lord Jesus the Christ, Who had given patience to the saint for that torture, sent an angel, and took his pure body out of the fire before them at noon-tide out of the city, and all its inhabitants beheld it; and he ascended up on high with it, with joy and glory and honour, till he vanished from their eyes. And he arrived with it at Jerusalem; and he hid it in a tree. And when all the crowd beheld this wonder, and remembered the multitude of wonders and of signs which God had caused to happen by his hands, of the healing of divers sicknesses, they all raised their voices, women and men, saying: "There is one God, the God of Philip the servant of Jesus the Christ. He is God, the God of heaven and earth, and the great, the High God, blessed by heavenly beings

f. 79 b and earthly beings, and by all the city and its surrounding districts together, Jesus the Christ. And they sent people who feared God to the top of the mountains; and they remained many days in the desert, going round about. And the citizens fasted and prayed, and humbled themselves before God, that He might restore to them the body of the saint.

And when God beheld the beauty of their dispositions, and their regret for what they had exceeded in the ugliness of their deeds, He sent that angel to tell them the place of the body of the disciple. And they took it, and journeyed with it to the city, with praise and glory and honour. And they wrapped it in fine raiment, and left it in a new coffin. And the completion of the martyrdom and conflict of the holy Philip was on the eighteenth day of Hathôr, and he was left in Carthagena[1] in peace. And glory be to Jesus the Christ, and His Father, and the Holy Ghost, for ever and ever. Amen.

And praise be to God always and for ever.

[1] MS. "Martagena."

THE PREACHING OF BARTHOLOMEW.

In the name of the Father, and the Son, and the Holy Ghost, the One God. f. 80 a
*The Book of the Preaching of Bartholomew the Blessed Disciple, and his
Preaching in the City of the Oasis, in the peace of the Lord Jesus the
Christ.*

And it came to pass, when the disciples were gathered together and
they divided amongst themselves the cities of the world, and the lot of
Bartholomew was to go forth to the land of the Oases, to preach amongst
them in the name of the Lord Jesus the Christ, that he said unto Peter,
the chief of the Apostles: "O my father Peter! I have neither gone into
this city, nor do I know the language of its people. I entreat thee to
remain with me until thou shalt have brought me unto it; and what is
His will, shall come to pass."

Peter replied, saying: "I shall not go out with thee alone but with the
company; I am commanded by the Lord to bring each one to his city."

And Peter arose and Bartholomew, and they both went forth, seeking
the city of the Oases. And they travelled in the desert, and they met
a rich man who had slaves, and ten camels with him. And when Peter
and Bartholomew saw him, they rejoiced at it, and went on to meet him;
and they said unto him: "Peace be on the owner of the camels." He said
unto them: "Peace be upon you."

Peter said unto him: "O thou man! unto what country art thou f. 80 b
journeying with these camels?" The man said unto him: "To the city
of the Oases." Peter said unto him: "Do us a favour, and carry us with
thee, and bring us to the city." The owner of the camels said unto him:
"And what cause hath led thee thither, when thou hast nothing to sell
in it?" Peter said unto him: "We are not going to sell nor to buy;
we are servants of a good God, Whose name is Jesus. He hath chosen
twelve men, and hath taught us commandments, and hath put into our
hands the healing of all diseases. And He hath commanded us to go
round about in the farthest countries, and to preach in His name, and
exhort the people not to persist in their error, but to turn unto Him, that
He may forgive their sins, and make them meet for His kingdom. And
therefore we seek to enter the city, that we may bring these commandments
unto them, which our Master hath taught us, that they may hearken unto

them, and may forsake their former deeds, and may repent, so that they may live for ever."

And when the man heard that speech, he said unto them: "If ye be some of the friends of Jesus, of Whom ye have spoken, we will not allow you to enter our city; because we have heard that ye lead the people astray, and ye separate women from their husbands; and ye say that f. 81 a except a man live in purity he cannot see God. And I am just coming from a friend who loves me greatly. When he saw me coming to meet him, he rejoiced over me, but this time he did not lift his head to greet me, on account of the grief in which he was. And I asked him what was the cause. And he told me that he had been in sorrow for ten days about his wife; for some of your people had come into the city, and had commanded the people [to do] all that you have said. And his wife had followed their speech, and had forsaken her husband. And I am afraid about myself, that if I bring you into my city, and you teach its people what your Master hath commanded you, my wife would hearken unto you, and would believe in your words, and would separate herself from me."

And when they had heard this from him, they resolved on going away, and they were grieved. And Bartholomew said unto Peter: "What shall we do, that we may succeed in entering the city? Give me counsel." Peter said unto him: "I will give thee counsel. But I fear that thou wilt meet with great trouble in this business, and thou wilt say: 'Peter counselled [it].' But this is thy lot, and I will not separate myself from thee by the will of the Lord Jesus the Christ, Who desireth the salvation of every man, until I bring thee unto it."

Bartholomew said unto him: "Arise, O thou beloved father! the f. 81 b Lord is helping [us]. Let us disguise ourselves, and gird our loins, and get before this man without his knowing it; and when he gets up to us, let us ask him to carry us on his camels to the city. And if he should enquire about our business in it, say: 'This slave who belongs to me, I will sell him in it.' And if he should say unto thee: 'What is his handicraft?' say: 'A vine-dresser.' And when I shall have entered the city which the Lord gave unto me to speak in it, I will do what He hath commanded me."

Peter said unto him: "The view which thou hast stated is good." And they did that about which they had agreed; and they preceded the man in the journey until he got up to them. And Peter said unto him: 'O thou good man! carry us with thee on these camels to the city of the Oases."

He said unto them: "And what is your business in it?" He said unto him: "I wish to enter it that I may sell this boy who belongs to me."

And when the man heard this speech from him he rejoiced with great joy, and he tied up the feet of his camels[1]. And he said unto him: "This is a blessed day, for I have been away from my home for many days, I and those who are with me, with these camels, seeking for a boy whom I might buy, and I have not found one; and God hath made thee pass near me." Then he said unto Peter: "Tell me what is his handicraft, that I may buy him from thee, and I will pay thee the price." Peter said unto him: "He is a dresser of blighted vines, skilled in their cultivation." The man said f. 82 a unto him: "I am seeking one like that, for I have many vineyards. I want him to be chief man in them."

And they agreed with each other about the price—thirty dinars. The man paid them to Peter; and he delivered Bartholomew to him. And he said unto Peter: "Wilt thou go with me to my house? Thou hast taken the price from me, and hast delivered up the boy to me, but I would fain honour thee in my home." Peter said unto him: "May God repay thee with a rich reward for what thou hast done unto me. Do thou it unto this boy, and do not tire him out, but be gentle unto him, and thou wilt praise the result of it greatly." And when Peter found how kind the owner of the camels was, he paid the money, which was the price of Bartholomew, to himself; and said unto him: "Let this be in thy keeping; if thou findest a needy man, pay some of it"; and he commanded him what was needful, and gave him [the salutation of] peace, and bade him farewell. And Peter returned.

And Bartholomew travelled with the owner of the camels, seeking the city. Then they went astray from the path, and all the water which they had with them came to an end, and the camels were tired, and some of them became separated from them, and died on the road. And the man wept, and those who were with him, saying: "Woe unto us! what hath befallen us because of this boy! Perhaps he was not a good boy when he f. 82 b was in his own country, and his master drove him away to this far-off land, where he is of no use to any one. And I do not grieve for the camels as I do for myself and for those who are with me, for we shall die of thirst in this desert." And Bartholomew wept openly. And he prayed in his heart, and did not wish that they should know that he was a disciple of the Lord, lest they should prevent him from entering the city. And he

---

[1] The Bedawîn usually tie up one fore-foot of a camel when they halt, to prevent it from walking away.

took hold of the camels and said : " In the name of the Lord Jesus the
Christ, the true God, let these camels rise, that these men may know who
I am, and that they may not imagine what is not convenient for them."
And immediately the camels rose up, and returned to life as they had been.
And the men were astonished and they said nothing ; and they rode upon
them, and journeyed.

And as they drew nigh unto the city Bartholomew dismounted, and
girded up his loins, and went on in front of his master.   And when they
reached the city, lo ! there was a blind man beside the gate, on whom the
spirit of God descended.   [And] he cried with a loud voice : " Have compassion on me, O Bartholomew ! disciple of Jesus the Christ ! give me the
light of mine eyes ; for thou art able to do this."   And when Bartholomew'
heard the speech of the blind man he was silent.   The man who had bought
f. 83 a   him said unto him : " Art thou one of the disciples of the Christ ? and
I have entered the city with thee ? and I did not know thee ? "   Bartholomew said unto him : " I will not say unto thee that I am a disciple of the
Christ until thou shalt have seen the wonders which shall appear in this city
at my hand."   And the blind man repeated his saying : " Have compassion
upon me, O disciple of the Christ ! give me the light of mine eyes."   He
said unto him : " May He Who hath commanded thee to speak give thee
the light of thine eyes ! "   And straightway his eyes were opened ; and the
astonishment of the man and of those who were with him increased.

And when that magistrate went into his house, he called his friends
the magistrates, and said unto them : " Come, see this boy, whom I have
bought, and who sayeth that he is a vine-dresser, skilled in the treatment
of the vines.   And a great wonder hath been shown by him on the way,
whilst we were journeying in the desert we mistook the path, and the
camels perished ; and he raised them up alive, as they had been.   And
when we drew nigh unto the gate of the city he made that blind man see
whom ye know sitting at the gate of the city.   What would ye advise me
to do with him ?   It is said that he is a clever worker, skilled in vines
which are blighted, so that their cultivation may be restored."

f. 83 b   His friends said unto him : " If he be a worker skilled in the treatment
of the vines, let him remain with thee, and try his workmanship, if it be as
hath been said ; and if it be not, thou canst sell him, and take his price."
Then he called all the labourers who tended his vines, and sent to bring
Bartholomew, and made him stand in the midst of them.   And he said
unto them : " I have made this man chief over you, and all that he sayeth
unto you, hearken unto him."

And Bartholomew went out to the vineyard in which he was to work, and he was busy all the day amongst the vines. And he entered the city at eventide, and remained teaching for the rest of the night, whom he could, for forty days; and not a single man hearkened unto him. And after the forty days Bartholomew besought the Lord, and said: "O my Lord Jesus the Christ! how long shall I remain in this city and not a single man listen to my speech? Put me to death, O my Lord! in this city, this day." And he stood and prayed in faith that it might be given unto him that a miracle might be shown at his hand. And after his prayer was ended, he said unto the blind man whom he had made to see—for he was with him, and had never left him: "Go into the city, and f. 84 a tell the magistrate, my master, to call thy friends, and go out to the vineyards, and thou shalt see this new handicraft which I have done to-day." And the man went as he [Bartholomew] had commanded him, to the city. Then the disciple took three roots from the vines and laid them upon canes, and at once when he had suspended them, they bore good fruit. And when the magistrate went with his friends, they saw the wonder which the disciple had done, every root which he had taken bearing leaves before he had left it upon the canes, and the grapes coming. And they threw themselves down before the disciple, and worshipped him, saying: "O our Lord! Who art thou? art thou God who hath appeared on the earth? Tell us which of the gods thou art, that we may bring thee a sacrificial offering. If thou art a man, tell us what sacrifice thou desirest that we should offer [for?] thee."

The disciple replied: "I am not one of those whom ye imagine; I am a servant of Jesus the Christ." And he commanded them to bring canes, that he might put the rest of the vines upon them. And the magistrate went, and brought him canes, and a huge snake which was amongst the canes fastened itself on his hand and bit him; and he fell upon the ground, f. 84 b in great pain. And they wept.

Bartholomew said unto them: "Why do ye weep? Is there no physician in this city to whom ye can send, that he may come and treat him?" And one of the slaves of the magistrate hastened and told his wife, and they came with a doctor to take care of him, and they found that he was dead. And his friends rent their garments; and they all wept for him. And the disciple was working amongst the canes, and he was singing. And some of those who were present said: "Look at this bad servant, he doth not weep for his lord; but he is very glad. And as for these sayings which he utters, we know not what it is." Others said: "He is not a bad servant, for we have seen wonders from him which our fathers neither saw nor heard about." And Bartholomew was diligent in his work until he finished it and washed his hands. And he said to those who were weeping: "Ye have wept enough. Go far away, that ye may see and behold the glory of our Lord and His strength." And they did as he commanded them, and withdrew from him. And he stretched out his hands, saying: "O God! Who ruleth all things, Who sitteth on the throne of His glory, Who hath created the heaven, and the earth, and all that therein is, by His beloved Son, Jesus the Christ, Who hath not left us [as] pledges

f. 85 a in the hand of our enemy Satan, and hath delivered us by His precious blood in Jesus the Christ, the pure Seed which beareth fruit in pure seeds; Who went out into the wilderness to seek the lost sheep until He restored it to the good fold. I entreat Thee, O my Lord Jesus the Christ! and I beseech Thee on behalf of this man whom a serpent hath bitten, that the serpent may return and take the poison which it has thrown into his body; and that he may live, to the glory of Thy name in this city."

And while Bartholomew was praying, the serpent appeared from the place in which it was, and stood before Bartholomew. And it said: "Thou hast charged me to take the poison out of this man; and I shall die, and he will live."

Bartholomew replied to it: "Thou wast not called in order to multiply talk, but that we may know who thou art and who is thy father." Then the serpent came near to the man, and took the poison out of him. Then the man arose alive, as he had been. And when they saw this wonder, they fell at the feet of the saint, saying, "Truly thy God is a mighty God. He hath power to make the dead live." And the magistrate who was alive stood and said: "Have ye seen this wonder which I have seen from this man whom I have bought? a God, thinking that he was a

f. 85 b man; I have bought a lord, saying that he was a slave."

And he returned to the disciple and said unto him: "I adjure thee by the name of the God, Jesus the Christ, thy God, Whom I saw standing with thee when thou didst raise me up from death, I adjure thee by His name; do not refuse the request which I make unto thee, but respond to it." The disciple said unto him: "If it be a good request, I will respond to thee, but tell me what it is." The magistrate said unto him: "I desire that thou shouldest do away with this vineyard, and destroy it; for it is the place in which thy blessing hath rested; and I will build a fine church, for this is the place in which I have died and come to life."

Bartholomew said unto him: "Let it be as thou hast said." Then he commanded the vineyard to be cleansed; and he brought straw, and drew a line upon the surface of the ground to the extent of the foundations of the church. And he commanded them to bring masons and all the architects, and the church was built with fine masonry until it was completed. And Bartholomew commanded that the multitude should be gathered together unto him, and he baptized them in the name of the Father, and the Son, and the Holy Ghost. And he took some of the grapes which were in the vine which bore leaves and fruit at the hands of the saint, and he squeezed it in a cup, and asked for clean bread, and made supplication, and gave thanks, and brake it, and gave to the multitude of the Body and pure f. 86 a Blood of the Lord. And he appointed unto them the magistrate whom he had brought to life as presbyter, and he appointed unto them deacons, and he abode for three months preaching unto them; and he healed all the sick who were amongst them, and committed them to the Lord, and went out from amongst them; they bidding him farewell in peace, saying: "There is no God but God, the God of Bartholomew, Jesus the Christ, He Who sent thee unto us that thou mightest deliver us from our sins." And he went forth from the city of the Oases, and journeyed to the city of Andînûs, that he might preach in it in the name of the Christ, to Whom be praise and glory for ever and ever.

THE MARTYRDOM OF SAINT BARTHOLOMEW.

The Martyrdom of St Bartholomew, Disciple of the Lord Jesus the Christ, and the completion of his testimony on the first day of Tût, in the peace of the Lord. Amen.

And when Bartholomew, the disciple of the Lord, went to the great cities built upon the shore of the sea, whose people knew not God, but were like the wandering sheep in the greatness of their ignorance; the blessed Bartholomew went in unto them and proclaimed unto them the Gospel of the Lord. And when he entered the city, he preached thus unto them: "Hearken, all ye inhabitants of the city, 'Blessed are the poor in spirit, for theirs is the kingdom of heaven. Blessed are the merciful, for they shall obtain mercy. Blessed are the peace-makers, for they shall be called the children of God. Blessed are they that hunger and thirst after righteousness, for they are those that shall be filled. Blessed are they that give to the poor, for theirs is the kingdom of heaven, and they lend unto God. Blessed is he who hath a wife, and is as he who hath no wife, they are those who shall inherit the earth.'"

Matt. v. 3, 7, 6, 9, f. 86 b

And when they heard this from the holy Bartholomew, God, the Sustainer of all, opened their hearts, [and] they received the commandments of God, Who desireth the life of the sinner, and his repentance, and his return unto Himself, that He may forgive him. Thus He gave unto all the people of this city a strong character, and a right conscience, from the eldest to the youngest of them. And they obeyed, and believed in God and the Gospel. And all the words of Bartholomew were sweet to their hearts like honey, and the honeycomb in the heart of all who listened to him. And all the city and all the region forsook the worship of idols and believed in God Who loveth the salvation of the race of Adam; Who formed their hearts for the sweetness of faith that He might save their souls and forgive them; and every one amongst them remitted all his friend's debts to him.

Ps. xix. 10

And when the people of the city and all the district called to Bartholomew he blessed their multitude, [and] many of the men and women loved God and obeyed His commandments, and forsook all the works of the devil in this fleeting world, and they loved purity.

f. 87 a

And the call of the saint was spread abroad to every place that was near. And all who heard the preaching of the Gospel believed in God with all their hearts and all their souls. And the name of Bartholomew and his preaching reached Agrippus the king. And when Iphia, the king's wife heard it, she withdrew herself from the company of the king and from all contamination with him.

And when the king heard that his wife had withdrawn herself from him and had accepted the words of Bartholomew who had commanded every one in the knowledge of the truth and the faith of Jesus the Christ [to do so], he sent in haste and brought him to his presence. And when he appeared, the king said unto him: "Art thou Bartholomew the wizard—a friend of Jesus?"

The disciple replied to him with great boldness and courage: "I am not a wizard as thou hast affirmed, O thou king! but all sorcery and every deed that is done becomes vain when Jesus the Christ is mentioned."

And the king commanded that he should be removed from his presence; and he said to those who were beside him to bring to him his wife. And Bartholomew went a little way aside from the king and stretched out his hands, and prayed the prayer of the Gospel, and said, "Amen." f. 87 b

Then a blind man came to him, who could see nothing with his right eye, and one of his hands had been withered since he was born, and entreated him to heal him. And when the disciple looked into the blind man's face, his eye was promptly opened, and it became like its fellow. And the disciple said unto him: "Give me thy hand, that I may speak unto thee, that the power of my Lord Jesus the Christ may appear, that every one may see and may believe in His name." And when the man pulled his hand out from his raiment, he found that it was straight like the other. And he went forth from the crowd, praising God and thanking Him, and preaching in the name of the blessed disciple. And he went about in all the countries, preaching in them, and telling their people about the beauty of God's dealing with him; and about the power which had been shown forth at the hand of Saint Bartholomew.

And Agrippus said unto the nobles of his kingdom and to all his servants: "If this disciple should remain alive in this country he will turn us all to his faith. And it will be best for us to kill him and to destroy his body so that it may no more be found." They answered him, saying: "As the king hath commanded," for their hearts were sorrowful; they did not wish him to be slain, for they rejoiced in him from what they had seen of the many wonders which God had done by his hands. They said unto the f. 88 a king: "If the king desireth this, let him drive him away from our country." And the people of the country were anxious for his deliverance from his [the king's] hands.   And he was wroth with a great wrath, and swore with great oaths that he would not hearken unto their speech, but would slay him in a cruel manner; and no one could answer him anything.

And Bartholomew continued to go about in all the neighbourhood, and to preach the good news of the Gospel in it, and to exhort the multitude, and to command them and teach them faith in the Lord Jesus the Christ.

After these things, a wicked man came to the king and said unto him: "Thou carest not that Bartholomew [should go] throughout all the country and contradict thy commandments and insult thy gods." And when he heard it he was wroth with a great wrath and sent two of the captains of his army and his men to seek for Bartholomew; and he commanded them that in whatever place he should be found, they should bind his hands and his feet, and throw him into the sea, so that his body might not be found. And the messengers journeyed on their way, and they found Bartholomew casting a devil out of a man who had been possessed with it for a long time, and teaching the multitude, and commanding them to believe in the

f. 88 b Lord Jesus the Christ.   And when the messengers drew nigh to the blessed disciple, he called to them with the [greeting of] peace, and said unto them: "The peace of the Lord be upon you, O brethren!"   And they stood gazing at one another, wondering at his meekness and the beauty of his love.   They answered him, saying: "Wilt thou go with us to the presence of the king? for he calleth for thee.   And if thou dost not wish [it], we will not compel thee to appear with us without thy consent; for we are sure that God dwelleth with thee in all thy circumstances."   And the disciple said to himself: "I must not resist the commandment of the Lord,

Luke xxi. which He said, 'Ye shall be brought before kings and rulers for My name's
12 sake,' and this is His will."   And he went with them to Agrippus the king. And when he looked at him, he said unto him: "Art thou he who hath raised a sedition in this city and all its districts, and doth separate women from their husbands?"   The holy disciple answered and said unto him: "It is not I who have raised a sedition in the city, and who separates women from their husbands; but God in Whom they have believed with all their hearts and souls, He it is Who hath given them purity.   And thou, O Agrippus! if thou wilt receive thy soul from me, thou shalt be saved, and shalt inherit the kingdom of heaven instead of this fleeting sovereignty."

f. 89 a   And when Agrippus heard this from him, he was wroth with a great wrath, because of what Satan had made him understand about the separation from his wife.   And he commanded the guards to fill a hair-sack with sand, and to put the saint into it, and throw him into the sea. And they did as the king commanded them.

And this came to pass on the first day of Thoth. And this was his death and he rested. And afterwards the water cast him on the shore of the city on the second day. And people who had believed in the Lord by means of him, took him and swathed him in a fine shroud, and put him into a good place. And praise be to the Father and the Son and the Holy Ghost, for ever and ever. Amen. And praise be unto God always and for ever.

THE PREACHING OF THOMAS.

The Preaching of Thomas the Disciple, which he proclaimed in the City of India, in the peace of the Lord Jesus the Christ. Amen.

And it came to pass after the Resurrection of Jesus the Christ from the dead that He appeared unto His chosen disciples, and said unto them: "May the peace of my Father rest upon you. And what He gave unto me, I have not hidden it from you. Assemble and divide the world into
f. 89 b twelve portions and let each one of you go to his portion. And fear ye not; I am with you, and I know all the sufferings that befall you, and the persecution from the world; but be ye patient with them, until ye shall turn them from error unto faith by My name. Remember the sufferings which befell Me and everything that was done unto Me for the sake of mankind."

And the lot of Thomas came out to the city of India. And he worshipped the Lord and said: "Wherefore hath my lot come out, that I should go forth to the city of India? for they are hard men, like wild beasts, and it will be difficult for them to receive the hearing of the words of the Gospel. But thou wilt accompany me, O Lord! to this country."

The Lord said unto him: "Behold, Peter is your guide; he will go forth with thee to this country." And the Apostles prepared to go forth, each one to the country which had come unto him in his lot. Peter was to go forth to the city of Rome, and the cities belonging to it: and Matthias to the city of Persia. And Thomas said unto Peter: "O my father! arise, go with me and my brother Matthias, until thou bring us to our cities." And he consented unto them about this, and went forth with them. And the Lord departed from them, ascending to heaven with glory. And it came to pass, after they had journeyed for forty days, they arrived at a city which had come by lot to Thomas and to Matthias. And when they had entered the city they sat down in the street of the
f. 90 a city like foreigners. And the Lord Jesus the Christ appeared unto them like a learned man, and said unto them, "Peace be upon you, O brethren!" And they said: "On thee also be peace!" And He sat down on their right hand, not far from them. Peter said: "O my father! let us go into this city and preach in it in the name of the Lord, for this is the first of the cities which we have reached: perchance we may be able to save its people,

and turn them to the obedience of God. For the Lord said: 'Whoso shall preach [in] many cities, he shall save many people, and he shall have a great reward in the kingdom of heaven'."

And while they were sitting, a man came up to them, one of the friends of Contûrîs, the king of India. And he looked at the disciples sitting like foreigners. He said unto them: "Whence are ye, O ye brethren?" They said unto him: "Ask for what thou dost wish." He said unto them: "It is nothing but good, for I see that ye are very fine men; and I am seeking for a slave who will be like you, that I may buy him."

Peter said unto him, "We three are servants of one Lord, whose name is Jesus the Christ, and He is present in this city. And when He shall appear, He will sell thee whomsoever of us thou desirest; for [in] our city and all the country round it the men are handsome."

And when he had said this—the Lord was listening to what they were saying to each other—immediately the Lord appeared unto them, and spoke to them in the language which they knew, and said, "Peace! O noble f. 90 b Peter and faithful learned Thomas, and meek Matthias! I have told you that I will not forsake you: but I will be present with you always as I have promised from my Father. I will go before you to every place to which ye shall journey."

And a friend of the king of India was present, who did not know the language in which our Lord was speaking to them. And afterwards the Lord appeared unto them like a rich man, and sat down on a place in the city. Peter said unto the man, the friend of the king, "Our Lord, about Whom I have told you, is present. Look at which of us thou dost wish, He will sell him to thee."

The man said unto the Lord: "Peace, O thou good man! Thine appearance witnesseth for thee, that thou art a nobleman. Art thou willing to sell me one of these thy slaves?"

The Lord said: "Which of these two dost thou wish me to sell thee? Now this one, the elder, was born in the household of my fathers; I will not sell him."

And the man looked at Thomas and admired him, for he was sturdy and strong in spirit. And he said unto him: "Sell me this one." The Lord said unto him: "His price is three pounds of gold."

The man replied unto him: "And I have bought him from thee," and f. 91 a he delivered the price to him. And he said unto him: "Write out the bill of his sale for me in the street of the city." The Lord said unto him: "Thou dost not need anyone to write. I will write for thee in my own hand; I will acknowledge to thee in it that this is the slave whom I have sold unto thee, O Deyâmus! friend of Contûrîs, king of India." And he finished the deed, as was right, and departed from them to heaven with glory.

And after this the Lord appeared unto Thomas and said unto him: "Accept thy price, and distribute it among the poor, and the orphans and the widows, in the place whither thou shalt go. I have sold thee for three talents of gold; for thou art a slave of the Trinity: the Father and the Son and the Holy Ghost." Thomas answered and said unto him: "May Thy grace be with me, O Lord!" And when He had said these words unto Thomas, He departed from him. And Thomas girded up his loins like a slave, and went to Peter and Matthias and said unto them, "Remember me in your prayers, and embrace me with a spiritual kiss, for this is the last of our meetings in this world." And they held each other's hands with [the salutation of] peace, and with a spiritual embrace; and separated. And Thomas went with his master; and Peter and Matthias went on their way.

f. 91 b   And the man asked Thomas about his craft. And he said unto him: "I am a mason, and I am a carpenter, and I am a doctor. As for the art of carpentering, I mend measures, and balances, and weights, and ploughs, which take away the briars and the thorns and the thistles and all that is needful for rooting them from the earth. As for the masonry, I build temples, and fortresses, and high towers which are suitable for kings. As for medicine, I treat the wounds which fester in the bodies."

And when the man heard this, he rejoiced and said: "Truly in such a manner the king will be suited." And after many days they reached the city of India. And the man went in unto the king, and told him about Thomas, and let him read the deed which the Lord had written with His hand. And when he saw it, he wondered at it. And he told him the crafts in which Thomas excelled; and this made him rejoice exceedingly. And he said: "Take this man, deliver him over to Lucius the captain; that he may pay him the money which he wants to build us a great fortress." And he went with him to him (Lucius) and told him all that the king had enjoined. And he delivered to him all that he needed, and Lucius went f. 92 a after these things to the city of the king; and he commanded his wife Arsânûni, and said unto her: "Let not this man serve like the slaves; but (rather) at his craft until I return from the king's presence." And after Lucius had gone, Thomas went to Arsânûni his wife, and read to her the Gospel of the Lord Jesus the Christ, and the prophecies of the prophets; and he said unto her: "O Arsânûni, I see that thou art in great grief.

Thou dost worship these idols of gold and of silver ; and thou sayest that they are gods, and they are not gods. And what thou doest unto them doth not profit thee. For they speak not, and they hear not, and they see not ; and if the earth were moved, they could not take care of themselves, but they would fall and would be broken. I entreat thee to go with me into the temple of those whom thou dost worship, that I may see their power." And she went before him to shew them to him.

And he lifted up his eyes to heaven and prayed, saying : " O God, who directest all things ! Father of my Lord Jesus the Christ, Thy beloved Son, and Thy Holy Spirit, Whom when all the devils had heard him, they were disturbed, Thou art the Shepherd of the sheep which wandered ; Thou art the good Shepherd ; Thou art the true Light which shineth in our f. 92 b hearts ; Thou art He by Whose name all creation is saved ; Thou hast sent me to this country that I may turn its inhabitants to Thee ; Thou art the Maker of all mankind, and of all the creatures which all humbly worship Thee ; Thou when Thou lookest at all the earth, the sea trembleth and all that is therein, and all its waves are silent when they hear Thy voice ; The serpents and all creeping things are subject unto Thee, for Thou dost nourish them. Yea, O my Lord and my Master Jesus the Christ ! (Thou art He) Who wilt show wonders and signs by my hand in the country, that Thy name be glorified, for to Thee be praise for ever and ever. Amen."

And while the disciple was praying, the foundation of the house in which she was, was moved, and all the idols fell to the ground on their faces, from their places, and the devils who dwelt in them cried out, saying : " Woe unto us, for our power and our fame is made vain, and no God is worshipped save Jesus the Christ, the Son of the Living God."

And when Arsânûni saw what had befallen her gods, she feared greatly, and she fell upon the earth before the saint. And he stretched out his hand and raised her up. And she laid hold of him and entreated him, and said : " O good servant of God, who hast come into my house ! f. 93 a art thou a man, or art thou a slave, or art thou a God ? And what is this Name which thou hast named, which is Jesus ? And when thou didst name His Name, the foundation of the house was moved, [and it] fell upon the ground, and all the gods in whom I have trusted fell upon their faces, and became like dust. Hide not from me this power of thine, O good servant of God ! And from this hour the worship of idols is destroyed in my house. And I am repentant, confessing, believing in thy God, the Lord Jesus the Christ, the Son of the Living God."

And Thomas, the blessed disciple, answered and said unto her: "Arsânûni, dost thou believe with all thy heart? Then forsake this fading world, so soon to pass away, and learn that thy pride in gold, and silver and beautiful raiment which perisheth, and which the moth eateth, and the beauty of the flesh, will decay, and whosoever boasteth therein shall be speedily destroyed. And one looketh after this beauty on a pained face and closed eyes, and a speechless tongue. And man goeth to his eternal home. Seek after God, O Arsânûni! and thou shalt find Him

f. 93 b not far from any one who seeketh Him with all his heart. The prophet said of God: 'I am the Living God who is near unto you, not far from thee, O Israel! and I am God; I desire not the death of the sinner, that he may return and his soul may live.' And he sayeth also about the return of the sons who have come back to me. And also he saith: 'Return unto Me, ye sons who have rebelled. Return ye unto Me, ye will find Me. He who seeketh, findeth Him. And whoso calleth upon Him, He will hear him'."

And when Arsânûni the wife of the magistrate had heard this, her heart was opened by the fear of God. God opened the eyes of her heart. And every one in her house and many of the citizens, believed in God. And she went into her chamber, and stripped off her fine raiment, and spread ashes beneath her and worshipped on her face, thanking God and saying: "I believe in Thee, O my Lord Jesus the Christ! the God of this foreigner, who hath come into my dwelling, and hath been a guide unto me into the path of life—I entreat Thee, O merciful Lord! Whom I knew not until this day, if Thou hast made me worthy of knowing Thee—O my Lord Jesus the Christ! Son of the Living God, forgive me all the faults that I have already committed, and the error in which I have been until this day from my worship of impure idols. Now I have returned unto Thee,

f. 94 a O my Lord Jesus the Christ! Thou art my Light, and my Saviour, Thou art my hope, and my strength, Thou art my refuge, in Thee have I trusted."

And when she had finished her prayer she went out to the disciple. And her face was changed because of the ashes. And she said unto him: "O good servant of God! arise, baptize me in the name of the Father, and the Son, and the Holy Ghost, by Whom thou hast saved me."

And the disciple rejoiced at her faith. And he said unto her, "O good woman! the grace of God hath rested upon thee."

She answered him, saying: "The faith of thy Lord hath dwelt in my heart, and my limbs, and my soul." And they both gave thanks to the Lord Jesus the Christ, Who had brought back the wandering sheep.

And he arose quickly and baptized her and all who were in her dwelling unto the Father and the Son and the Holy Ghost. And he took pure bread and a cup wherein was wine, and gave thanks and brake and gave to the multitude who had been baptized, the honoured Body of the Lord, and His blood. And he was praying all night long with the Psalms of David, he and all the brethren who had been baptized. And they brought to him every one who had a disease of any kind, and those who were possessed with devils, and the blind, and the lame, and the lepers, and he healed them all.

And he went out every day in the midst of the city, preaching in the f. 94 b name of the Lord Jesus the Christ. And he preached the holy Gospel, and said unto them: "Let the sick people come unto me; I will heal them without price. I desire no reward from any man." And they came unto Arsânûni, the wife of the magistrate, who had believed in him. And all the citizens became believing Christians. And he recited the Gospels and the Prophets in their presence; and taught them the precepts of religion. And afterwards he baptized them all in the name of the Father and the Son and the Holy Ghost. And he continued to dwell amongst them in the city for the space of four years. And their faith in the Christ became stronger: Lucius being absent near the king. And when he returned to the city, his wife and all the inhabitants of the city went out to meet him—and he looked from afar at his wife—she being dressed in mean garments—he was grieved about it with a great sorrow, and thought that everything in his dwelling had been stolen. And he called one of his slaves, and said unto him: "Hath anything happened in my house?" He said unto him: "Nothing hateful hath happened, but everything is good since thou hast been absent from it." And he entered the bath to wash himself, and went to his dwelling. And he called his wife Arsânûni, and when she appeared he talked with her in the fashion of men of the world; and invited her to intercourse with him. She replied, weeping: "O my lord! God hath rooted out of my heart this wicked f. 95 a inclination in which there is no profit; and as for to-day[1], it is by the will of the Lord." He answered her in fierce anger: "What speech is this which I have never heard from thee? and why art thou changed since I first knew thee? But to-day woe is me! Hath not the foreign slave who hath come unto us in these days bewitched thee?"

Arsânûni replied to him, saying: "It cannot be as thou sayest of him, O my lord! because all the doctors seek to heal bodies; but he healeth

---

[1] BUDGE, *Ethiopic version*: "and this day is the sabbath of God."

bodies and souls; and do not say an evil word about him; but hearken thou also to his words."

And when Lucius heard that from her, he was filled with the rage of a devil; and he replied to her: "If he be a practising physician let him heal himself from the torture which shall befall him from me." And he straightway commanded the guards to bring him the tanners who were in the city; and they brought them.

And he called Thomas and said unto him: "O thou wicked slave! thou wizard! where are the works and the handicrafts which thou hast said that thou couldest do? Where are the temples which thou art building for the king? Where is the fortress? where are the ploughs, and the measures, and the balances which thou didst say that thou wouldest make? Where is the craft of medicine, and the good of thy treatment?"

f. 95 b   Thomas answered him: "I have finished all my workmanship, and have made it complete."

Lucius said unto him: "Thou art jesting with me. I will torture thee, O thou wicked slave! to the death."

Thomas said unto him: "I assure thee of the truth without torture, for until this time thou hast not learnt it and I will tell thee the truth. The temples and the fortresses which I have built are the souls which have come; they are the fortresses which I have repaired for the Heavenly King to dwell in. In them are the ploughs; they are the holy Gospels, which root up all evil from the heart of the believers who seek after God with all their hearts. And the treatments which are of the art of medicine, these are the Holy Mysteries which root up all evil imaginations, and pains, and longings from all those who seek for purity. These are the treatments and the handicrafts which God hath taught me."

Lucius said unto him: "O thou wicked slave! What speech is this?" And he commanded concerning him that he should be bound, and that four stakes should be driven into the ground, and that he should be bound to them and stretched out in his presence. And he commanded the flayers to flay off his skin. And he said unto him: "I will torture thee, and I will not let thee die quickly, except as I wish." And all the citizens wept, saying: "Woe unto us! what can we do with this righteous man f. 96 a who hath healed us from all diseases? If we lay our hands upon him, his God will be wroth with us, and His wrath shall descend upon us; and fire shall come down from heaven to burn us up; and if we do not do what this hypocrite hath commanded us, he will kill us. And we have seen many wonders from this holy man on the day when this wild boar entered the field of the widow woman ; and the men could not drive it away. And the woman went and did obeisance to this righteous man, and besought him, saying : 'O my Lord! help me.' And he had compassion on her, and went out to the field of this widow woman, and her fruits did not perish. And the boar did not go out, and fire came down from heaven and burnt him. And we are much afraid of his God."

The saint replied to them, saying : "Arise! fulfil the commandment which he hath commanded you. Well do I know that ye are constrained against your own opinion from fear of this ignorant magistrate."

And Lucius commanded that his skin should be flayed off. And the disciple raised his eyes to heaven and cried with a loud voice, saying : "O my Lord Jesus the Christ, Son of the Living God! help me in this tribulation." And Arsânûni heard the voices of the flayers, and the multitude who were weeping. And she looked from a window in her dwelling and f. 96 b saw the disciple being flayed, and she was greatly troubled. And she fell on her face, and died. And immediately Lucius cried : "This my wife hath died because of thee, O thou wicked slave! But I will spend all my energy upon thee, that I may know all the evil deeds that thou hast done." And when the father of Lucius' wife and her brothers heard it, they appeared and stood round her, weeping over her, crying and saying : "Woe unto us! Why hast thou died because of this foreigner? but our hearts rejoice over thee because thou hast died for the faith of the Christ, and the commandment of His blessed disciple."

Thomas answered and said unto them : "Hush! do not weep, for if she be dead in my Lord, I will raise her up." Lucius said unto him : "Say not that the torture is finished. I will torment thee at my pleasure ; and I will leave nothing possible to thee." And he commanded them to bring him vinegar and salt, and he put it over the body of the saint. And the disciple cried, saying : "O my Lord Jesus the Christ! help me in this tribulation. For my heart and my body and my spirit are very weary. O my Lord Jesus the Christ, the Compassionate, the Merciful, bring Thy help nigh unto me. Remember that I am a foreigner, my want of friends, and my loneliness. I have no father, nor mother, nor brother, nor f. 97 a kinsmen in this city. And I have no one who knoweth me in it. Jesus the Christ! Son of the Living God! Thou art my help, on Thee is my reliance ; and Thou art my Saviour ; Thou hast sent me to this city, and I did not resist Thy saying, O my Lord, and my God! I have hated all things for Thy sake, father and mother, and kinsfolk, and all that was mine, I have left all this and have heard Thy voice. Thou, O my Lord! didst send me to this city, O Lord, for the salvation of its people; and behold, Thou seest what hath befallen me in it. And as Thou hast suffered for me, O Lord, I am ready to endure all toil that may come upon me in it with gladness. Remember the time when Thou didst appear unto my brethren the disciples, at Thy Resurrection from amongst the dead; and I was not with them. And when they said unto me that they had seen Thee, and I remembered Thy words which Thou hadst said: 'Try the spirits, for many shall come in My name, and shall lead astray many.' I said unto my brethren, the disciples, 'Except I see the Lord, and see the print of the nails in His hands and put my finger on the print of the spear-thrust in His side, I will not believe.' And Thou didst appear unto me, and didst show me what I sought from Thee, and the certainty of Thy resurrection; and didst reprove my little faith. And as Thou hast suffered for me, because of this, I entreat Thee, O my Lord! that Thou wouldest forgive me, for Thou art a good God, merciful, and Thou receivest those who return unto Thee with all their hearts."

And while he was saying that, and weeping, the Lord had compassion on him, and appeared unto him in a shining cloud; and said unto him: "Let thy heart rejoice, O my beloved Thomas! And be strong; for thou art victorious over thine enemy, and all who shall oppose thee. Verily I say unto thee, that all trial and torture have befallen thee for the sake of mankind, that I may deliver them from the hands of the enemy, and they are not like one hour of My appearance unto thee, and My reception of thee, and My seating of thee on My right hand in My kingdom. For thou art called 'The Twin.' Thou art beloved by Me. Be patient, for thy reward is large, and thy glory is great with My Father. And many wonders shall be shown by thy skin. Let thy heart be strong and hasten to show thy right faith in my Godhead in this city which is to the east of thee which is named Cantôrīa. And thou shalt turn its people to the faith in My name. And the whole world hath been filled with the grace of My Father, and His mercy to mankind for the sake of My blood, poured out for the salvation of the world."

And when the Lord had said these words unto him, He embraced him and touched his body, and healed him from the wounds that were in it, and departed from him.

And Thomas arose quite whole; [and went] till he reached the place in which was the wife of Lucius and he layed his flayed-off skin upon her, saying: "In the name of Jesus the Christ, and His Father and His Holy Spirit, the voice which called Lazarus, it is He who will raise thee." And

(marginal references)
Matt. xxiv. 5
John xx. 25
f. 97 b
f. 98 a

she straightway opened her eyes and looked at the disciple standing near her head, and she stood up immediately and did obeisance unto him.

And when Lucius saw this wonder, and the great miracle which had been shown by him, he arose terrified, and did obeisance to him, saying: "Truly there is no God but thy God, Whom thou servest. I entreat thee, O good servant of God! that thou wouldst forgive me all the evil that I have done unto thee in mine ignorance." And Thomas raised him up, for they all believed. And he said unto him: "Fear not; God will not punish those who repent and confess their sins." And in that hour he believed, and all the nobles of the city. And he commanded them to bring bread and the cup, and he prayed, and gave to them all the Holy Mysteries and made them Christians. And he laid for them the foundation of the church, and appointed Lucius to govern them, and enjoined on f. 98 b them all the laws of religion, and commanded them the precepts of the Gospel; and remained with them a month. And every day he preached to them from the Holy Scriptures, and said unto them, "If it be the will of the Lord, I will return unto you. And the Lord hath commanded me to go unto the cities which are to the east of you." And he went forth, and they took leave of him weeping and saying: "Stay not long away from us, for we are a new plant." And the disciple prayed and blessed them and gave them [the salutation of] peace.

And he went to Cantôria to preach in it as the Lord had commanded him. And when he reached it, and was within its gates, he met an old man weeping vehemently, with his clothes rent, looking ill. And he said unto him: "O old man! why do I see thee in this great sorrow and much weeping? thou hast pained my heart." The old man said unto him, "Get away from me, O my brother! for my affliction is great." The disciple said unto him: "I entreat thee to tell me thy condition; and perchance my Lord Jesus the Christ will put it right by my hand."

The old man said unto him: "Hearken unto my tale; I have six sons; I betrothed the eldest of them to the daughter of a magistrate of the city, to be his wife. And when the time of the wedding came, he said unto me: 'O my father! do not concern thyself about my marriage; for I shall not take a wife, and I have renounced this world, and all its desires.' And when I heard this from him I said in my heart: 'Perhaps he is f. 99 a stupid, [that] he has spoken these words.' And I said unto him: 'The time draws near when I wish to take thy wife for thee, and thou sayst this unto me!' He said unto me: 'Truly by the greatness of the King who is King of kings, Jesus the Christ, if thou dost force this upon me I will go out into

the desert, and thou shalt not see me after this day.' I said unto him: 'Tell me what thou hast seen?' He said unto me: 'I will tell thee. I was, O my father! during this night asleep, and I saw a young man, beautiful of countenance, and his raiment was shining like the sun, and a sweet scent issued from his mouth and filled the house with the odour of its fragrance. And a kingly crown was on his head; and in his right hand was a rod of gold. And when I saw him, I was greatly afraid of him, and I fell beneath his feet as dead. And he stretched out his right hand and raised me up; and said unto me: Take heed unto thyself, and hearken not to any one who counsels thee to marry. But keep thy body, that thou mayst be pure, and thou shalt be My successor[1], and a ruler over the Church. This My disciple, Thomas, is coming into this city, he will lead thee into the faith, and will give thee the sign of victory; and will make thee
f. 99 b meet to receive the Holy Mysteries. Know that I am God. I became incarnate for your sakes, and ye ought to make no delay about your salvation and your life. And when He had said this unto me, He put His right hand on my head, and blessed me and ascended to heaven with great glory till He vanished from mine eyes. And because of this, O my father! I shall not neglect the gift of which God hath deemed me worthy, lest the King be angry at this and destroy me because of my resistance to Him.'

"And when I heard this speech from my son I was silent, and I said to myself, 'Perhaps the God of this city hath appeared unto him.' And I called people from amongst the chief men of the city and I told them all that my son had said unto me. And I sent them to the father of the girl, and they told him all that they had heard from me. And he was wroth with a fierce wrath, and he said unto me: 'Thou hast put a slight on my house, and hast trifled with my daughter by these deceitful words.' And he went in unto the king and slandered me, both me and my child his servant. He said that we had stolen the property of the temple. And the king sent out and slew all my children;—their number was six—in one hour. And this is the cause that thou seest my weeping and my grief, and I have also debts (for money) which I had borrowed and had paid to the
f. 100 a girl, and it is now required of me. And since the death of my children I am afraid of my creditors. I know not any way to pay them their money. Would that one of my sons had remained alive to help me in paying the debt I owe!"

And when the disciple heard this from him, he said: "Weep not, O

[1] Or "Khalifa."

thou old man! I have heard thy weeping, I am Thomas. Bring me to the place in which thy sons are. And my Lord Jesus the Christ will give them life." And the old man journeyed along with him to the place in which their graves were. And many people followed them, saying: "If this wonder should take place, verily we will believe in the God of this man." And when they reached the place, the disciple gave the skin which had been flayed off to the old man; and said unto him, "Go thou into the grave and lay this skin upon all thy sons; and say: 'In the name of the Father, and the Son, and the Holy Ghost, arise, O my sons! and return to life as ye were.' I may not do this, lest it be said that I am a wizard."

And the old man did as the disciple had commanded him. And he laid the skin upon his sons, and there were nine persons beneath his sons in the grave-yard before his sons, and then they all arose. And the number of them was fifteen souls. And they went forth to the place in which the blessed disciple was; and they did obeisance to him, saying: f. 100 b "We entreat thee, O disciple of the Lord! to give us baptism, the seal of life." And when the multitude saw these wonders, they cried out with a very loud voice, saying: "Truly there is no God but Jesus the Christ, the Son of the Living God. One is the God of Thomas." And some of them hastened to the temple of Apollo, and told the priest of the temple all that had happened. And when the priest heard the name of Jesus he rent his clothes, and said: "Woe is me! for he is one of the disciples who have gone forth from the land of Judaea, journeying about in all the world; deceiving the people and all who hearken unto them. And they are disciples of a wizard man, whose name is Jesus. We have heard of him that Pilate crucified him. And these stole his body, and went about in the world saying that he was risen from the dead." And he said unto them : "Arise all of you with us, let us go out to him and reprimand him and tell him that his sayings are not true. And all that he doeth is by means of sorcery."

And the priest arose, and the multitude with him [and went] to where Thomas was. And they found him in the street of the city, and the crowd assembled near him. And he was casting a devil out of a man who was possessed with it. And the priest said unto Thomas: "What art thou doing in this place? O deceiving wizard! Was the land of Judaea not enough for thee, and its inhabitants, that thou hast come to this city? f. 101 a Who is Jesus? If he were God, why did he not save himself from slaughter? so that ye had to steal his body and bear witness to all mankind that he is risen from amongst the dead. And know that the people of this city are learned; they are not like other people whom thou mayst deceive." Then he turned and faced the multitude, and said unto them, "Let each one of you take a stone in his hand and throw it at this wizard; and let us kill him, so that he may not find any way of deceiving the people after this time." And they bent their backs to take up the stones and stone the saint. And their hands were withered among the stones, and they could not stand up. And they cried with one voice, saying: "We entreat thee, O good servant of God! to beseech thy Lord, that He may forgive us and allow us to rise and stand up on our feet, and we will believe in thy God; and do not punish us for our ignorance."

And the blessed disciple prayed, saying: "I thank Thee, O my Lord Jesus the Christ! that Thou hast not been unmindful of my request; and Thou hast shown Thy glory unto this multitude who are gathered together before Thee. And I entreat Thee to send, by Thy command, heavenly power from on high, that this unbeliever may be suspended head down-f. 101 b wards in the air, because he hath reviled Thy holy name." And speedily the priest was suspended in the air head downwards in the presence of the multitude. And when he looked at the high power of God, and at what was being done to him, he cried, while he was suspended, " I believe in Thee and I confess, O Jesus the Christ! Thy dominion, that Thou art God in truth; the gods which are made by the hands of men are not worthy of our calling them gods, only Thou alone art God; Thou art God before all ages. And Thou art Lord of heaven and earth, and of what is below the earth. Jesus the Christ! Thou art my trust and Thou art my King, and Thou art my hope."

And when the priest had confessed to this faith, while he was hanging head downwards, and the crowd gazing at him, he was let down to the earth. And the multitude believed and were saved, and they besought the disciple to baptize them, in the name of the Father, and the Son, and the Holy Ghost, the One God. And when he saw the strength of their faith he took them to the temple, and pulled down all that was therein from the places where the idols were seated; and he made the temple a church. And he appointed that priest as their bishop, and the six brethren, sons of the old man, presbyters and deacons, those whom he had raised from the dead. f. 102 a And he left them in the church to serve the holy place.

And he remained in the city for some time, teaching them the faith and all the precepts of religion. And many wonders were shown by his hands, and his skin was borne upon his shoulder. And he went about with it to every place whither he travelled. And afterwards he went forth

from amongst them, from this city praising God. And after these things
the Lord appeared unto him and took his skin and fastened it upon
his body as it had been; and embraced him and comforted him, and said
unto him, " Ride thou upon this cloud to thy brethren, it will bring
thee unto thy brethren, the disciples, in peace. I am present with you
in every place; for ye are those whom My Father hath chosen to proclaim
My divinity in the world."

And the Lord departed from him to heaven with great glory. And
Thomas mounted upon the cloud as the Lord had commanded, and it
went swiftly with him until it brought him to the mountain of Madyânîn;
and he found the disciples assembled, and Paul in the midst of them; and
Mary the Lord's mother. And he embraced them with a spiritual kiss,
and they reminded each other of the wonders which God had wrought by
their hands. And they remained for [eight?][1] days assembled together
with each other, giving glory to God; to Whom be praise, and glory and
honour, for ever and ever. Amen.

[1] Ethiopic " eight."

THE MARTYRDOM OF SAINT THOMAS.

The martyrdom of Saint Thomas, the disciple of the Lord Jesus the Christ; and his conflict which he finished on the twenty-sixth day of Pachōn, in the peace of the Lord. Amen.

And it came to pass, after Thomas the disciple had gone forth to the city of India, and had proclaimed the faith amongst them, and had preached to them the precepts of the Holy Gospel, and Lucius the magistrate had flayed off his skin; and he had remained for some time carrying it on his shoulder; and had gone about in all the countries laying it upon the dead and upon the sick; and the Lord had opened their hearts and they had believed; and he had built them a church; and had established for them the precepts of religion; and had appointed them a bishop and priests; and had given them the Holy Mysteries; he went forth from amongst them in peace.

And the Lord appeared unto him and restored his skin as it had been. And he went afterwards to the city of Zabadka in Macedonia. And he preached amongst them about the knowledge of God. And when the magistrates heard it, they met him [in] anger, and laid hold of him, and put him into prison. And Tertanâi, the wife of the king, came to him, and Margīta his daughter, to the prison. And it was locked, and many of the believers followed them.

And the door was opened to them; and they called the disciple. And he went out to them, and said unto them, "O my brethren, and my children, and my beloved servants of the Christ, and ministers of the Lord! hearken unto me to-day, unto my words and my last teaching to you. For I shall not see you in this world after this day, whilst I am in the body. For the Lord hath willed to remove me from this world, and to take me out of this trouble into rest. For He gave up His life for our sakes that He might save us from slavery to Satan; and He chose us to be disciples unto Himself; and made us meet to preach in His name in all the world. And my conflict is ended, and I have delivered the message as He commanded me. And He hath willed to bring me from the trouble of this world, and to give me the reward which I have deserved from Him. For He is very rich in gifts, and will give me His grace without price, and [also] to those who ask Him. For I am a servant of Jesus the Christ, a doer of His will. And He hath willed what ye have heard from me, and take heed that ye do not allow Satan to draw nigh unto you in any way. And be wakeful, looking for the coming of the Lord, that He may receive you into His kingdom."

And when he had said this, the women went down, and he went into the prison. And they mourned and wept; and they knew that the magistrates, if they got the saint into their power, would destroy him. And when he had gone into the prison, the doors of the prison were shaken, Cod. 75 and they became again shut in their [former] state. And when the Fonds warders saw a thing like this, they cried one to the other, and were f. 73 b confounded, and amazed. And they said: "This man is a wizard; he hath opened the doors of the prison; and he wishes to bring every one in it out. And he hath not found out the way to do this. But let us go to the king, and tell him this affair; and that his wife and daughter have come unto him." And while they were talking, Thomas answered nothing. And when the morning came they approached the king and said unto him, "O our lord! put this wizard out of this prison; and place him in another prison, for we cannot guard him. This is the second time that we have seen the prison doors open; and it is he who openeth them. And thy wife and thy daughter are always visiting him." And the king looked at the bolts which were on the prison door, and sealed it as it was; and said unto them: "Ye speak falsely: neither my wife nor my daughter visits him." And they swore unto him that they did f. 74 a visit him.

And the king sat down in a [certain] place and commanded them to bring the saint to him; and they stripped off his clothes and bound his waist with an apron, and made him stand before the king. And the king said unto him: "Art thou a slave or a free man?"

And Thomas said unto him: "I am the slave of a Lord over Whom thou hast no power."

The king said unto him: "Didst thou not flee from thy country, and D. S. didst come to this place?" f. 104 a

He said unto him: "I came to this place that I might turn this multitude from error, and I shall depart from this world by thy hand."

The king said unto him: "What is the name of thy Lord? and from what country art thou?"

Thomas said unto him: "My Lord is the Lord of heaven and earth, thou canst not hear His hidden Name, but His revealed Name is Jesus the Christ."

The, king said unto him : " I do not wish thy destruction ; but I have had patience with thee and thou art waxen great in the wickedness of thy deeds ; and thou hast made thy sorcery manifest in this city, until every man in India hath heard [of it]. But I will slay thee, so that all thy sorcery shall cease ; and thy name shall be forgotten, and thy sorcery, by all the country."

Thomas said unto him : " My ministration shall be firmly established after my departure from this world." And Mastâus the king took counsel how he could slay him, for he was afraid of the crowds who were surrounding him ; for amongst them were many of the magistrates who believed in the preaching of the saint, and of the nobles of the f. 104 b city, and many from the country. And the king arose and took him outside of the town ; and with him were many of the army bearing weapons. And the rest of the crowd imagined that the king wished to talk to him about something between themselves ; and they went aside from him. And when he was two miles distant from the city, he delivered him to fifteen of the soldiers, with his son and many of the chief citizens. And he commanded them to go with him to a high mountain and to kill him on it. And the king returned to the city.

And when the multitude knew, they set out one before the other in the steps of the saint, seeking his deliverance. And the soldiers who were with him made haste to slay him. And two of them stood on his right hand and two on his left, having spears in their hands. And the chief magistrate stretched out the spear in his hand against him. And the disciple said : " The hidden mystery which is finished, which is by the supernal gift, is that weariness of body shall not have power over me ; for four are ready to destroy my earthly temple like unto the four elements which are its component parts."

And when he reached the place in which he was to be killed, he said unto them : " Hearken, at my departure from this world, let not the eyes f. 105 a of your hearts be blind, and your ears deaf. Believe in God Whom I have preached unto you. And let His words enter your hearts and your ears ; and be every day of your life in purity and freedom, which is the life that will bring you near unto God."

And he said unto Masâsawi, the son of the king, " Thou art a servant of Jesus the Christ ; give these swordsmen what will enable them to let me pray unto my Lord."˙ And he commanded them to do this. And

the blessed disciple stretched out his hands, and besought God saying:
"The Lord, my hope and my guide, and my Saviour, Who strengthened
me and made my heart ready for His obedience. Thou art He Who
hast given me patience from my youth, and hast been in place of life
unto me, and hast kept me from defilement and destruction. Thou art He
Who hast given me knowledge, that I might not be defiled with women.
And I have kept my temple sacred to Thee. My mouth and my tongue
shall not achieve Thy praises because of Thine abundant mercy unto me.
Mine eyes have not looked to the taking of riches; for Thou didst say:
'The wealth of this world is loss. Do not choose it.' And I have
wished for poverty in this world; so that I might become worthy of Thee.
Thou hast opened Thine everlasting kingdom to me, unto the end of the f. 105 b
age; and to all who believe in Thee. I have fulfilled Thy will and Thy
commandments. Trials were multiplied upon me, and I endured tribulation.
And that was sweet unto me because of Thy name. For Thou art
my hope, and to Thee my soul hath clung; and my trouble shall not be
in vain. Receive my supplication and do not cast me away from Thy
face. The plants which are for honour, which Thou hast sown in me,
let not the enemy root them up. And the talents which Thou hast
given me I have committed them to the money changers[1] and the profit
on them became ten thousandfold[2] more. I have forsaken this world
and have followed Thee; mine eyes have looked for Thy salvation. I
have fulfilled the commandment which Thou didst give me; and the
message with which Thou didst send me, I have delivered it; that I might
be Thy resolute servant, fearing Thy name. I have girded up my loins
in all right things; my steps were wide in the path of the Gospel of
Peace. I have ridden upon the plough and have not looked backwards,
lest it might be crooked. The earth hath blossomed, and the time of
the harvest draweth nigh; that I may receive the reward. I have finished
the toil which hath brought me to repose. I have kept the first trouble[3],
and the second and the third, that I might see Thy face, and worship Thy f. 106 a
glory. And I have despised the flesh, that I might be satisfied with good.
I have fulfilled all Thy will and I have not turned backwards. I have
pressed forward that I might not be a stone of stumbling to others;
that I may receive a crown of glory and the heavenly reward. Let
not the serpent stand in the way, and let not the adders rise up against
me. And let not the powers of darkness come near to me, but may

---

[1] Literally "owners of tables."   [2] *i.e.* ten hundredweights.   [3] Possibly "watch."

they keep far away from me. For Thine is the praise, and to Thy Holy Father and Thy life-giving Spirit. Amen."

And when the blessed one had finished his prayer, he returned to the officers and said unto them: "Finish the will of your king." And four of the soldiers came prepared; and they pierced him with spears. And he fell upon the ground and yielded up the ghost immediately. And the brethren wept for him, those who were present. And they brought clean shrouds and sumptuous raiment and swathed him and left him in the graves of the ancient kings. And Sirfûr and Tanîs stood beside the grave that day; and they did not enter the city. And the holy Thomas appeared unto them and said unto them: "Behold! I am here alive. Why do ye sit and guard me? My Lord Jesus the Christ, my King, hath accepted me. And I have received all the promises which f. 106 b I had hoped for. Rise up from this place, and know that in a little while ye shall go forth from this world. And be not slack about the salvation of your souls, for ye will come unto me."

And Matthâûs the king and Hersânûs took their wives, who were Tertanâi and Atbaniâ, and punished them severely that they might consent to leave purity for their sake and return to cohabitation. And they did not consent to it.

And the saint appeared unto them, and said unto them: "Do not forget my words which I said, and the Lord Jesus the Christ will help you." And when Matthâûs and Hersânûs knew that their wives would not consent to their desire they left them to be according to their wish and choice.

And all the brethren were assembled, and the one was telling the other all the precepts of the Lord; and they were rejoicing in the gift of God and the grace of the Holy Ghost. And Asîs, the son of the king, was possessed with a devil. And the king meditated and said: "What shall I do? This is [because of] my opposition to the disciple. I have not received his words." And he went to the grave to take a rag of the shroud from his body, and hang it on the neck of his son. And he was saying that he would believe if God were to cure him. And Thomas appeared unto him, and the saint said: "Thou didst not believe in me when f. 107 a I was alive, O Matthâûs. Dost thou believe in me when I am dead? But fear not, the Lord will have compassion upon thee, for He grudgeth not His gift."

And when he had opened the grave he found nothing of the saint's body, for he had been taken secretly to Eden. And he took a little dust from the place where the body of the saint had been and tied it on the throat of his son and said : " I will believe if on supplication to the saint, this unclean spirit should go out from my son." And immediately the devil went out of his son.

And the king believed and did obeisance before Arsaphorus the priest ; and besought him and his brethren to seek forgiveness from God for him. And the priest said to the brethren, " Pray for the king, lest God slay him, and bring down on him all his sins." And they did this with gladness and joy because of what they saw of the king's faith. And God Who loveth mankind ; the King of kings, and Lord of lords, gave Matthâûs the king a true faith and a firm hope. And his faith and his goodness were noised abroad in all the countries, and he honoured all the brethren ; and he praised the Father and the Son and the Holy Ghost. And Thomas the disciple received the blow of the four soldiers with four spears ; and thus he finished his conflict in the highway of the city of India ; in the twenty-sixth day of the month of Pachôn. f. 107 b And praise be to the Lord Jesus the Christ with the Father and the Holy Ghost. Amen.

THE ACTS OF MATTHEW.

The Acts of Matthew the disciple which he did in the country of the Kahenat[1], *in the peace of the Lord. Amen.*

And Peter and Andrew were on their return from the country of El Barbar. And they had established them in the faith, and had taught them the precepts of religion. While they were journeying on the road Matthew met them. And they embraced one another with a spiritual kiss; and he said unto them: "Whence have ye come?" They said unto him: "From the country of El Barbar." Matthew said unto them: "And I also have come from the country of the Blessed." And each one of them told him what sufferings had befallen him. Matthew said unto them: "The city in which I have been, the Lord Jesus the Christ is present with them every day: and He keepeth a feast with them. He setteth up His throne in the midst of their church in the early morning, and He teacheth them His precepts. And when I entered their city, and preached amongst them, and proclaimed the Gospel in His name, they said: 'We know this Name.' I said unto them: 'Who hath taught it to you?' They said unto me: 'Be patient, and trouble not thyself until the morning; thou shalt look on Him Whom thou hast preached unto us.' And when the

f. 108 a   morrow came the Lord Jesus the Christ came riding upon a shining cloud, and all the powers of heaven praising Him. And when I saw Him, in the abundance of joy I exulted in the Holy Ghost, and cried, saying: 'Ascribe ye glory to the King of kings; and exalt His greatness to all generations.' And we remained three days praising Him in the church. And when the three days were ended He blessed us and ascended to heaven with great glory.

"Then I said unto them, 'How have ye become worthy of this honour? that the Lord Jesus the Christ should keep a feast with you?' They said unto me: 'Hath not the tale of the nine tribes and a half reached thee, which the Lord caused to enter the Land of Promise? We are they. When it is mid-day, Gabriel, the angel of the Lord, cometh unto us; and there come with him the hundred and the four and forty thousand infants whom Herod slew; they defiled not their garments in

---

[1] *i.e.* "priests."

the world. And when they sing praise we sing praise with them, and when they say Alleluia, we say it with them. But as for gold and silver we do not wish for it in our country. We eat no flesh and drink no wine in our country ; but honey is our food and our drink. We do not look on the faces of our women with desire; the first boy who is born we present him as an offering to God, that he may serve the f. 108 b temple all his life, when he is three years old. Our drink is not the water from wells dug by the hands of men ; but the water which we drink is the water which overfloweth from Paradise. We do not wrap ourselves in clothing made by the hands of men ; but our clothing is from the leaves of trees. Our country heareth no lying speech, and no one knoweth of it. No man weds two wives in our country; and no boy dieth before his father. And the younger speaketh not in the presence of the elder. Lions dwell with us in our country ; they hurt us not, and we hurt them not. When winds blow, we smell from them the scent of the garden of Paradise. There is no cold in our country, and no snow, but a breath of life ; and it is temperate.'

"And when I had heard [this] from them, I longed to dwell in their country ; and my eyes were dazzled from hearing the sweetness of their speech."

And Peter and Andrew praised God for this, and besought Him to reveal unto them to what place they should go. And the Lord appeared to them and said unto them, " My peace be upon you, O My pure disciples! whom I have chosen before all mankind. Be strong, and believe ; for I am dwelling with you always ; I will never be absent where ye are." And they worshipped down to the ground. And they said : "We bless f. 109 a Thy name, O Lord! and we thank Thee always. Command us on which way we should go."

And the Lord commanded Peter to go forth to the city of Rome, and Andrew to the city of Masya, and Matthew[1] to the city of Kahenat. Matthew[1] said unto the Lord : " I know it not, and I have never entered it." The Lord said unto him : " Art thou still of little faith ? go on this path, which will bring thee to their city." And then a cloud arrived, and carried Peter and Andrew until it brought each one of them to his place wherein the Lord had commanded him to preach. And Matthew[1] walked a little way, and he lifted up his eyes to heaven and prayed, and said : "O Thou, the Holy Lord, Jesus the Christ, my Lord! Who taught Abraham, and fulfilled His oath to Isaac ; and established His testimony

---

[1] MS. "Matthias."

to Jacob, and His grace to Joseph, and Thou didst keep the nation forty years in the desert; a cloud overshadowed them by day, and the pillar of fire shone for them by night; and didst destroy their enemies beneath their feet; and Thou didst bring them up out of the Red Sea; and didst bring them into the Land of Promise, which Thou didst swear to their fathers, Abraham Isaac, and Jacob, be Thou a guide to me on this destined road."

f. 109 b   And immediately a cloud came and bore him until it arrived at the city of Kahenat. And when he saw the city, he rejoiced and resolved to enter it. And he saw before him a young man, a shepherd; and he overtook him. Matthew said unto him: "Tell me, O thou young man! thou shepherd, which is the road that leadeth into this city." And he said: "This is the road; but thou canst not enter it when thou art in this dress; for it is not like the dress of our countrymen. Thy garments are not clean. If thou art fain to enter it, strip from thee this dress, and put on the dress of the priests. And shave the hair of thy head and of thy beard. And gird up thy loins and take the bough of a palm-tree in thy right hand. And put palm-leaf sandals on thy feet, that thy dress may be like theirs, and thou mayst enter the city."

And when he heard this his heart was grieved, and he returned on the path by which he had come. And he did not wish to go into the city.

And the young man who had conversed with him was Jesus the Christ. And when he had returned a little on his way He stretched out His hand and turned him backwards, and said unto him: "Matthew, whither goest thou?" He said unto him: "How dost thou know me? and who told thee my name?"

f. 110 a   The young man said unto him: "I know thee, O Matthew! Turn and go into the city. I am Jesus, thy God. Do what I have told thee. And let not thy heart be sorrowful. For if thou doest it not thou wilt not be able to enter the city."

And he did as Jesus had commanded him; and He walked along with him till He brought him to the gate of the city. And He said unto him: "Be strong, O Matthew My disciple! and be steadfast and patient. Severe torture shall come upon thee from this city, and long imprisonment; and afterwards they will burn thee with fire. Fear not, and be not troubled, and tremble not and despair not. For the king will turn and believe in Me, and all the inhabitants of the city, by means of thee. And the fire which they shall kindle wherewith to burn thee shall delight in burning Apollo their god. And be thou patient, and call upon My name;

and I will answer thee. And I am with thee always; and I am not far from thee nor from thy brethren the disciples, wherever they may be." And the Lord said this, and departed from him to heaven with glory.

And Matthew arose and entered the city, and he asked its people: "Where is the temple?"

They said unto him: "From what country art thou?"

He said unto them: "I am from Egypt."

They said unto him: "What is the reason of thy coming, and what seekest thou?"

He said unto them: "I shall look at your gods, and at how they f. 110 b teach you."

They said unto him: "Our god teacheth us nothing, and we do not hear a sound from him; and we know not who eateth the sacrifices which we offer unto him, but people who are entrusted with his service take them from us."

And he said unto them: "Are ye not of the priesthood?" They said unto him: "Yea, but not of the foremost in the service of the gods."

He said unto them: "Are all your gods of one rank?"

They said: "Nay, the greatest is Apollo."

He said unto them: "Apollo loveth the rich, and hateth the poor, these are scales in which there is nothing even. And I would fain speak with him, and say unto him: Why doth he love the rich and hate the poor? and they all worship thee, and thou shouldst respect them all."

And when they had heard his words they separated into two companies: and they said: "Let us accompany him, that we may hear his words." And they walked with him till they brought him to the temple. And they brought the priest who was in it. They said unto him: "This man hath arrived from Egypt; come out and talk with him."

And when Matthew looked at him he embraced him with a spiritual kiss, and he was anxious for his salvation. And when the lips of Matthew touched the lips of Armîs the priest, the hand of God rested upon him and he said unto the disciple: "Whence art thou? and whence hast thou come? for since thy kiss and the grip of thy hand great grace hath f. 111 a rested upon me. Tell me who thou art, O my lord?"

The disciple said unto him: "I am of a good tribe, priests of the Living God."

And Matthew rejoiced at the grace which had rested upon Armîs by his words. And Armîs said unto him: "I would fain know how thou didst find the road to arrive at this city."

He said unto him : "My God made me reach it."

He said unto him : " How was that ?"

He said : "He took my hand, and made me stop at the gate of the city."

He said unto him : " I would fain see thy God."

He said unto him : "If thou dost believe on Him and dost keep my precept, and art certain about all that I say unto thee, and art convinced that it is true, I will allow my God to converse with thee ; for my God looketh not on an impure person, only on him who is pure both without and within."

He said unto him : " And where is the place of thy God ?"

He said unto him : " He is in my country."

He said unto him : " And where is thy country ?"

Matthew said unto him : " He is in a clean country ; whose streets are justice, and its roads righteousness.   My country is a country of righteousness, and its inhabitants die not.   There is no darkness in my country, but it is all light.   And my God is He Who giveth light to all who are in it.   And death hath no power over my countrymen.   My country is all f. 111 b furnished with seats; the sweet scent in the midst of it is great; the trees never wither ; not one of the inhabitants of my country hath a wish to sin, but they are all just men.   There is no slave, but all of them are freemen. My God is merciful and pitiful ; a giver to the poor until He maketh them rich.   There is no anger in my country, but they are all in harmony; there is no hatred in my country, but they are all united.   There is no rebellion in my country, but they are all of one mind.   There is no deceit in it, but they are all humble.   There is no sound of wailing in it, but joy and delight."

And when Armîs had heard this he said unto Matthew : " How sayst thou, ' There is nothing that defileth in my country'?"

Matthew said unto him : " Because my God is pure."

He said unto him : " I would fain go out with thee to thy country."

Matthew said unto him : "Thou shalt enter my country, and thou shalt see my God, partaking with me in the faith of my Father, and in His Holy Mysteries!"

And at the end of the day Armîs said unto Matthew : "Wait for me until I go and light the lamp of Apollo before we go and sup."

Matthew said unto him : " Is it thou who dost light the lamp of thy god ?"

Armîs said unto him : " It is not the lamp only, but I wash him and bedeck him that he may be beautiful.   And I carry him from place to place."

Matthew said unto him: "It is my God who giveth light unto me, and all who serve Him shine with the light at all times, and whoso feareth f. 112 a Him, the light surroundeth him; and every one who glorifieth Him is clothed with the light."

Armîs said unto him: " I will go with thee to thy city."

Matthew said unto him: "We need not go forth, for I called on my God, He appeared unto me, and when He cometh unto me the temple shineth with light."

Armîs said unto him: " I would fain see this wonder."

And Matthew raised his eyes to heaven and spake thus: "I entreat Thee, O my Lord! my God! Ruler of all things, Father of my Lord and my God Jesus the Christ, King of Glory, Robe of the pure and King of just men, and Light of the blind, and Brightness of the world; the quenchless Lamp, the Light which is never overtaken by darkness, the Axe which breaketh every fruitless tree, the Fire that destroyeth all fabricated gods; Tree of Life, Giver of life to all mankind; my God and my Lord, Jesus the Christ, may Thy mercy overtake me, and hearken unto my entreaty. Send Thy light upon us to comfort our souls, and may Thy mercy arise upon us all."

And when Matthew had finished his prayer, a great light dawned upon them.   And when Armîs saw it he fell upon his face.

And there was a great earthquake in the city, from the abundance of f. 112 b the light.   And in the earthquake Apollo fell upon his face and was broken to pieces.   And nothing remained of all the images that were in the temple; for they were all shattered.   And Matthew took hold of the hand of Armîs, and raised him up, and said unto him: "Look at thy god, he could not be saved; how can he save others?"   And Armîs arose, and went into the place of Apollo, and found that he had fallen and was broken.   And he trampled on him with his feet and said unto him: "Apollo! couldest thou not be saved? how canst thou save others?   It is good that thou hast called on this Name which is [that of] thy God."

Matthew said unto him: "Come out and leave this contemptible thing fallen on its face."

And Armîs came out and laid hold of the hand of Matthew and said unto him: "Come with me into my dwelling, and let us eat bread." Matthew said unto him: "We will eat, but tell Apollo to prepare something for us that we may eat."   Armîs said unto him: "When he was in

his glory and majesty, he did nothing of this kind; and how when he is
f. 113 a shattered and has been trampled and spoiled under the feet of man [can he
do it?"]

Matthew said: "My God can send us something to eat."

Armîs said unto him: "I believe thee in all thou sayest, because of the
light which I have seen resting upon us; but I desire to see this food which
He will send to us."

Matthew said unto him: "I will bring thee what thou hast asked for."
And Matthew raised his eyes and his hands, and made supplication, saying:
"O God of the sinners who repent! Who turnest erring souls to the
knowledge of Himself; Purifier of souls and of bodies together; the Word
which came down from heaven, the Manna which fell from the sky in the
desert; the loud Voice which [resounded] over all; the Guide of wanderers;
the Ladder which reacheth to the sky; the Food which the children of
Israel ate in the wilderness in the Fast and the Passover; Quickener
of souls and of bodies; Thou, O my Lord Jesus the Christ! art He who
hast made me meet for this spiritual service. Send Thy glory and Thy
blessing and Thine honour upon me for ever and ever."

Then a shining table appeared unto them, and upon it were three
loaves white as snow, and a skin of wine. Matthew said unto him:
"Thou art not allowed to eat of this food until Thou become a partaker
in the faith and the Holy Mysteries."

Armîs said unto him: "Haste thee and make me fit to receive it."

f. 113 b   And he preached unto him the Word of life; and prescribed to
him the knowledge of the faith; and baptized him in the name of the
Father, and the Son, and the Holy Ghost; and gave him some of that
sacred bread. And Matthew prayed, and the table was lifted up to
where it had been. And Matthew and Armîs went out, and came to
where Apollo was, and they closed the temple. And they went together
unto the house of Armîs. And Matthew preached unto them about the
faith, and baptized them all in the name of the Father, and the Son, and
the Holy Ghost. And there was great joy in the house of Armîs. And
on the morrow the king came to enter the temple, and he found the door
closed. And he commanded Armîs the priest to come. And when he
stood before him, the king said unto him: "How hast thou dared to lock
the door of the temple? and shut up the place of Apollo the great god?"

Armîs said unto him: "Apollo is not able to save himself, how shall he
save any one else?"

The king said unto him: "And who is able to save?"

Armîs said unto him : " He, Jesus the Christ, Son of the Living God, the Saviour of souls, the Resurrection of the dead, the Glory of the Righteous, Who hath destroyed all the wickedness of the enemy, and the deceit of Satan under His feet."

The king said unto Armîs : " Whence hast thou learnt the name of Jesus ?"

He said unto him : " Matthew, his disciple, is he who brought to me f. 114 a the knowledge of Him : and caused His light to shine on me and on all my household."

And when the king heard this from him he was wroth with a fierce wrath ; and he commanded that Armîs and Matthew should be bound with ropes on their feet ; and they were dragged through all the city until their bodies were wounded, and the blood flowed from them, and their flesh stuck in the streets. And they were beaten with rods. And the king commanded that they should be thrown into prison. And the king went into the temple, and found all the statues in it shattered, and Apollo broken in pieces. And he rent his clothes, and cried with a loud voice, and [so did] all those who were with him. And he commanded Armîs and Matthew to be brought, and to be burnt with fire. And immediately there was a great earthquake. And all the images which were in the houses of the citizens fell from their pedestals, and were shattered. And a loud voice cried out, " There is no God but Jesus the Christ, Son of the Eternal God." And the city became two factions, one faction of Apollo, and the other of Jesus. And the faction of Apollo said : " Let these wizards be burnt with fire." And those who believed in Jesus said : " Ye have no power over them." And the king f. 114 b commanded plenty of wood to be brought, and fire to be kindled in it, to burn Matthew and Armîs therein alive. And those who believed brought all weapons of war, and kept them away from Armîs and Matthew. And they said : " Ye have no power to burn the disciples of the Lord except it were just."

The king said unto them : " Why have ye rejected Apollo ?"

They said unto him : " Because he is unable to save [himself] from the destruction which came upon him ; he and all the idols which were in our dwellings have been shattered. How can he save anyone else ?"

And the king commanded that the two disciples should be burnt, and should not be spared for a single hour. And the friends of Jesus and the friends of Apollo made an uproar in the city, and immediately Matthew cried with a loud voice, speaking thus: "O ye brethren! it is not meet that ye should please men, and provoke God to wrath."

And whilst he was speaking, a man came from the palace of the king, and told him that his only son had died. And he made haste to go to his dwelling, he and those who believed in Apollo. But the friends of Matthew, those who believed in the Christ, stayed with the disciples, and there were four hundred persons with them, and Matthew preached to them and exhorted them and said unto them, "Let your faith be genuine, that ye may see a new wonder."

f. 115 a   And Matthew went to the place where the king was, and said unto him: "I see that thou art sad at heart for the death of thy son. Call on Apollo that he may make him alive for thee."

The king said unto him: "Which of the gods is able to raise the dead?"

Matthew said unto him: "My God, Jesus the Christ, the Son of the Living God, if thou wilt believe in Him, shall raise thy son alive."

And the king swore with a mighty oath and said unto him: "If I should see this wonder from Jesus thy Lord, and the resurrection of my son from the dead, I will not worship Apollo, or any one of all the idols."

And when Matthew had heard the saying of the king, he glowed with the power of the Holy Ghost; and he raised his eyes to heaven; and stretched out his hands; and made supplication thus, saying: "I bless thee O Lord of all time! who never failest: I worship the high dwelling above all height; I give Thee glory, Thou who didst not spare Thine own self, but didst give Thyself up for our sins; until Thou hadst redeemed us and made us partakers in the truth. I thank Thee alone, Who canst raise the dead. I beseech thee, O Father of our Lord Jesus the Christ! Ruler of all, send from Thy height and Thy sublime power and break the sting of death; shatter all its power; may the shield-bearers of
f. 115 b   Hell fall, and its guards fail; and its deceits and its temptations be confounded. Crush the seed of the serpent. Send Thy high power, O my Lord Jesus the Christ! and raise this youth; that this king may believe, and all the inhabitants of this city." And when Matthew had finished his prayer, he stood where the dead man was and took hold of his hand, saying: "I say unto thee in the Name of Jesus the Christ, arise in health."

And straightway the lad sprang up, and laid hold of Matthew's feet, and said unto him: "I beseech thee, O good servant of God! to baptize me, and make me partaker in the Holy Mysteries. And do not make me return, O my lord! to Hell."

And when the king saw this wonder, he sprang up in haste, and commanded every one who was in the city to be baptized ; and all his own household, by the hand of Matthew, in the name of the Father, and the Son, and the Holy Ghost. And there was great joy in the city. And the king took Apollo out, and burnt him in the fire which he had kindled to burn Saint Matthew in. And the fire never ceased with Apollo till it had made him ashes. And this is the cause of the faith of the citizens in the Lord by means of the blessed Matthew.

And afterwards the Lord Jesus the Christ appeared to him, and said unto him : "Be strong, O blessed Matthew ! and let thy faith be confirmed. f. 116 a Dost thou not remember the words which I spake unto thee ? Be not troubled, and be patient, and fear not. For I have souls in this city who shall believe in me by means of thee."

Matthew said unto Him : "Yea, O Lord !"

The Lord told Matthew and Armîs to baptize the multitude and to purify them. And when the Lord had finished His sayings, He departed to Heaven with glory.

And all the citizens saw Him. And they did this, and baptized them. And the king and the citizens overthrew the temple of Apollo. And they built a church in place of it ; and Matthew consecrated it. And he appointed them a priest and deacons ; and gave them the Gospel. And he remained amongst them for some time, until their faith was strengthened, and he went away from them in peace. And when he was outside of the city, he turned back with his face to them and said unto them : "The grace of the Lord and His peace rest upon you for ever and ever. Amen."

And praise be to God always and for ever.

MARTYRDOM OF SAINT MATTHEW.

f. 116 b   *The Martyrdom of Saint Matthew the Apostle, the Evangelist, which took place on the twelfth day of Phaophi, in the peace of the Lord.   Amen.*

And when Matthew the Evangelist had come to Jerusalem and the land of Judea, he wrote his Gospel in the Hebrew tongue; and he went out to Parthica, and preached the Gospel of the Christ to them; and confirmed them in the true faith.   And when he knew that their faith was strengthened, and [that of] all who were in that country, he went out from amongst them rejoicing and exulting in what God had given him of their faith.   And he journeyed in that country from the frontier of Berinat, and preached amongst them, and evangelized them with the Word of God the Life-giver; and His birth from the pure Virgin, the Lady Mary, the Mother of God in truth; and His death; and the beginning of the genealogy which was the Christ's; teaching every one that God dwelt in the body which He received from the Virgin Mary without intercourse with a man.   And He was united with it, but He was not confounded, and was not mingled, and was not divided.   And Saint Matthew visited the prison and cured all who were in it without recompense.   And the cure which he gave to every one was his saying: "In the name of Jesus the Christ may you have healing."   And straightway his saying was accomplished.   And he healed all who believed in God by his means.

f. 117 a   And once upon a day [Matthew] went into the prison, and he found in it a man of whom much money was required, on whom the gaolers inflicted a severe punishment.   And when he looked at him and at his torture, and his much weeping, he had compassion on him, and said unto him: "Why do I see thee in this great grief and much weeping?"   He said unto him: "I am the slave of Festus, and I was trusted and acceptable in speech with him.   And he committed much property to me; and commanded me to go over the sea, and trade with the same.   And I fulfilled his commandment and went forth; and sailed on the sea.   And the sea was tempestuous against me, and a mighty wind was stirred up in it; and the boat sank, and all that was in it.   And I despaired of life in this tribulation.   [And] God sent a little boat which brought me out to the shore of the sea. And I returned to my lord, Festus, to tell him all that had happened. And he said unto me in wrath: 'Whence hast thou come?' And I told him all that had befallen me on the sea. And he was wroth with a fierce wrath, because of [his] great love of money. And therefore he threw me into the prison and required of me that I should repay him some of the money."

And when Matthew had heard this from him, he was very sorrowful and said unto him: "Weep not, and be not grieved; but believe that God dwelleth in the heart of every man who believeth in Him." The man said unto him: "And what dost thou desire me to do, for I am f. 117b in great sorrow? Verily I say unto thee, O good servant of God! that many times I have wanted to kill myself for the greatness of the torture which is inflicted on me." The disciple said unto him: "I will tell thee this great secret; but swear to me that if what I tell thee be fulfilled thou wilt believe in God all the days of thy life." And the man threw himself down before the Apostle, and said unto him: "God be my witness, that if a bit of bread should come to me by thy hands through what thou hast commanded me, I will believe in the Christ who was crucified." The disciple said unto him: "If on the morrow thy lord Festus should inquire for thee, and should bring thee out of the prison to punish thee as is his wont, and if when thou seest him he command concerning thee that thou be punished, say unto him: 'I entreat thee, O my lord! to spare me to-day; and perhaps God will open [a way] to me, and the hearts of the people of this city will have compassion on me to help me to my deliverance.' And perchance there will appear in his judgment-hall some one who will be surety for thee for two days. And if he release thee, go to the place where the boat sank; thou wilt find everything of thine that perished lying, take it and deliver it to him. And pay what thou owest. And be free, thou and thy household."

And on the morrow Festus sent and brought him out of the prison, f. 118a and commanded that he should be set up for punishment, in anger. And he entreated him for a respite, as the disciple had commanded him. And he consented to what he asked for. And he went out to the place in which the boat had sunk, trusting that all which the disciple had said unto him would be fulfilled. And he looked to the right on the shore of the sea and he found a great bag[1] filled with dinârs; and he took it, and returned to the city blessing God, and thanking the holy disciple.

And he went in unto Festus and delivered the bag[1] to him. And

[1] Or "ragged cloth."

he opened it, and counted up what was in it, and found therein two thousand dinârs. And Festus said unto him: "What is this?" He said unto him: "This is the price of the boat which sank in the sea, and of all that was in it."

And he said unto him: "And whence hast thou got this money?" And he told him the story; his condition, and what the disciple said unto him, and his discovery of the money; and Festus said unto him: "What is this silly talk which I hear from thee? perhaps thou hast gone out to a place where thou hast bored into it and plundered it, and thou hast come hither with it."

The man said unto him: "Nay, by the truth of my Lord the Christ, the God of Matthew, I have not bored through any place except the one I have told thee of. This is the truth. And if thou desire to see him,
f. 118 b behold he is in the prison healing every sickness, and casting out devils."

And while he was saying this, behold, a bad man came who hated good, and cried, saying, "Hearken, O company of Romans! I will tell you about the sedition which hath appeared in this city. A man, a foreigner, preaches in its streets about a new god, whose name is Jesus the Christ, the Nazarene. And if thou dost permit him [to do this], O Festus! chief of the city, he will ruin the city and all who are in it."

And Festus reported this to the king. And when the king heard it, he was wroth with a fierce wrath against the disciple. And he said unto those of the guards who were present: "Go out quickly to where ye will find him; take off his head, and throw his body on the ground, that it may be food for the fowls of heaven." And they went out from his presence; and they did as the king had commanded them; and they took off his head, and left his body prostrate for the birds of the heavens to eat. And God, Who loveth mankind, sent two good men to take his sacred pure head with his body; and they wrapped it in a clean shroud and put it in a tomb which belonged to their fathers.

And when the man whom the disciple had been the means of
f. 119 a delivering from Festus heard that the disciple had endured all this and had died, he remained three days mourning for him. And when twelve days after the death of Saint Matthew the Evangelist, disciple of the Lord Jesus the Christ, were fulfilled, the completion of his martyrdom was on the twelfth day of Phaophi. And praise be to the Father, and the Son, and the Holy Ghost, the Life-giver, now and at all times, throughout all ages. Amen.

THE MARTYRDOM
OF JAMES THE SON OF HALFAI.

The Martyrdom of James the son of Halfai, and completion of his conflict on the tenth[1] day of Machîr, in the peace of the Lord.   Amen.

It came to pass when James the disciple had gone into Jerusalem, to preach the Holy Gospel in it, and all the wonders of the Godhead; that every one who heard his words might believe in God with a pure heart, and that his soul might be saved,[2] he thought in his heart how the crowd might hear him and believe.   And he went into the temple where the multitude were assembled.   And he found a great crowd of the Jews gathered together; and he began to preach the Gospel in the midst of them with great joy and gladness in the presence of them all.   And he continued his speech, and explained about faith in God, testifying that the Only Son of God is the Word of life, the God of all ages; f. 119 b Jesus the Christ He is the Son of God in truth; eternally with the Father before all ages.   And He is in the Father, and the Father in Him. He it is Who is the Word of the Father when He said: "Let us make man in our likeness and our image"; and He dwelleth in heaven with His Father; and He is upon the throne of the cherubim; and the seraphim ascribe glory to Him.   And He it is Who is on the right hand of power on high.   And He dwelt in the womb of the Virgin Mary.   And He is the Lord Jesus the Christ, to Whom Mary the Virgin gave birth; and He is the God Who was made man.

And this is his confession amongst that assembly without the fear of any man.   He testified about His birth, and he testified about His death, and His resurrection from amongst the dead; and His ascension to His Father Who is in heaven.   And He taught to every one who was present faith in the Christ.   And when the multitude heard that from him they were angry with a great anger, which was from their father the Devil who dwelt in them, against the disciple of the Lord Jesus the Christ.   And they all helped one another; and took his blood upon themselves; every one who was present and heard his words.   And they seized him and brought him before the Emperor Claudius, and false witnesses rose up against him. f. 120 a

---

[1] The Sinai Codex, 539, has "ninth."
[2] MS.+ "and."

L. A.   P

And they said unto the Emperor: " This man is a seducer, he goeth about the country and the cities and saith: ' I am the slave of Jesus the Christ'; and he prevents them from obeying the Emperor." And when the Emperor heard this about the blessed disciple, he commanded that he should be stoned with stones that he might die. And the Jews stoned him as the Emperor had commanded. And such was his martyrdom. And the blessed disciple entered into rest, James the son of Halfai[1], on the tenth day of Machîr[2]. And he was buried beside the temple in Jerusalem. And praise and glory be to the Father, and the Son, and the Holy Ghost, for ever and ever. Amen.

[1] Cod. Sin. Arab. adds " brother of Matthew."
[2] Cod. Sin. Arab. has "ninth."

THE PREACHING
OF SIMON THE SON OF CLEOPHAS.

The Preaching of the holy Simon, the son of Cleophas, called Jude, who is Nathanael called the Zealot. And he became bishop of Jerusalem after James the Lord's brother. In the peace of the Lord Jesus the Christ. Amen.

It came to pass when the disciples were gathered together to the Mount of Olives, that they might divide all the cities of the world, [that¹] while they prayed and blessed God, the Lord Jesus the Christ was present f. 120 b in the midst of them, and said unto them: "May the peace of My Father rest upon you, O My pure disciples!" And they cast lots, and the lot of Jude the Galilean came out that he might go to the country of Samaria; and preach amongst them about the Gospel of the Lord Jesus the Christ. Simon answered and said unto the Lord: "Thou wilt be with us, O our Lord! in every place wherein we dwell, and we will be patient in all that may happen unto us. And let my father Peter go out with me; that he may bring me to the land of Samaria."

The Lord said unto him: "Peter's lot is to go out to the city of Rome, that he may preach in it. But let him go out with thee until he bring thee [thither] in peace. And after thy proclaiming the Gospel, and thy preaching amongst them, thou shalt return to Jerusalem after the death of James the Just, and thou shalt be bishop in it after him. And thou shalt finish thy conflict as James the Just finished his in that place. Behold now, O my friend Simon! go out with him in strength, for I shall be thy companion." And the Lord blessed him and all the disciples; and He ascended to heaven in great glory. And after the ascension of the Lord to heaven, Simon arose and prayed; and he went down to Jerusalem, and Peter was with him, and he journeyed to Samaria, and preached amongst them in the name of Jesus f. 121 a the Christ,² the good news of the Gospel. And Simon went into the midst of their synagogue, and preached amongst them in the name of the Lord Jesus the Christ. And when the Jews who dwelt there heard [it] they rose up against him and smote him with painful blows, and returned with him to the outside of the city. And Peter kissed him and took leave of him, and went out from his presence. And Simon returned and remained in their

¹ MS. "and."   ² MS. adds "and."

synagogue for three days, and preached amongst them in the name of the Christ. And some of these people did not believe. And at the end of the third day, the son of the ruler of the synagogue fell sick, and his name was James, and he died. And one of the men who believed in what Simon had said went to the father of the dead boy, and said: "Behold! a disciple of the Christ is here; call him that he may pray over the lad." And the man went in haste, and called the disciple of Jesus the Christ. And he came joyfully and stood over the dead boy; and said unto his father: "Believe in Him Who was crucified, that He is the Son of God, [and] thou shalt see the glory of God."

The father of the boy said unto him: "If my son should rise from the dead, so that I may see him alive, I will believe in the crucified Jesus, that He is the Son of the Living God."

f. 121 b   And the disciple turned away his face to the east, and said: "O my Lord Jesus the Christ! Who wast crucified under Pontius Pilate, Thou art He Who hast made me worthy of this—that I should preach in Thy blessed name,[1] Thy suffering for our sakes, that Thou mightest redeem us from the hand of the Enemy;[1] look upon this dead boy; and by Thy will command him to rise, that Thy name may be glorified to-day in the midst of the multitude in this city that they may believe in Thy holy name." And when Simon the blessed disciple said this he turned to where the dead boy was, and said: "In the name of the Father, and the Son, and the Holy Ghost, rise, and stand up alive. And be thou whole, so that every one who is present may believe in the name of my Lord Jesus the Christ." And straightway the boy opened his eyes, and rose, and sat up. And he commanded that they should offer him something to eat. And when the crowd saw this wonder, they all came forward and bowed down to the earth to the disciple; and they believed in God, saying: "There is one God, [and] Simon is the disciple of Jesus the Christ, the Son of the living God."

And the parents of the boy threw themselves at the feet of the
f. 122 a   disciple, and said: "O our lord! how may we be saved?" He said unto them: "Believe with all your hearts (and) ye shall be saved." And he exhorted them from the holy Scriptures; and he baptized them in the name of the Father, and the Son, and the Holy Ghost; and he gave them the Holy Mysteries; and commanded them to build the church; and appointed them a bishop, who was the ruler of the synagogue, whose

---

[1] The MS. adds "and."

name was Marcellus[1], and a presbyter and deacons; and he gave them the holy Gospel. And he stayed with them a month, teaching them the word of God; then he returned to Jerusalem. And when the Jews killed James the Just, the disciples were in Jerusalem. They took Simon and made him bishop in Jerusalem. And he taught them the word of God; and made known to them what was in the Gospel, and the salvation of their souls. And the Jews were angry with him; and he was in Jerusalem praising the Lord at [all] times and all seasons. Amen, Amen, Amen.

And praise be to God always and for ever.

[1] The Sinai MS. has "Cornelius."

THE MARTYRDOM OF SIMON.

f. 122 b   *The Martyrdom of Simon, son of Cleophas, disciple of the Lord Jesus the Christ. And he finished his conflict on the ninth of Abîb[1], in the peace of the Lord. Amen.*

And after the death of James the Just, Simon the son of Cleophas, who was called Jude, was made bishop of Jerusalem. And he lived a hundred and twenty years, and he loved to have his blood shed at the end of his life for the name of the Lord Jesus the Christ. And he built churches in every place in Jerusalem; and he appointed them a presbyter[2] and deacons. The first church which he built was in the name of the Lord Jesus the Christ; and the second in the name of the Virgin Mary, who gave birth to the Lord upon earth, that He might deliver mankind from the slavery of Satan, and make them meet for His kingdom. And the third was in the name of Michael the Archangel, the Interceder for mankind, that wrath may be turned away from them, and mercy may rest upon them. And the fourth was in the name of the disciples. And he wished that the faith of the Jews might be brought to nought, and their polluted worship, and their wicked synagogue. And he preached the Word of God to every one, until the churches which he had built were

f. 123 a   frequented; and the knowledge of God appeared to all the people, from the oldest to the youngest, both men and women. And all of them believed by means of the disciple; until all the people of the city forsook the synagogue of the Jews, and followed the truth which the disciple taught them with the authority of the Lord Jesus the Christ. And when they heard of the work of the blessed disciple, and that he wished to destroy their religion and their idol, they gathered themselves together, both old and young: and they took counsel together to slay him, as he was an evil-doer. And they assembled in wrath and anger; and they put him in chains, and delivered him over to the Emperor Trajan. And they together bore witness against him before the Emperor, and said: " He is a wizard." The Emperor trusted them in all that they said;

---

[1] *i.e.* July. The Sinai MS. says, "in the tenth day of the month of May." The Ethiopian, "on the tenth day of the month Hamlê," *i.e.* July 4 (cf. Budge, p. 75).

[2] Sinai MS. " presbyters."

and he was wroth with the disciple, and said unto him : " I say unto thee, O evil-doer! it hath been told me that thou art a wizard, thou hast bewitched every one in this city." The disciple said unto him: " O thou Emperor! I am no wizard ; and I know not how to practise the art of witchcraft ; but I am a slave to my Lord Jesus the Christ, the God of all creation, and the King of kings; the great, the mighty God, Who destroyeth all the gods of the heathen." And when the Emperor heard that, he was wroth with a fierce wrath ; and delivered him over to f. 123 b wicked people that they might crucify him. And the Jews gathered themselves together against him. And they brought the blessed disciple out to be crucified, as the godless Emperor had commanded, upon the cross. And they tortured him until he died. And he finished his martyrdom on the ninth day of Abîb[1], by the will of God, the Ruler of all ; to Whom be glory and honour for ever and ever. Amen.

---

[1] i.e. July. The Sinai MS. "on the tenth day of the month of May." Ethiopic, "on the tenth day of the month of Hamlê."

THE PREACHING OF THADDEUS.

In the name of God, the Pitiful, the Compassionate.   The Preaching of the blessed Thaddeus which he proclaimed in Damascus and the island[1] *And he finished his testimony on the second day of Abîb*[2], *in the peace of the Lord Jesus the Christ ; to Whom be glory for ever.   Amen.*

It came to pass when the disciples were assembled on the Mount of Olives, and had divided the world, that they might go out and preach amongst them the Gospel of our Lord Jesus the Christ, [that] the lot of Thaddeus was to the cities of Syria.   Thaddeus said unto Peter : "Go with me to this country."   Peter said unto him : "Be patient with me ; and I will make thee to arrive in peace."   And while they were talking, the Lord Jesus the Christ stood amongst them like a young man, beautiful

f. 124 a of countenance, and said, "Peace be unto thee, O Peter, Ruler of My Church !   Peace be unto thee, O Thaddeus the beloved ! go and fear not, why dost thou doubt?   I will dwell with you until ye shall have finished your administrations."

He said unto Him : "Yea, O Lord !   Thou wilt be with us while we are preaching in every place."   And the Lord gave them the [salutation of] peace ; and departed from them, ascending to heaven in glory.   And they took counsel together, and journeyed in the peace of the Lord Jesus the Christ.

And when they drew nigh unto the city, Thaddeus said unto Peter : "I would fain know what shall befall us in this city."   Peter said unto him : "I have no knowledge ; but behold, I see an old man ploughing in the field.   Let us go to him and say unto him : 'If thou hast a bit of bread, give us something that we may eat.'   And if he shall say unto us : 'I will give it you,' know that good will befall us.   And if he shall say 'Nay,' know that we shall have trouble in this town."

And when we came up to him, Peter said unto him : "Peace be upon

---

[1] The Sinai MS. has, "This is the Preaching of the blessed Jude, brother of the Lord, who is Thaddeus, which he proclaimed in Syria and the island."   "The island" is a geographical term for Mesopotamia.

[2] *i.e.* July.   The Ethiopic has "in the second day of the month Hamlê (Budge, *i.e.* June 26). The Sinai MS. has "in the nineteenth day of Hazîrân."

thee, O thou old man! If thou hast bread, give us something that we may eat."

The old man replied to him: "I have nothing here, but sit ye down with these oxen while I go and bring you what ye need."   f. 124 b

Peter said unto him: "If thou wilt bring us what we may eat, we will sit beside the oxen." And he said unto him: "Are the oxen thine?" He said: "Nay, but I have borrowed them." He said: "Tell me, is the field thine?" He said unto him: "Yea, it is mine." Peter said unto him: "Go in peace."

And when the man was gone, Peter said: "It is unbecoming in us to stand idle here with these oxen; while the man has gone to deal kindly with us." And Peter girded up his loins, and laid hold of the plough, and called to the oxen to plough.

Thaddeus said unto him: "O my father! what great work is this that thou doest? Thou art an old man; and thou art exalted to a high position, and there is a great heavy burden on thy shoulder. Thou canst not accomplish it thus. As for us, O my father! thou art the greater [and] thou dost work whilst I sit and rest." And he took the plough from Peter and ploughed; and Peter took a basket of wheat and blessed it; and said: "O my Lord Jesus the Christ! let Thy blessing descend upon this field." Thaddeus said: "O my Lord Jesus the Christ! let Thy blessing rest upon the earth and appear in this field." And they worked [over] thirty paces, until the old man returned.

And straightway the seed sprouted and became ears full of wheat corn. f. 125 a And the old man returned to the field and saw what the two disciples had done. He said unto them: "O my lords! who are ye? tell me whence ye have come; that I may follow you to every place whither ye may go" And he fell at the feet of the disciples, and said unto them: "Truly ye are both gods who have come down from heaven to earth."

And Peter raised him up, and said unto him: "Stand up, O man! we are not gods, but disciples of God. He hath given to us a spiritual doctrine, that we should teach it to the people; and should proclaim among mankind that they may repent of their sins, and inherit everlasting life." The man said unto them: "What shall I do, that I may have everlasting life?" Peter said unto him: "Love thy God with all thy heart and all thy Matt. soul and all thy mind. Hast thou a wife?" He said unto him: "Yea." xxii. 37 He said unto him: "And sons?" He said: "Yea." He said also: "Thou shalt not kill; and thou shalt not commit adultery; and thou shalt not cf. Matt. swear falsely. What thou wouldest not that men should do unto thee do vii. 12

it not to any man like thyself. And if thou doest what I have commanded thee, thou shalt inherit life everlasting."

f. 125 b   The old man said unto him : "Though I have done [this], what shall I do for you as a reward for the good which ye did unto me? ye have made my field to sprout in such a way out of its season. I will leave these oxen standing and will follow you to every place whither ye may go." Peter said unto him : "This is not the way in which thou shouldest act. Take the oxen, and return them to their owners ; and tell thy wife about thy state; and prepare something for us to eat in thy house. For we wish to stay in this city to-day; and we have made supplication unto our Lord Jesus the Christ for it."

And the man took a bundle of ears in his hand from the field which the two had sown ; and he went into the city with the oxen. And when he entered its gate the people saw him with a bundle of ears in his hand. They said unto him : "Whence hast thou these green ears, this being the time for ploughing ?" And he returned them no answer. And he drove the oxen joyfully until he had returned them to their owners. And he returned to his dwelling, and prepared in it what was needful for the coming of the two disciples.

And his story came to the magistrates of the city ; and they sent to
f. 126 a   him, saying unto him, "Whence comes this bundle, these green ears, to thee? Tell us the tale, or else thou shalt die an evil death."

He said unto them : "It matters not to me, since I have found life. And if ye desire to know the truth, hearken. Two men passed by me while I was ploughing, and they said unto me : 'If thou hast any bread, give it us that we may eat.' I said unto them : 'I have nothing here, but sit ye down beside my oxen until I go and bring you what ye want.' And when I had gone to my house, and had got bread for them, and had returned to the field, I found that they had sown it : and full green ears had sprouted, and I gathered this from it. And they are outside of the town."

And the magistrates said unto him : "Go and bring them to us." The man said unto them : "Have patience with me for a little while, for I have prepared my dwelling for them, that they may go in and rest in it. And when they appear ye will see them." And he returned to his dwelling.

And Satan disturbed the hearts of the magistrates ; and they wept[1] and said : "Woe unto us![2] Perhaps these two men are some of the twelve wizards

---

[1] The Sinai MS. omits "wept."
[2] The Suriani MS. says "unto them."

of whom we have heard that they go about in every place and deceive the people with their magic. What shall we do? We shall not allow them to enter our city." And some of them said: "Rise, let us go out unto them and f. 126 b slay them." Others said: "We cannot slay them; for we have heard that Jesus their God doeth for them what they ask from Him; lest they bring down fire upon us, or a flood to destroy us. But [though] we cannot slay them, let us not allow them to enter the city. We have heard of them that they hate fornication. Let us take a woman, a harlot, and strip her, and place her at the gate of the city. And if they wish to enter the city, they will look on her, [and] they will go out, and will not return to destroy us in entering it."

[1]And they brought her, and did this thing[1]. And when the disciples arrived at the gate they looked at the naked woman standing opposite them, with her evil deeds. And Thaddeus said unto Peter: "O my father! look at this woman, how Satan hath deceived her, that she should tempt the Lord and His servants." Peter said unto him: "The matter concerneth thee, command what thou wouldest about her." And Thaddeus prayed and said: "O my Lord Jesus the Christ! I entreat thee to send Michael the archangel to suspend this woman in the air by the hair of her head, that we may enter the city. And when we desire to go out, let her down." And straightway the woman was suspended by the hair of her head, and the magistrates saw her; and they did not perceive who was holding her. And she cried out f. 127 a with a great cry, and said: "May God do me right against the magistrates of this city! It is they who have taught me this evil. And if I had been sitting in my house, being in my sins, so that the Lord's two disciples might enter the city, and save all the sinners: they would have saved me also from my sin. Come, O ye young men whom I have hurt by my fornication! arise and beseech the Lord's disciples on my behalf: perhaps they will have compassion on me."

And while the woman was saying this, not one of the citizens believed; because Satan had hardened their hearts. And Peter said unto Thaddeus: "Rise with us, let us pray and beseech God to help us; for Satan hath led the hearts of the multitude astray." And they arose and prayed and said: "O God the Lord! Ruler of all, Who hast taught us to call upon Thee in the time of tribulation, and hast said that Thou wouldest answer us; be gracious, O Lord! and have compassion upon us; and strengthen us for the war with Satan who hath risen up against us in this place." And

---

[1] The Sinai MS. "And they brought the harlot, and stripped off her clothes, and placed her at the door."

while they were entreating, Michael the archangel came down to them, and chased away the bad spirits who filled the souls of the citizens. And Peter went out, and Thaddeus, and walked in the streets of the city, and preached in the name of Jesus the Christ. Then all the citizens believed, for no one who was corrupting their hearts remained. And the woman who had been suspended in the air [believed]. And after this they appointed them a bishop and priests; and they baptized them all in the name of the Father and the Son and the Holy Spirit. And they made the woman who had been suspended in the air to serve the church. And they healed the sick, and opened the eyes of the blind, and they made the dumb to speak, and the deaf to hear, and the lame to walk[1]. And they drove away a devil, and he returned to his craft, and crept into the heart of a boy, a rich young man, who loved money, and excited him against the two disciples, and sent him to them. And when he appeared he did obeisance to them, saying: "O good servants of God! what do you wish me to do, that I may live?"

Peter said: "Love the Lord thy God with all thy heart and all thy soul; and do not steal, and do not kill, and do not commit impurity, cf. Matt. vii. 12 and do not swear falsely. And what thou wouldest not that men should do unto thee, do not thou unto them." The youth said: "If I keep all this, shall I be able to work miracles like you?" They said unto him: "Tell us thy condition. Hast thou a wife?" He said: "No, I am a man, a merchant, and I have much property, tell me what is my duty to do with it."

Peter said unto him: "Go and renounce [thy] property, and distribute it amongst the poor." And when the youth heard that, he was wroth against him with a fierce wrath, and he rushed on Thaddeus and [tried to] choke him. And he said unto him: "Dost thou advise concerning me, that I should destroy my property?" Thaddeus said unto him: "The Lord spake in this wise about one who was like thee, 'That a camel could go into the eye of a needle, but not a rich man into the kingdom of heaven.'" And his wrath against Thaddeus increased, and he choked him most violently, seeking to kill him. And had it not been for the power of God preserving him, his eyes would have flown out from the force of the choking. And Peter said unto him: "Why dost thou strangle the disciple of Christ because of a true word which he hath said unto thee? Dost thou wish to renounce what is thine? Renounce what thou wilt, no man

---

[1] The Sinai MS. adds, "and the dead arose, so that they all believed, and entered into the knowledge of God—may His name be glorified!"

forceth thee. If thou sayest that it is not true about the camel and the eye of the needle, bring a camel and a needle." And immediately a man passed by them having a camel with him. And they laid hold of him and asked for a needle from a man who sold needles[1]. And the two stood and stretched out their hands and prayed and said: "O our Lord Jesus the f. 128 b Christ! unto Whom belongeth power over all things, we beseech Thee to hearken unto our entreaty, and to manifest Thy power, so that the multitude may learn that all things are obedient unto Thee. Yea, O Lord! hearken unto the supplication of Thy servants, and may this camel go into the eye of the needle, that Thy name may be glorified." And Peter said unto the man who held the camel: "In the name of my Lord Jesus the Christ the Nazarene, enter thou and thy camel into the hole of the needle." And straightway the man and the camel went into the eye of the needle.

And when the multitude saw this wonder, they lifted up their voices and said: "There is no God but God, the God of these two disciples, Peter and Thaddeus." And when the rich youth saw this, he rent his garments, and smote his face, and said: "Woe is me, what have I done!" And he put his face upon the ground at the feet of the two disciples, weeping, and he begged them to take all that he possessed, and to distribute it amongst the poor and the needy, and to seek pardon for him from God. And they consented to what he asked ; and they exhorted him and taught him the commandments, and the precepts of religion, and they baptized him in the name of the Father, and the Son, and the Holy Ghost, f. 129 a him and all his household[2]. And they gave them the holy Mysteries, the Body of the Lord, and His pure Blood. And they built a church for the citizens, and they appointed them a bishop and priests, and they wrote the Gospel for them, and all the commandments, and they went out from amongst them, they bidding them farewell in peace. And this is the reason of their faith in the Lord Jesus the Christ.

And as for Thaddeus, he fell asleep after a while on the second of Abîb[3], praising the Father and the Son and the Holy Ghost, henceforth and always, and for ever and ever. Amen.

---

[1] The Sinai MS. adds: "And the man wished to help the disciples. And he sought for a needle with a wide eye. Peter said unto him: 'God bless thee, my son! and accept thy faith from thee. I seek a needle with a very narrow eye; that the glory of God may appear, and His power in this city.' And he did as he [Peter] had commanded until he found a needle, as it had been said unto him, with a very narrow eye. And the disciples stood," etc.

[2] The Sinai MS. has "all the citizens."

[3] =July. The Sinai MS. has "on the nineteenth day of Hazirân"=June. The Ethiopic "on the second day of the month Hamlê."

THE PREACHING OF SAINT MATTHIAS.

In the name of the Father, and the Son, and the Holy Ghost, the one God. The Preaching of the Blessed Matthias, disciple of the Lord Jesus the Christ, with which he preached the Gospel in the city whose people are cannibals ; and he finished his conflict on the eighth day of Phamenôth, in the peace of the Lord Jesus the Christ. Amen.

It came to pass when the disciples divided the cities of the world, [that] Matthias took out the city whose people are cannibals. And in it they neither eat bread nor drink water ; and they have no food save the flesh of men, and their blood. And they seize every foreigner who enters this city, and they tear out his eyes, and they weave spells about him that his reason may go, and they feed him on grass like the cattle, and they put him in a dark place for thirty days ; then they bring him out and eat him.

And when the Blessed Matthias entered this city, they laid hold of him and blinded him by a treatment of theirs which they knew ; and they fed him on grass. But he did not eat it because the power of God was with him, dwelling in him. And they cast him into prison. And he prayed and besought the Lord Jesus the Christ, and said: " O my Lord ! for Whose sake we have renounced the world and have followed Thee, verily we know that there is no helper but Thee. Behold what they have done to Thy servant ; they have made him like the beasts. Thou, O Lord ! knowest what hath been, and shall be. And if thou willest that I should die in this city, let Thy will be done. But, O Lord, give me light of mine eyes ; and do not give them power over me to eat my flesh like [that of] the beasts."

And when he had finished his prayer, his eyes were opened, and he saw all the world as it had been ; and a voice called to him, saying unto him : " Be strong, O Matthias ! and fear not ; I will not depart from thee : but I abide with thee in every place whither thou shalt go. But be patient until six days are completed. I will send Andrew unto thee, and he shall bring thee out of prison."

And he thanked God and glorified Him, and his soul rejoiced. And he remained in the prison as (the Lord) had commanded him. And when the citizens entered the prison to take some one out to sacrifice, he closed his eyes that they might not see him. And they had a custom when they put a man in the prison, the first day they put him in, they wrote a label and

f. 129 b

f. 130 a

hung it on his neck. And when thirty days were accomplished for him, they sacrificed him according to the custom. And they did thus to Matthias.

And on the thirty-sixth day of his imprisonment the Lord appeared unto Andrew in the city of El Barbar and said unto him : "Arise, go out to Matthias in the City of the Cannibals, that thou mayest bring him out of prison, for in three days the citizens will seek to eat him."

Andrew said, " I cannot reach him in this time, but send an angel to bring him out of the prison, for I shall not reach it in these three days." f. 130 b

The Lord replied unto him, " Hearken, O thou, whom I have chosen ! who canst say unto the city, ' Come hither, and all its inhabitants[1].' Arise, thou and thy disciple[2], to-morrow ye shall find a ship ready, embark in it ; it will bring you thither." And the Lord gave him [the greeting of] peace, and ascended to heaven in glory.

And Andrew stood, as the Lord had commanded, on the shore of the sea. And the Lord had prepared for him a spiritual ship ; and He was sitting in it like the captain; and angels were the sailors. And when Andrew drew nigh to the ship, and perceived the Lord sitting (and he did not know it), he said unto Him : " Peace be unto thee, O captain of the ship ! "

The Lord said unto him : " May the peace of the Lord rest upon thee ! " Andrew said unto him : " Wilt thou carry us with thee to the country whose people are cannibals ? " And the Lord, Who was like the captain, said unto him, " Every one fleeth from that city, and ye are going to it."

He said unto him, " We have business, and because of it we must go thither."

Andrew said unto him : " I beseech thee, O beloved brother ! to convey us, and we have no means to pay thee for it, but we will eat with thee of thy food." The Lord, Who was in the likeness of the captain of the ship, f. 131 a said : " If ye two will eat of our bread, and ye have nothing wherewith to pay us the fare of the boat, tell me who ye are." Andrew said unto him : " We are disciples of a good Lord, whose name is Jesus the Christ, twelve disciples. He chose us, and gave us commandments, and sent us to preach in His name in the world, and commanded us not to possess gold nor silver, nor anything of the currency of this world : and not to be anxious about bread. And therefore we are as thou seest us. And if thou dost consent to us, and wilt convey us, thou wilt do us a kindness. And if thou wilt not do it, tell us, that we may seek another ship."

---

[1] A word has been lost here.
[2] The Syriac and Ethiopic versions have "disciples" *passim*.

He said unto them: "Embark in the ship, I am willing to carry you, rather than people who would pay me the fare. This is a great joy, if I am worthy that ye should sail with me, O disciples of the Christ!"

Andrew said unto him: "God bless thee with spiritual blessings!" And Andrew and his disciple embarked and sat in the ship.

And the Lord said unto one of the angels who resembled sailors, "Bring bread to these two brethren that they may eat, for they are come from a far country." And he did as He had commanded him.

And the Lord said unto Andrew: "Arise, O my brother! and thy disciple; eat bread before we go out to sea." And the disciple of Andrew f. 131 b could not speak for fear of the sea.

And Andrew turned and said unto him: "May my Lord Jesus the Christ make thy reward good in the kingdom of heaven! Be patient with me for a little while, and I shall not eat until my disciple shall eat."

And they went upon the sea; and they had never before sailed on it. Andrew said: "Arise and go down to this place, that thou mayest go whither thou hast been sent." And the Lord said unto one of the angels who were in the likeness of sailors: "Put up the sail of the ship." And he did it. And the Lord took hold of the rudder like the captain of the ship; the angels standing at His side, [with] Andrew and his disciple sitting in the middle, [and] he consoled them and said: "Fear not, O my child! the Lord will not forsake us. As for the sky, He hath lifted it up, and the sea, He hath raised all its water; and everything, He hath created it. Fear not, for He is present with us, as far as the place whither we are going; as He hath promised us." And when Andrew had said this, he prayed, entreating the Lord that his disciple might sleep, and that they[1] might not fear the sea. And this took place speedily. And while they slept he took their souls up to Paradise, and they ate of its fruit. And when he knew that they were sleeping, he said unto the Lord, f. 132 a "I entreat thee, O good man, to tell me about this voyage which thy boat is making; for I have not seen anything like it; and I have sailed on the sea many times; [but] I never have sailed in a boat like this. Truly I am as if I were sitting on the land, and the ship doth not rock; though we have come out into the midst of the sea. The sailors can do nothing with the gear of the ship, and neither can others."

The Lord Jesus the Christ said: "All the time we have sailed over the sea, no voyage like this hath been seen. When the ship knoweth that a disciple of the Christ is in it, it is not shaken as at all other times."

[1] From this point, in the Arabic text, Andrew's one disciple becomes two.

Andrew said: "Blessed be the name of my Lord Jesus the Christ! Who in His merciful kindness hath enabled me to sail with a man who knoweth His name."

The Lord said: "If thou art a disciple of the Christ, tell me why the children of Israel do not believe in Him, and do not say that He is God. I have heard of Him, that He hath shewn wonders to His disciples on the Mount of Olives."

Andrew said unto Him: "I will tell thee His miracles. He opened the eyes of the blind; and the dumb spake; and He made the deaf hear; and He cast out devils; and raised the dead; and He placed five loaves of barley bread upon the grass, till they became enough to satisfy five thousand men, besides the women and the children. And beyond that afterwards, the twelve baskets of the superabundance of the bread. And with all this they did not believe in Him."

Matt. xiv. 19
Mark vi. 41
Luke ix. 16
John vi. 10

The Lord said unto him: "Perhaps He did not do these wonders in the presence of the chief priests, and therefore they did not believe, but they rose up against Him."

f. 132 b

Andrew said unto Him: "But in their presence He did not shew His power, and also in secret He worked amongst them."

The Lord said unto him: "What was the secret thing?"

And whilst they were talking they drew nigh to the city. And Andrew slept. And the Lord commanded the angels to carry him and his two disciples, and the provender on to the shore of the sea; and He ascended to heaven in His glory.

And when he awoke he beheld the city, and he did not see a trace of the ship. He said: "Have I been sitting with the Lord, and I knew it not? I will look, and the Lord will speak unto His servant. This is a blessed day for me. When my ship shall sail I shall behold Him who hath humbled Himself for whom?"

Then his disciples awoke; and he said unto them both: "Arise, we have been sailing with the Lord, and we knew it not." His disciples said unto him: "Once when I prayed we saw shining eagles; they overshadowed us, and took our souls up to Paradise; and we saw the Lord sitting upon a throne, and the angels round about Him. And I saw you, the twelve disciples, and the twelve angels round about you. And since then until the time we awoke we have seen many wonders."

And Andrew rejoiced when his two disciples had seen this spiritual vision. And he arose and drew a circle on the ground, and said: "O my Lord Jesus the Christ! I will not depart from this place until Thou shalt

L. A.   R

appear, for I know that Thou art not far from me. Forgive me for what
my heart hath thought in my folly. I entreat Thee that Thou wouldest
appear unto Thy servant." And the Lord appeared unto him outside
f. 133 a of the city like a youth fair of face; and said unto him: "Andrew, my
beloved." And Andrew fell upon the ground, and said: "I thank Thee,
O my Lord Jesus the Christ! What have I done, that Thou shouldest
appear unto me on the sea?"

The Lord said unto him: "Fear not, I have done this unto thee
because thou hast said: 'We shall not reach the city in three days.'
I wished to teach thee that I am Almighty; and that nothing is too hard for
Me. Arise, go into the city, take Matthias out of prison and all who are
with him there. And much suffering shall come upon you in it. Be patient,
for I shall abide with you. Remember that I am compassionate; and be ye
like unto Me: and remember that it hath been said, that by Baʿelzebul
I cast out devils. I could, more quickly than in the twinkling of an eye,
command the earth to open and take them down to the depths, but I was
long-suffering, for I know that the Evil One dwelleth with you upon the
earth; and I know [by] your patience in suffering in this city many in it
will believe in Me."

Andrew said unto Him: "Be with me, O Lord! and I will do all that
Thou dost command me."

And the Lord gave him [the greeting of] peace, and ascended to
heaven with great glory.

f. 133 b   And Andrew arose and his two disciples, and they went into the city,
and no one perceived them. And they came to the gates of the prison.
And when they took hold of the prison gates they were opened unto them,
and they entered and found Matthias sitting, singing psalms, and they
greeted him. Andrew said unto him: "Sayest thou that after two days
thou shalt go out and be sacrificed like the beasts? and thy flesh shall be
eaten? And hast thou forgotten these mysteries which we saw from the
Lord? which if we were to speak about it the very heaven would be shaken."

Matthias said: "I have known that, O my brother! but I said: Perhaps
the Lord hath willed thus, that I should finish my conflict in this city.
Hath not His voice been heard in the Holy Gospel, when He saith, 'I send
Matt. x. you forth as ewe-lambs among wolves'? But as for me, on the day I
16 was thrown into prison, I called on the Lord, and He appeared unto
me and said unto me: 'Fear not; when the days are fulfilled, I will send
Andrew unto thee; he shall bring thee out of prison—thee and those who
are with thee.' And lo! thou art come, and I see what thou hast done."

And Andrew saw in the midst of the prison the men who were tied up
like the beasts : and he cursed Satan and all his hosts.   And Andrew
and Matthias began to supplicate the Lord, and He heard them.   And f. 134 a
they laid their hands upon the men who were in the prison ; and
opened their eyes, and their senses returned unto them.   And they
commanded them to go out of the city ; and they told them that they
would find a fig-tree in the path, under which they might sit until the
disciples returned unto them.   And the men said unto them : " Come ye
out with us, lest the citizens should come and make us return."

The disciples said unto them : " Go ye out in peace ; nothing unpleasant
shall befall you."   And they went forth outside of the city ; and they
found a fig-tree, as [the disciples] had told them.   And the number of
them was a hundred and forty-nine men.

And the two told Rufus and Alexander, disciples of Andrew, to go
out of the city.   And Andrew and Matthias and their disciples arose and
prayed, and entreated the Lord to send a cloud to convey Rufus and
Alexander, the disciples, and to bring them to Peter.   And the Lord sent
a cloud ; it carried them.

And Andrew and Matthias went forth into the midst of the streets of
the city, and they sat down beneath the covering of the street[1] that they
might know what was going to happen.   And the citizens sent officers to the f. 134 b
prison to bring them the men whom they were about to sacrifice, as their
custom was, every day.   And they found the doors of the prison opened, and
the guards dead, and their number was six men, and there was no one in
the prison.   And they returned and told the magistrates.   And they said :
" What shall we do ? can we remain to-day without anything to eat ? "   And
they took counsel about what troubled them.   " Either we shall eat the dead,
or we shall bring out the old men of the city and they shall cast lots, and
on whomsoever the lot falleth he shall be sacrificed and eaten, until the
messengers return to us."   For they had persons whom they sent in a ship
to gather people together from every place to their country, that they might
eat them.   And they had a lake in the city ; [so that] when they wished to
sacrifice a man or a woman, they might be slain in it, and the blood might filter
away into a pool in the midst of it.   And when they had brought them to
the place, and had taken up knives to cut them up, Andrew saw them.   And
he stood and made supplication : " O my Lord Jesus the Christ, Lover of
mankind ! may these knives which are in their hands be broken."   And f. 135 a

---

[1] We may suppose that the narrow street was lightly roofed over with canes or bamboos, as a
protection from the sun.   Cf. Dozy, vol. I. p. 663.

straightway their hands were withered, and they could not move them. And when the magistrates saw what had happened, they wept and said: "The wizards who brought the men out of the prison are they who have bewitched these men, so that we have no power over them." And the old men of the city, whose number was three hundred and sixteen men, came together. And they made them cast lots, and the lot fell upon six, that they should be sacrificed and eaten. And one of the six whom the lot had constrained said: "I have a son, take him and release me." And the officers said: "We will not take him unless we inform the magistrates." And they informed them and they said unto them: "If he should deliver his son unto you instead of himself, release him." And he delivered his son unto them. And when they had laid hold of the boy to slay him, he wept in his father's face, and said unto him: "I entreat thee, O my father! let me not be killed while I am a boy; but let me live that I may become like thee. And when I am an old man like thee, let them eat me." And the boy cried and said unto the officers: "Ye are hard of heart; but it is my father who hath delivered me over unto death."

f. 135 b   And it was the law of their city that every one who died should be cut up and eaten. And they brought those upon whom the lot had fallen. And Andrew made supplication unto the Lord and said: "I entreat Thee, O my Lord Jesus the Christ! as Thou hast answered me about the dead; hearken to my supplication about these living ones, and let no one have power to slay them." And their swords became as wax before the fire. And when the magistrates saw that, they wept bitter tears and said: "Woe unto us! what hath befallen us?"

Then Satan appeared unto them like an old man, and cried and said: "Woe unto you! ye will die of hunger; for ye cannot eat your dead after this; they will remain lying in the midst of your streets until they are decayed; and ye will not be able to eat them. Arise, seek for this man Matthias and kill him. For if ye kill him not, ye will not be able to do what ye want. For he it is who brought the people out of the prison; and he is in this city; seek for him and slay him, so that your condition may be prosperous."

And when Andrew saw Satan talking thus with them, he said unto
f. 136 a him: "O Enemy of our Lord! may God, Whose name is exalted, put thee down under our feet." And when Satan heard these words he said: "I hear the voice, but I do not see the body." And Andrew appeared to him and said unto him: "Yea, is not thy name called Sāmil[1]? O thou

---

[1] Or "blind," Syriac ܣܡܝܐ.

blind one! for thou art blind; thou dost not see the servants of God." And Satan cried with a loud voice and said: "Behold the men! lay hold of them." And the multitude went before and locked the gate of the town while they were seeking and saying: "Matthias and Andrew! seize them for us, that we may do unto them what we will." And the Lord commanded the two disciples, saying: "Arise and appear. that they may know the weakness of their power." And they went out from under the covering and they said unto them: "We are those whom ye seek." And they rose up against them and laid hold of them, and said unto them: "We shall do unto you as ye have done unto us." Some people said: "Let us take your heads and give them to the chief priests." And others said: "Nay, but let us cut them into small pieces, and distribute their flesh among all the citizens." And they dragged them through all the city until their blood flowed on the path; and they cast them into prison, and bound f. 136 b them, and left them in a dark place. And they set many strong men to guard them. And when the two entered the prison they prayed and said: "O our Lord Jesus the Christ! let not Thy help be far from us. Thou hast commanded us not to hasten; and let not the enemy rejoice over us."

Then the Lord appeared unto them and said: "I am abiding with you." And He said: "Fear not."

And whilst they were in the prison Satan took with him six of his friends; and they appeared unto them, and spake forcible words against them, and said: "Ye have fallen into my hands; and who shall save you from me? Where is your power wherewith ye prevailed over me in all the cities, and laid waste the temples which were mine? I shall allow them to slay you as I slew your Master."

And he said unto his friends: "Arise, slay these people who have resisted you; so that ye may have rest from them, and that every place may be yours." And the devils rose up against the disciples, desiring to kill them. And they made the sign of the cross on their faces; and they f. 137 a fell upon the earth. And their father Satan said unto them: "What hath befallen you?" They said unto him: "We saw a sign in their hands, and we were afraid of it. And if thou hast power against them, act, for we are frightened." And they went away ashamed.

And when the citizens awoke in the morning they brought out the two disciples, and dragged them through the city. And they made supplication to their Lord, saying: "Have compassion on us, O Lord! for we are flesh and blood, and we know that Thou art not far from us." And they heard a

Matt.
xxiv. 35
voice calling them, in Hebrew, saying: "Andrew and Matthias, the heaven
and the earth shall pass away; but My word shall not pass away." And
the citizens went with them to the prison; and they said: "They shall die
this time." And the disciples made supplication, while their blood was
streaming on the ground, saying: "O our Lord Jesus the Christ! help us
and save this city and all who are in it." And immediately they saw the
image of an idol of stone standing on a pillar in the midst of the prison,
and they made the sign of the cross over it. And they spread out their
hands and prayed; and they drew near to the pillar on which was the idol.
And they said unto it: "Be afraid of the sign of the cross, which we make
over thee, and make water to flow out from beneath it abundantly like the
f. 137 b water of the Flood upon that city and all its inhabitants." And water
gushed out at once from beneath it in abundance intensely salt, and it
began to drown the city and all its inhabitants. And the citizens took their
children and their cattle and they tried to get out of it. And Matthias
said: "O my Lord Jesus the Christ! give an answer to the supplication of
Thy servant; and send Michael the Archangel with a dark cloud upon
this city; so that no man may go out of it."

And when Matthias knew that the Lord had answered him, he struck
the pillar and said: "Finish what I have commanded." And the water
rose higher until it reached to the necks of the people, and it almost
drowned them. And they wept and said: "Woe unto us! perhaps this
wrath that abideth on us is because of the two good men, the servants of
God, whom we have thrown into prison; and of our cruel conduct to them.
Behold! we shall die an evil death in this water; but come along with us,
let us cry out to their God and let us say: 'We believe in Thee, O God!
the God of these two foreign men. Save us from this water.'"

f. 138 a   Then Andrew answered and said unto the pillar: "The time of the
flood is gone; and now is the time for sowing in the hearts of the
citizens. Truly I say, that when I shall have built a church in this city
I will put thee in it."

And the water straightway stood still which was gushing from beneath
the pillar. And when the citizens saw it, six of the elders of the city with
some young men accompanying them rose up and went to the prison—
the water being up to their necks. And when they saw the two disciples,
their hands were stretched out making supplication to God. And they
went out to them, and the water was divided before them. And when the
elders saw this they were afraid and cried, saying: "Have compassion on
us, O servants of God!" And amongst them was the old man on whom

the lot fell that he should be sacrificed; and who had delivered up his son and saved himself. And Matthias said unto him : " I am amazed at thee when thou sayest : 'Have compassion on me,' and thou hadst no compassion on thy son. In this hour the water shall return to the depth of the earth and thou shalt go down with it, and the six men who sacrificed the people ; so that the state of him who hated his son, and of those who slew the people, may be seen." And he said unto the young men who accompanied the elders : "Go ye to the spot in which the people were sacrificed, so that f. 138 b the water may return unto its place." And they went with the disciples, the water flowing away from before them. And they stood beside the lake and prayed. And straightway the earth was opened, and it swallowed up the men who had been sacrificing the people, and the old man who had delivered up his son to death, and all the water which was in the city ; and all the citizens saw this, and were greatly afraid. And they said : " They will say : 'Let fire come down from heaven to burn us up because of the wrong which we have done unto them.'" And they said unto them : " Fear not, and believe with a true faith. Ye shall see the glory of God. And we shall not leave those whom the earth hath swallowed in it ; but we shall raise them up." And Matthias and Andrew commanded that every one who had died from the water should be brought unto them, that they might pray over them, and that they might rise. And they could not do it because of the multitude of the dead.

And the disciples made supplication unto the Lord, and He sent a rain from Himself upon the dead ; and they all arose. And after these things the foundation of the church was laid ; and they built it. And they gave them the commandments of the Gospel, and the Law and the Gospel ; and f. 139 a they baptized them all in the name of the Father and the Son and the Holy Ghost. And they gave them the holy mysteries ; and they healed all the sick. And they said unto them : " Take heed to what we have commanded you till the end of your lives ; and teach your children who shall come after you. And make supplication unto the Lord that He may take away from you the custom which ye have of eating man's flesh." And he gave them the right feeling that their food should be like the food of men. And afterwards they (the disciples) departed from amongst them ; and they bade them farewell, saying unto them : " O good servants of God! abide with us for a while, so that we may rejoice in you: for we are new plants." They said unto them : "Grieve not, and fear not ; we shall not stay long away from you, by the will of God."

And as they were going out from [the city] the Lord appeared unto them like a youth fair of face. And He said unto them : "Have pity on the inhabitants of this city; and accept their request; and abide with them for some days. For I have heard their petition unto you when they said : 'We are new plants.' And why did ye command the six men and send them into the depths?"

And they said : "Forgive us, O our Lord! we will return unto them, and will make them rise from the depths by Thy name." The Lord said f. 139 b unto them : "Return unto the city, and abide in it for seven days; and go forth from it ; and thou Andrew, go unto the city of El-Barbar." And they both said : "O Lord, bless us!" And He blessed them ; and ascended to Heaven with glory. And they entered the city, as the Lord had commanded them ; and they abode in it for seven days. And they raised up those whom the earth had swallowed ; and they confirmed their faith, and strengthened their knowledge of the Lord's commandments. And they went out from amongst them as they were giving glory to God, Who had not left them in error. And the men went out with them, bidding them farewell and saying : "There is one God, the God of Andrew and Matthias, Jesus the Christ, to Whom be glory and honour ; and to His Father, Who upholdeth all things, and [to] the Holy Ghost, the Giver of life for ever and ever. Amen."

THE MARTYRDOM OF MATTHIAS.

The Martyrdom of Matthias, disciple of the Lord Jesus the Christ, and his conflict which he finished on the eighth day of Pharmouthi·; in the peace of the Lord. Amen.

It came to pass, when Judas Iscariot had betrayed our Lord Jesus f. 140 a the Christ to be crucified, that Satan and his hosts might be vanquished by the sufferings of the Lord Jesus the Christ, King of the heaven and the earth, unto the wicked Jews; he went and hanged himself; and lost his honour; and fell from the rank of the Apostles. And Matthias was appointed in his place. Matthias went out to preach in the city of Damascus, because his lot came out to preach in it.

And he said: "O ye men who have gone astray and are wandering in your sins! who know not God your Creator, why have ye left the true God, and ye serve stones made by the hands of men? And ye would like all men to go astray like you. Give up the worship of idols; and put error and the vileness of your deeds far from you. And come unto God your Creator; and accept my words. I will bring you near unto God your Lord; and He will make you meet for His kingdom. Come unto me, I will teach you the way of the angels; and I will feed you with the Bread of Life; that ye may live for ever. Renounce the gods which are made by the hands of men; and awake from the deceit of Satan, that ye may be truly the servants of God, Jesus the Christ, f. 140 b the Lord of heaven and of earth, the Everlasting Word; the Word of the Living God; Who dwelt in Mary the Virgin; without seed or union of man; Who bore the sufferings until He saved mankind from slavery to Satan; Who is unseen in His glory and His height; Who hath no father upon earth as in the bodily birth of children; but He is always in heaven with His Father without separation; and He ruleth all by His wisdom; Who took dust from the ground and made thereof our father Adam, the first father; the God in Whose hands are the spirits of [all] creatures; He Who loveth you and will make you meet to approach Him. And if ye return with a true faith, and a whole mind, He, and His Father, and the Holy Ghost—for He is a Trinity in Persons, One

L. A.   S single Godhead ; One in substance. And the first thing that He hath commanded you is, that ye keep yourselves free from pollution, and that ye do not increase your intercourse with women ; so that God may look upon your purity, and may bless you with heavenly blessings, and may have compassion on you in the day of judgment."

And when the people of the city heard this from him, Satan took f. 141 a possession of their hearts by his deceit and his wicked deeds. And they said one to the other : " Certainly this man is one of the twelve wizards who go about in the countries and separate women from their husbands." And they took counsel together, and laid hold of the disciple, and bound him, and placed him on an iron bed. And they kindled a fire beneath him, until the smell of his body issued [from it]. And each of them saw it, and they wondered when the flame of the fire shot up above the bed to a height of fifteen cubits. And those who were around him said: " If he were a wizard he would have perished. And after three days the evil of his deeds will appear."

And after three days they found him on the top of the bed with his eyes open. And they felt his body, and they found it whole; no decay had reached it. And no smell of burning was in it ; and his clothes were not singed. And when they saw this wonder which was from God, many of the citizens believed in God, and said: " This man is a god." And seven days passed away; and on the eighth day the saint was lying on the bed; and all the citizens saw him ; and they believed with a true faith; and f. 141 b trusted the words of Matthias the disciple. And those who did not believe his sayings remained for four-and-twenty days stirring up the fire below the bed, day and night. And the Lord Jesus the Christ did not allow anything unpleasant to reach His disciple, Who had preached in His name; for he had suffered for His name. And after these things they took him out from the midst of the fire, and they saw that his body remained; and his face was as bright as the body of an infant, and all who beheld him said : " This man hath not been in the fire"; for his body was whole from the hair of his head to the nails of his feet. And all who were in the city believed, and in all its borders they cried: " There is no God in Heaven and upon the earth, but God, the God of Matthias, disciple of Jesus the Christ; Who saveth all who trust in Him, and believe in His holy name."

And Matthias the blessed disciple commanded that they should destroy all the temples of the idols and that [these] should be thrown into the sea, that nothing more of them might be found; because of the wicked works which had been done in them. And he built a church for them ; and he

baptized all the citizens, men and women and youths in the name of
the Father and the Son and the Holy Ghost, the United Trinity, the f. 142 a
Undivided, the Unchangeable. And after the baptism he consecrated the
church for them. And he preached to them the laws of life; and taught
them the true faith; and the commandments of the Gospel. And he
went out from amongst them; and they all bade him farewell in peace;
for he had taught them the way of truth, and had brought them out of
error to the guidance of the religion of our Lord Jesus the Christ. And
after his preaching and his teaching the Gospel, he fell asleep in one
of the cities of the Jews which is called Malâwân on the eighth day of
Pharmouthi, by the grace of God, Who loveth mankind; the Father of
our Lord Jesus the Christ; to Whom be glory and honour, and praise
henceforth, and at all times, and for ever and ever. Amen.

THE PREACHING OF JAMES THE JUST.

In the name of God, the Pitiful, the Compassionate. The Preaching of James, Disciple of the Lord Jesus the Christ; the Just, who was called the Brother of the Lord in the flesh. And the lot which came out for him was to teach in Jerusalem. And after his preaching to them he became
f. 142 b *Bishop of Jerusalem. And he fell asleep therein in the name of the Lord Jesus the Christ. Amen.*

It came to pass when the disciples were assembled to divide the cities of the world amongst themselves, the Lord Jesus the Christ appeared in the midst of them and said unto them: "My peace be unto you, O my sincere disciples! as my Father hath sent Me into the world, so I send you, that ye may preach in the inhabited earth about the knowledge of My Heavenly Father." Then the disciples prayed together, the Lord being in the midst of them. And they cast lots; and the lot fell upon James, that he should preach the Holy Gospel in Jerusalem and in all its district. Then he worshipped the Lord and said: "Thou knowest, O Lord! that the Jews seek to slay us, when we preach about Thy resurrection and Thy Holy Gospel. And I do not resist Thy command, nor the lot which hath come out for me; but I know that the Jews will not hearken to my words which I shall speak unto them. And I entreat Thee, O Lord! that Thou wouldest send me unto the Gentiles like my brethren. And I will do all that Thou dost command me. And I will endure all that may befall me of suffering for Thy name's sake."

f. 143 a   Our Lord answered and said unto James: "Thou must needs preach in the place which came out as thy lot. Behold, Peter, My chosen one, I have made him care for you. And thou must needs become Bishop of Jerusalem. And thy words shall be listened to, and thy good conflict shall be accomplished; and thy grave shall be in it. Arise then, and fulfil what I have commanded thee."

James said unto him: "Let my father Peter be a helper unto me: and I will endure all that may befall me, for the sake of Thine honoured Name."

And the Lord gave them the [salutation of] peace, and ascended to heaven in glory. And the disciples were filled with joy by the power of the Holy Ghost; and they prayed upon the Mount of Olives.

Then Peter said unto the disciples: "Go with us with our brother James that we may seat him upon the throne of the bishopric."

And Peter arose, and all who were with him, and they stretched out their hands and prayed, and said: "O God! Who rulest all things, Governor of the whole creation! hearken unto us. We know that Thou art not far from us: nor from whatsoever word we entreat of Thee. Give to our brother James power to govern Thy nation which Thou hast committed unto him to rule according as Thou hast commanded."

And when they arrived, they saluted one another, and brought James f. 143 b into Jerusalem. And he preached in the name of the Lord Jesus the Christ; and many of its people believed in his proclamation of the Gospel. And when some of the Jews saw James preaching in the name of the Christ they would fain have killed him. And they found no way to do it, because of those who believed in the Lord by means of him. And when he knew this, he went out to the villages which were around the city, and preached the Gospel to them in the name of the Lord Jesus the Christ. And when he was going into one of the villages he found an old man, [and] said unto him: "I wish thee to let me lodge with thee." The old man said: "Come in [and] rest until to-morrow." And the disciple went with him to enter his house. And, behold, there was on the road a man possessed with a devil. When the devil saw James the disciple, it cried and said: "What hast thou to do with me, O disciple of Jesus the Christ? Hast thou come hither to destroy me?"

He said unto him: "Shut thy mouth, O thou unclean spirit! and come out of the man." And straightway it came out of the man like fire. And when he saw this wonder, he fell at the feet of the disciple, and said: " I am not worthy that thou shouldest enter my house; but teach me what I should do, that I may be saved; I and all my household."

And then the disciple praised the name of God, our Lord Jesus the Christ, and said: "I thank Thee, O my Lord! Thou hast made my way f. 144 a easy."

And he returned to the old man, and spoke unto him the words of salvation; and he exhorted him, and taught him the name of the Lord Jesus the Christ. And he went into his house, and the old man gathered his people together: and the disciple preached unto them, and taught them the faith: and baptized them in the name of the Father, and the Son, and the Holy Ghost: and made them partakers in the Holy Mysteries— the Body of the Lord and His pure Blood. And the people of the village heard of it; and they brought before him all the sick of divers diseases : and the possessed : and he healed them all. And he appointed unto them a presbyter and deacons. And he appointed unto them the old man as bishop, and committed unto him the Gospel of the Lord Jesus the Christ ; and he went out journeying into all the country round about Jerusalem to preach in it. And when they believed, he returned unto Jerusalem ; and they all came into his presence, praising the Lord Jesus the Christ, and His Father, and the Holy Ghost, the Holy Trinity, henceforth and for ever and ever. Amen.

THE MARTYRDOM OF JAMES, THE LORD'S BROTHER.

Cod. Vat.
Arab. 694

This is the Martyrdom of James the Brother of the Lord; which he f. 148 b *finished on the twenty-third of the first Teshrîn[1], in the peace of the Lord. Amen.*

And when James the Just, the blessed, Brother of the Lord, returned to Jerusalem, and preached amongst them in the name of the Lord Jesus the Christ in that city, many believed on Him because of the wonders and the miracles which God wrought by means of him—may His name be blessed! The Lord deemed him worthy of the rank of a Bishop in Jerusalem. And when he had become Bishop, God made many healings of diseases manifest by his hand. And the ruler of the city was a great lover of money; and he hated the saint, because of what Satan, may God curse him! showed him against them. And he had no child; because God, may His fame be glorified! was recompensing him for his many sins. But nevertheless his wife besought God—praise be unto Him!—that He would grant her a child; and she did good unto all who were in want, and her alms never ceased from the holy Churches without the knowledge of her husband, because of his great greed. And once upon a day she was very sad because of what was in her heart in asking for a child. And when her beseechings were multiplied and her desire was not granted, because f. 149 a God—may He be glorified and magnified!—knew what of good there was to her in it.

And on a certain day the believing woman was standing, when there came to her the fame of Saint James in his religion; and how God was—may His power be glorified!—dwelling with him in all his deeds. She arose with joy and gladness and went unto Saint James. And she was sound in the faith, for God—praise be to His name!—through the prayer of the saint, had given her her desire.

And when the saint knew that Theopistē, the wife of the Prefect, wished admittance to him that she might be blessed by him, he wondered exceedingly; and he said, "This is a serious thing," for he knew the wickedness of her husband. And he allowed her to have access to him. And when she came into his presence, she knelt down and did obeisance at his feet, and said: "I entreat thee, O holy father! to receive thy handmaiden, and

---

[1] *i.e.* October.

hearken unto her words. I have lived with my husband for twenty years, and have had no child. I am grieved exceedingly at this state of things."

Saint James said unto her : "Dost thou believe that our Lord Jesus the Christ is able to give thee a child ?" She replied with all her heart, and said unto him : "I believe." And he said unto her : "If thou dost believe, be it unto thee according to thy faith." And she bade him farewell, and delivered unto him the blessing that she had with her, that he might distribute it amongst the needy. And she received his blessing, and f. 149 b returned to her house. And she gave glory unto God, and the fame of the saint was increased.

And after these things God—may He be praised!—answered her petition, and gave her her request. And she conceived and bore a male child and called him James, like the name of the saint. And she took her child and much money, and went to the saint ; and was blessed by him. And she said : "O good servant of God ! God hath heard thy supplication, and hath given me what I asked for. And it is this child which thou seest on my hand ; and he is by the blessing of thy prayer. And I entreat thee, O thou holy one ! to bless him."

And the saint took him from her hand, and blessed him with all his heart, and returned him to his mother ; and restored her to her house in peace. And when [this] reached the Prefect her husband, he was wroth with a fierce wrath, because of what his wife had done. And he gathered to himself the nobles of the city and said unto them : "Ye are negligent ; and this bishop is corrupting the city for us ; and leading all its people astray, desiring that everyone round about us should be of his faith and doctrine."

And they all arose and took counsel [saying] : "What shall we do with him ?" Some of them said : "The feast-day is near, and if ye wish, some one will watch for him in the temple." For many people were called James, but there was no James the Just among them except this one ; because f. 150 a God chose him from the womb of his mother like Jeremiah the prophet. He drank no wine all the days of his life ; and he ate no food from which blood issued ; and he never put a razor upon his head ; and he never washed in a hot bath ; and he never wore a coat ; but all his life he was wrapped in a mantle. And he was always in the temple intent on prayer and supplication to God—glory be to His name !—that He might forgive the sins of the nation ; until his feet swelled from much standing and worshipping, and for this reason he was called James the Just. And all the Jews—may God curse them !—know that he was just, pure ; and he was amongst them in the house of the devout. This James was the youngest of the sons of Joseph the carpenter. And Joseph had four male children, and two daughters. And all the children of Joseph were married except this James. And he was orphaned of his mother. And when the Lady Mary was espoused to Joseph, she found James: and he was the youngest in his house; and she brought him up and taught him the fear of God. And therefore the Lady Mary was called the mother of James. And when he became Bishop in Jerusalem, many of the people believed in the Lord Jesus the Christ by his means; because they knew his purity. And there was a great tumult among the Jews and the Scribes and the Pharisees; because the people said that James was the Christ. And they drew nigh f. 150b unto James and desired to deceive him, and said unto him: "We beseech thee to consecrate all the nation; for they are doubtful about Jesus, that He is the Messiah Who is to come. And all this people will be present at Jerusalem at the Passover; speak thou to them and make their hearts docile, for we know that thou wilt not say aught that is false; and all the people will accept thy speech; for thou art like a Prophet amongst them, and we will bear witness to them about all thine integrity and will tell them that there is no hypocrisy about thee. Do thou agree to our request, and they will all accept [it] from thee. Go up to a pinnacle of the temple, and stand so that all the people will hear thy voice."

These are the tribes of the children of Israel; they went up, and many of the Gentiles. And all the scribes and the Pharisees desired that James should say unto them that Jesus was the son of Joseph, and he (himself) was his brother. And they commanded a herald to order the crowd to be silent, that they might hear the words of James the Just. And they all cried, " It is our duty to listen and not to oppose," because all the people were going astray with the evil of their deeds; and the Jews were longing for faith in Jesus the Christ, Who had been crucified. "Tell us now, O f. 151a thou Just One! who is Jesus the King?" James answered in a loud voice and said unto them: "Why ask ye me about the Lover of mankind? Behold He is seated in His majesty on the right hand of the Father; and He it is Who shall come on the clouds of heaven to judge the quick and the dead."

And most of the nation believed in what they had heard from James; and they praised the Lord the Christ, saying: "Hosanna to the Son of David!" And when the priests and the Pharisees heard these words, they were ashamed in the presence of the people; and were filled with rage against James. And they returned and cried to him, saying: "Tell us, whose Son is Jesus?" He said unto them: "The Son of God in truth—the Father—glory be to His name! Who begat Him before all the ages.   And it is He Who was born of Mary the Virgin in the latter days.   I believe in Him, and in His Eternal Father, and in the Holy Ghost, the Equal, the Everlasting Trinity for ever and ever."

And when the chief priests and the scribes and the Pharisees heard these words from him, they gnashed their teeth at him, and stopped their ears lest they should hear the word of God—may He be exalted and glorified!—at

f. 151 b   the mouth of Saint James.   And they took counsel together and said: "Alas for what we have done! for we have made him testify to all the people that Jesus is the Christ, the Son of God; but let us go up to him and kill him, lest all the nation should believe in the Christ."   And the

cf. Isaiah
iii. 10   prophecy of Isaiah the prophet was fulfilled, when he said: "The righteous shall prosper; it shall not be hard for him to become the Anointed One over us; and they shall eat the fruit of their wicked deeds."   And they went up to him in a rage; and they threw him down and stoned him.   And he fell prone upon his face, and knelt upon his knees like Stephen the first of martyrs: and he made supplication unto God—the God of mercy— saying: "O God of mercy! forgive them, for they know not what they do." And they stoned him while he was praying after this manner.

cf. Jer. v.
31   And one of the priests of the sons of Ahab, about whom Jeremiah the prophet bears witness, cried out to them, saying: "Have pity for a little; what is this that ye are doing to the good man of God? he maketh supplication unto Him—may He be magnified and glorified!—that He would forgive you."   And one of them, a fuller, who had not turned at his words, took the piece of wood with which he beat the clothes, and struck the head of James the Just with it, and he yielded up the ghost, on the eighteenth day of Abib.   And his martyrdom was ended; and he was buried beneath the walls of the temple.

f. 152 a   And James the Just was a disciple and a martyr and Bishop of the Jews.   And he died for the name of the Lord Jesus the Christ.   And after his death, a mighty wrath abode upon all the Jews, the inhabitants of Jerusalem.   And this was chiefly upon those who had been the cause of the murder of James the disciple.   And Vespasian surrounded them, and plundered them, and took them captive, and their humiliation increased daily because of the wickedness of their deed to the Lord Jesus the Christ, the King, and to His saints.   And may there be to us all, the Christians whom He calleth by the new name, that we may find mercy and forgiveness in the terrible position when the Lord Jesus the Christ cometh to judge the quick and the dead.   To Whom be praise and glory henceforth and at all times, and for ever and ever.   Amen.   Amen.   Amen.

The stories which follow have been copied from MSS. in the Convent of St Catherine on Mount Sinai.

THE MARTYRDOM OF SAINT MARK.

This is the Martyrdom of Mark the Evangelist in Alexandria at the end of the thirtieth year of the sufferings of our Lord the Saviour Jesus the Christ. And the completion of his martyrdom and his conflict was on the twenty-fifth of the month of Nisan, in the peace of the Lord. Amen.

Our Lord Jesus the Christ, the Word of the Father, Who was before the ages, Who became flesh for our sake, Who is the God who made us, Who redeemeth mankind and ruleth them by His grace, appeared unto His pious disciples at His resurrection from the dead; and said unto them : "Go ye and teach the world, and all the nations; and baptize them on the name of the Father, and the Son, and the Holy Ghost." And they were scattered among the cities, and the villages; and distributed all the world among themselves. And amongst them there was a man named Mark; and his lot came out unto Egypt. And he went forth preaching the Gospel of our Lord Jesus the Christ, as the blessed Apostles had commanded him, the pillars of the Holy Church. And this saint began to preach in Libya and the cities around it, and to proclaim the Gospel of our Saviour the Christ. And all the people of this country were worshippers of idols, drunkards, with every impurity, busied with vice, going to destruction by the works of the enemy. And the Blessed Mark the Evangelist preached in the power of the Lord Jesus the Christ, and enlightened them in those five cities. In the beginning he spoke to them the word of God. And he did great wonders amongst them. He healed their sick, he cleansed their lepers, he chased away the evil spirits by the grace of our Lord. And many believed in the Lord Jesus the Christ by his means. And he broke down their idols on the spot; and baptized them in the name of the Father and the Son and the Holy Ghost. And grace was made manifest upon them: and he resolved upon a journey to Alexandria, that he might sow the good seed from the treasures of the divine word of God. And he bade the brethren farewell, and saluted them, and said unto them : "The Lord hath said unto me in a vision, 'Go unto the city of Alexandria.'" And the brethren were blessed by him, and they made him embark in a ship and they said unto him : "The Lord Jesus the Christ be with thee in all thy ways."

Cod. Sin. Arab. 539. f. 201 a

Matt. xxviii. 19

f. 201 b

And on the second day the Blessed Mark arrived at Alexandria, and he descended from the ship, and went into [a place called Pentapolis ; and from there he entered][1] the city. And in that place his sandal was torn ; and the blessed Apostle saw a man sewing up rags, and repairing. And he gave up his sandal to him that he might mend it. And while the shoemaker was sewing at his sandal he pierced his left hand deeply with the awl in passing it through. And he said ; "In the name of God. There is one God." And when the Blessed Mark heard the shoemaker say, "There is one God," he said to himself, "The Lord hath prepared my way." And straightway he spat on the ground and kneaded clay with his spittle, and anointed the hand of that shoemaker, and said : "In the name of the Lord Jesus the Christ, Son of the Living God for ever."

f. 202 a   And straightway the man drew back his hand, and it was made whole. And he understood the power of the word, and knew that he (Mark) was a foreigner and was not of the country. And he said unto him : "I entreat thee, O man ! that thou wouldest come and alight at the house of thy servant, that we may eat bread together, for thou hast done a merciful deed to me this day." And the Blessed Mark rejoiced and said : "The Lord give thee the Bread of Life from Heaven."

And the man took the Apostle and went with him joyfully to his dwelling. And when Saint Mark entered the shoemaker's home, he said : "The Lord make a blessing rest here." And they prayed together ; and after the prayer they reclined and ate and drank and rejoiced exceedingly. And the man, the master of the house, said : "O my father ! I would fain have thee tell me who thou art ; and what is that powerful word which I have heard from thee."

And Saint Mark said unto him : "I am a slave of the Lord Jesus the Christ, the Son of the Living God."

And the man said unto him : "I am longing to see Him." The Blessed Mark said unto him : "I will tell thee about Him." And Saint Mark began to preach, and said :

"The beginning of the Gospel of Jesus the Christ, Son of God, son of David, son of Abraham." And he told him also about the prophets. And the shoemaker said unto him : "O my Lord ! I never heard of this book before, out of which thou dost preach. Will the sons of the Copts be wise ?" And the Blessed Mark gave him instructions about the Christ.

---

[1] The words in brackets are an insertion on the margin of the manuscript, so far as I can judge, in the same hand.

And he said unto him: "The wisdom of the world is foolishness with f. 202 b
God." And the man believed in God by the word of Mark. And he I Cor. iii. 19
(Mark) continued to do wonders and signs; and he enlightened him
and all his household. And the man was called Anianus. And because
of him many people believed in the Lord. And the citizens heard that
a Galilean man had come. And they said: "A man hath arrived in this
city who will destroy the sacrifices of the gods and their worship." And
they sought for him that they might kill him. And they hid an ambush
for him, and traps. And the Blessed Mark knew of what they had resolved
about him. And he made Anianus a bishop, and three presbyters with
him; the first was called Meliân, and Sâbînus, and Kerdônâ. And
seven deacons; and he appointed eleven for the service of the church.
And he took them, and fled with them to these five cities; and abode there
for two years. And he strengthened the brethren and appointed bishops
over them also, and priests in all the five cities.

And he returned unto Alexandria, and these brethren arrived who
had been enlightened by the grace of God. And they built a church
for them, which was upon the shore of the sea, lower down than the
Canal[1]. And the Just One rejoiced in his work, and he knelt in worship
and praised God. And he abode there for a time. And those who
believed in the Christ increased; and they mocked the heathen and the
worshippers of idols. And the heathen learned about the affairs of the
Christians, and they waxed wroth against them exceedingly because of the f. 203 a
wonders which they had done. The sick were healed, the lepers were
cleansed, the deaf heard, and the blind were made to see. And they
meditated the destruction of Mark the Evangelist; but they could do
nothing against him. And they squeezed their tongues with their teeth
from hatred. And they assembled in the temple of their idols; and they
cried and said: "What shall we do with this sorcerer?" And the Blessed
Mark was present on the first day of the Holy Passover. And that was
on the twenty-ninth day of Pharmouthi. And the heathen were seeking
him, and they did not at first find him. And on that day the messengers
of the multitude came to him; and he was standing offering a divine
prayer at the time of the mass. And they took him and put a rope on his
neck, and they dragged him along the ground and the pavement, and they
said: "Drag the Buffalo to the field." And Saint Mark was praising and
thanking the Christ, saying: "I thank thee, O my Lord Jesus the Christ
because I have been counted worthy of this pain for thy Name." And his

---

[1] The Khalîg.

flesh was strewn upon the ground; and his blood was flowing on the pavement; and the stones were wet with it. And in the evening they cast him into prison that they might consider by what death they might destroy him.

And when it was midnight, and the doors were locked upon him, f. 203 b and the guard sleeping at the doors, behold! the prison was illumined, and there was a mighty earthquake. And the angel of the Lord descended from heaven, and touched him, and said unto him: "O Mark, servant of the Lord! Thy name is written in the book of life in heaven. And thy memory shall never be forgotten, and the angels are protecting thy spirit, and thy bones shall not go down into the earth."

This vision appeared to Mark, and he raised his hands toward heaven and said: "I thank Thee, O my Lord Jesus the Christ! because Thou hast not rejected me, but hast made me meet to be with Thine Apostles. I entreat Thee, O my Lord Jesus the Christ! that Thou wouldest receive my spirit in peace, and not shut me out from Thy grace."

And when he had finished his prayer, the Lord Jesus the Christ appeared unto him as He had been seen among the disciples in the light which taketh away pains; and said unto him: "Peace be unto thee, O Mark the Evangelist!" The Blessed Mark replied and said: "Praise be unto Thee, O Jesus the Christ, my Lord!"

And when the morrow came, a multitude of the citizens again assembled; and they brought him out of the prison, and put a rope on his neck; and they also dragged him and said: "Drag the Buffalo to the field." And they dragged the Blessed Mark; and he was thanking f. 204 a God even more than the first time; the strong God. And he said: "Into Thy hands I commit my spirit, O Lord." And then the Blessed Mark gave up his ghost.

And the multitude of the heathen kindled a fire to burn his body. And by the guidance of the Lord Jesus the Christ, there was a great sandstorm and a very violent wind, until the rays of the sun were covered over; and the sound of loud thunder. And there was rain, and sleet[1] with hail till the evening, until it flowed down the valleys, and many people of the heathen perished. And they were terrified, and they left the bones of the saint, and fled. And chosen men came from the priests, and took the body of the Blessed One from the place where it had been thrown; and went with it to the spot in which they had finished the prayer. And this pure one was of middle height, with dark blue eyes, and

[1] Literally "wet."

large eyebrows, with curly hair, full of divine grace. And the priests put
him on a bier, and they buried him according to the custom of the city ;
and they put him in a place hewn out ; and made a commemoration for
him and a rejoicing in the Christ. And they placed him in the eastern
side of the city. And the Blessed Mark, the first Evangelist, suffered in
Alexandria, which is in the province of Egypt. And he finished his
martyrdom for the name of our Lord Jesus the Christ on the twenty-fifth
day of the month of Nisân[1], and of the Greek months in April ; and of f. 204 b
the Coptic months in Pharmouthi ; in the days of the Emperor Aghâyûn,
Tiberius Cæsar. Because of this may the Father be praised ! and the Son
and the Holy Ghost, henceforth and for ever and ever. Amen.

[1] *i.e.* April.

THE MARTYRDOM OF SAINT LUKE.

This is the Martyrdom of Luke the Evangelist which took place in the eighteenth year of the first Teshrîn[1]; in the peace of the Lord Jesus the Christ. Amen.

It came to pass that when the disciples had divided the cities of the world, the lot of Peter was the city of Rome; and some of the disciples abode with him. These were their names: Titus, from the city of Galilee and Luke from the city of Antioch. And when the blessed Peter fell asleep in Rome, in the time of Nero the Emperor, they were scattered to preach the Gospel of the Lord Jesus the Christ in all these countries. And Nero Caesar, the Emperor, seized Paul, and took off his head in Rome. And as for Luke, he fled from the face of the Emperor: and he preached in [all] the countries and all the cities which were in these coasts. And he was the scribe of Peter, to write about all the good acts with which he preached in the name of the Lord Jesus the Christ. And God f. 205 a wrought many wonders by his hand. He healed the sick; he opened the eyes of the blind; and the lame walked; and he cleansed the lepers; and he made the deaf hear; and he healed all the divers kinds of sickness in the name of our Lord and our God Jesus the Christ. And when his hearers went out into these countries, the believers were multiplied in them by means of him. And he built many churches and monasteries in every place; and those who believed in our Lord Jesus the Christ were multiplied every day; and they were devoted to the worship and the teaching of Saint Luke.

And when the priests of the idol temples saw the beauty of the faith of the Gentiles, the devil entered into them, and they took counsel —they and the Jews who dwelt in that city. And they assembled in the temple which is in the great city of these countries, and it was on the twentieth day of Thoth. And when they were gathered together with the Jews in the temple, the priests adorned their idols with the pictures, and the lamps and all the scents. And all the nobles of the palace were present, and the chiefs of the palace sat upon thrones, and the eldest of their priests came forward and said: "Some sorcerers of the twelve men and some

[1] *i.e.* October.

of the seventy whom Jesus who is called the Christ made His disciples, have entered our city, and they have preached about miracles in every place; and all the Romans have been led away to their teaching, by the abundance of their deceitfulness and their sorcery. And the Emperor Nero hath slain a multitude of them. And this Luke fled from the presence of the Emperor; and he hath led astray many people of the f. 205 b cities and the provinces."

Then a Jew stood up, his name was Isaac, and he was conspicuous among the community of the Jews who were in that district. And he said: "Before I came into these countries I was in Jerusalem with an excellent man whose name was Gamaliel, and the chiefs of the nation, Hannas and Caiaphas and Alexander, and Decalius, had seized a man named Jesus, and had sentenced Him to death; and they hung Him upon the cross, and slew Him, and left Him in the tomb. And He rose from amongst the dead on the third day. He it is in whose name this man, whose name is Luke, preacheth."

All the people replied to him with one voice and said : " How could this man whose name was Jesus, arise from the dead ? " And when the name of Jesus was named by them in the temple, the idols all fell and were broken like earthen vessels. And when the priests saw the destruction of their gods, they rent their garments, and tore out their hair, and went out into the city of Rome to seek help from the Emperor, saying: "How many more sorceries will he do in the name of Him who is called Jesus ? "

The Emperor said unto them : " I have slain every one who believes in this name in all my countries, except one man named Luke, and he f. 206 a escaped from my hand."

The multitude answered him: " Behold ! he is in our city; he hath led its inhabitants astray by his teaching faith in Jesus. And in the city he healeth the sick of divers diseases ; [with] many cures." And when the Emperor heard [it,] he was very wroth, and gnashed his teeth, and commanded that some of his captains should come and go out with two hundred soldiers of his army, and should bring him forth into his presence. And Saint Luke was sitting teaching the multitude the precepts of the Gospel. And when he had finished his speech, the multitude dispersed to their business, and the saint arose and went forth towards the sea. And on the shore of the sea he met an old man seated for catching fish. And he said : " Come near unto me that I may speak unto thee about what it is thy duty to do." And when he drew nigh unto him, and perceived the grace of God which was in his face, he knelt down and did obeisance unto him. And the saint raised him up and said unto him : " Behold ! the Emperor hath sent his friends and his soldiers to me to bring me unto him. And I have learnt that he is commanding that I should be slain. And the will of God, may His name be glorified ! shall be done. And these books—take them, and put them in thy house, in a clean place ; and they will teach thee the path of life."

And the man received the books from him in trust. And the power of God rested upon him, and he went and preached in the name of God in every place. And his name was Theophilus. And he became beloved and chosen of God in all things.

f. 206 b And while Luke the disciple was in this state, the army of the Emperor arrived at the city, and they laid hold of the saint, and went with him to Rome to the presence of the Emperor, he being chained. And Saint Luke was blessing the name of God in his soul. And the Emperor commanded that he should be imprisoned in the gaol till the morrow. And when the morrow came, he commanded him to be brought ; and he stood before him, being chained. And he never ceased from singing praises at all times and saying: " I thank thee, O my Lord Jesus the Christ ! that Thou hast made me meet for this honourable station." And when he reached the Emperor he said unto him : " Art thou Luke who hast made a sedition in all the cities of the Romans, and hast destroyed the worship of the gods by thy sorcery ? "

cf. Matt. v. 11, 12. Saint Luke replied to him and said : " Our Lord Jesus the Christ said in His Holy Gospel: ' When they persecute you, and every idle word is said about you for My name's sake, rejoice and exult, for your reward is great in heaven.' The works of my father Peter are good works, those which I have learnt from him. But as for sorcery ; I know it not ; and what I do know is the name of my Lord Jesus the Christ." The Emperor said unto all the people of his kingdom who were present, " Let not the name of Jesus be mentioned in my Council." And when he named the

f. 207 a name of Jesus the Christ, immediately all the images and the talismans which were in his council-chamber fell down which he believed to be gods.

And when the Emperor and all who were present with him saw the miracle which Saint Luke had wrought, they cried and said : " Put this man out of our country." And the Emperor straightway commanded that he should be set up for torture ; and that he should be beaten with whips until his blood flowed like water upon the ground ; and that his right arm should be cut off ; and he struck his arm with a blow and severed it.

And the Emperor said unto him : " This is the hand with which thou hast written the books wherewith thou hast led the Romans, the people of my kingdom, astray."

Saint Luke said unto him : " Think not that my God is weak ; I will show thee His power." And he prayed and said : " My Lord Jesus the Christ, for Whose sake we have renounced the world and have followed Thee, Thou art the Saviour of souls. Think not of what error goeth forth from me, whether I know it or know it not, for I am but flesh, and do not work this miracle for which I ask Thee because of me, who am a sinner; but for Thy holy name and Thy supreme power : that the Gentiles may not say, ' Where is their God on whom they call ? ' Grant this favour unto Thy servant, that my arm may return whole as it was ; for Thine is the power for ever and ever. Amen."

And when the saint had finished his prayer, he stretched out his left hand, and took hold of his right hand which had been cut off, and fastened it in its place, and it became whole again as it had been, by the f. 207 b power of our Lord and our God, Jesus the Christ. And when the Emperor beheld this wonder, he and all who were present, they were confounded and said : " See the power of the art of this wizard ! "

The saint said unto him : " May God keep me from being a wizard ! But I would fain have thee know the power of my Lord Jesus the Christ. And I do not loathe the death of this world." And the saint turned and took hold of his right hand with his left hand, and made it to be again cut off. And when Anatolius the Vizier saw this wonder, he believed in the Lord Jesus the Christ, he and his wife and his household and all his servants ; and their number was two hundred and sixty-seven men. And the Emperor commanded that their names should be written down. And he passed the sentence upon them that their necks should be struck [off] in one day. And this happened on the eighteenth day of the month of Phaophi. And he commanded that the neck (head) of St Luke should be struck, and that it should be put into a hair sack filled with sand, and be thrown into the sea.

And when the Blessed One heard this sentence, they went forth with him to the seashore to take off his head. And he said unto the officer " I entreat you by the right of one over the other, that ye wait for me a little while, that I may pray to my God."

And thus did he make supplication and say : " My Lord Jesus the Christ ! Who hath created all things in His wisdom according to f. 208 a His will, the heaven, and the earth, and the sea, and all that moveth in them, grant power unto Thy servant and give him pardon; and place my portion and fortune with my father Peter."

And when the saint had finished his prayer, one of the officers who was blind of one eye drew nigh unto him. And he approached the saint that he might take off his head. Then was his eye opened. And he knelt down on the ground and said unto the saint: "Forgive me, O good servant of God! for I have sinned against thee." And the swordsman drew his sword and struck off the head of Saint Luke, and separated it from his body, and [that of] the other officer whose eye had been opened. And they finished their testimony together. And they put the body of Saint Luke in a hair sack, and made it heavy, and flung it into the sea. And God made it possible, may His glory be exalted! that the waves should throw it on an island. And a man who believed in God found it and took it out, and wrapped it in a fine shroud. And the martyrdom of Saint Luke the Evangelist was finished on the eighteenth day of the first Teshrîn, in the time of the accursed Emperor Nero. To our Lord and our Saviour Jesus the Christ be dominion and power and praise and glorification and holiness and the everlasting eternal kingdom for ever and ever. Amen.

THE STORY OF JOHN, SON OF ZEBEDEE.

This is the story of John the son of Zebedee, a preacher of the Gospel Cod. Sin. Arab. 539. f. 96 b *and the beloved of our Lord the Christ, one of the Twelve Disciples.* *May his prayers protect us! Amen.*

When the Holy Ghost rested upon the disciples on the day of Pentecost, they were filled with the Holy Ghost; and this was after the ascension of our Lord the Christ to heaven. And they spoke all languages, and they dispersed themselves into all countries, and proclaimed the truth of the Gospel, the faithfulness of the Christ, the Word of God, in order that the people might believe. Then, when Simon Cepha had begun his speech, they all said: "The Christ commanded us before His ascension cf. Matt. xxviii. 19. Mark xvi. 15, 16. f. 97 a into heaven and said: 'Go ye, all of you, and preach the Gospel to the people, and baptize them in the name of the Father, and the Son, and the Holy Ghost. And whoso believeth, shall be saved; and whoso denieth, shall be damned.' And it is our duty to disperse ourselves amongst all the countries; and the worshippers of idols in which devils dwell shall hearken. And we shall tread down the Enemy, and all his powers with our feet."

And when the Apostles had finished these words they separated one from the other. And when John the son of Zebedee, the Apostle, went forth from Jerusalem, the grace of the Lord accompanied him. And his lot had come out for the city of Ephesus. And he had a cross, and after three days he planted it in the ground before him. And John worshipped and prayed and said: "O my Lord and my God, Jesus the Christ! now Thy promise to us is fulfilled. Thou hast given to us according to Thy pleasure, and Thou hast delivered us from Sheol; for Thou art our refuge at all times when we remember Thy birth, which was from the Virgin; and Thy conduct among men; and Thy being lifted up on the cross; and Thy death; and Thine entrance into the grave; and Thy resurrection after three days; and Thy ascension to Thy Father in heaven. And now give us the victory over Satan the Enemy. And I am going to the countries which Thou hast prepared for us in Thy dear grace, that I may turn the people from their error, and that they may receive the Holy Ghost, Who proceedeth from Thy Father and dwelleth in us; and Who will destroy

f. 97 b the idols of error ; and I will build Thee a temple to Thine honour in the city of images."

And when John the son of Zebedee had finished his prayer, the Lord answered him from heaven, saying : "I have loved thee, and I will not disappoint thee ; and I will not leave thee in their hands. I am with you all until the end of the world. And fear not, O son of Zebedee! go and preach, and be not anxious about what thou shalt do or what thou shalt say."

And when the speech of the Lord was finished, John arose from his prayer, and journeyed, being gentle in soul. And John was clothed in the fashion of the people of Palestine ; and he walked barefoot. And he journeyed on that road for forty-eight days ; preaching the fame of the gospel of the Christ. And some of the people said that he was mad. And some said : "Leave him alone, for he is a foreigner, he hath come from a far country, and he knoweth not our mighty gods. And if he should come in beside us, and go out again he will love them and will sacrifice unto them." But some people of the city, which was named Asia, heard of him and believed in what he said ; and two hundred souls of them were baptized in a night ; and he taught them the way of truth. Then he went out of Asia to the country of idols ; and his food was bread and beans with a little lentils ; and this he bought for its price from city to city. And his drink was water. And when Saint John arrived at the city of

f. 98 a Ephesus—as we have found written in the house of Nero the Godless, and he lifted up his eyes and looked at it, and behold! a [smoke went up] from the city of Ephesus. And on that day there was a feast, and they were sacrificing to their idols and to their devils. And he was amazed at this, and he said : "What is this smoke which hath veiled the eye of the sun?" And while he was walking, he reached one of the gates of the city, and he lifted up his eyes and saw the image of Artemis standing over the gate, painted in colours, and on her lips gold and ·dyes, and over her a veil of gold brocade ; and a candle burning before her. And when John the Pure saw her he left her. Then he wept over the people of the city. Then he went thence till he returned to four of the gates ; and at all these he saw as at the first one. And while he was standing at the second gate, he saw an old woman standing before the idol and worshipping it. And John said unto her : "O thou woman! what is this image which thou art worshipping ?" And she said unto him : "This image which thou seest is Artemis our god who came down from heaven, and she it is who nourisheth all the people." And John the Pure cursed her and said unto her : "Be quiet;

for as for thee, thy mind hath gone through the sacrifices to idols; but this is the daughter of Satan."

And when the old woman heard his words, she stooped down to the ground, and filled her hand with dust, and flung it in John's face. Then the f. 98 b saint withdrew a little space, and bowed down to the ground, and cried out to his Lord, and said: "O Lord! hearken unto my prayer, and make mine entrance into this city easy, that I may be in a certain place by Thy good pleasure." And he went in on the right side of the city gate and saw there a bath, and went towards it. And behold! a man was there, named Secundus, and John the Evangelist spoke to him in the language of that country, and said unto him: "O thou man! perhaps thou wilt hire me for the work of this thy bath." Secundus said unto him: "Yea, for how much wilt thou work with me every day?" John said unto him: "Give me what thou wilt." And he stipulated with him for a hundred obols a day. And he brought in wood and dung for the stokers of the bath, and he collected muck for them from every place.

And he remained with him for forty days, and took his wages day by day. And Secundus the owner of the bath said unto Saint John, "I would fain have thee tell me what thou doest with thy wages which thou art taking from me; for I see thee barefoot, naked. Leave it with me that there may be more; and thou mayest buy thee therewith what thou needest, what is fitting for thee, for thou art a foreigner."

And John said unto Secundus the native born: "Because my Lord hath said unto us: 'Do not possess gold, nor silver, nor brass, nor two coats.' f. 99 a And I cannot oppose His command, lest He be wroth with me."

Secundus said unto him: "And who is this thy master? What is his name? tell it me, for he will not fail to come and attack me. Or perchance he is a harsh man; and will force me to do something that will be hard on me. This will be a fault on my part, that I should have a slave without the consent of his master."

And John said unto him: "Fear not, O son of freemen! that my master will be wroth with me."

And Secundus said unto him: "And why didst thou not tell me from the first, as thou didst work with me, that thou art a slave?"

John said unto him: "Because this my Master is in heaven, and He accomplisheth [all that He willeth] in heaven, and in earth, and in the seas. He is the Creator of what is seen and what is not seen. And He it is Who sent the prophets to preach to His creatures. And some of them were slain, and some of them were stoned. And in the last times—I mean at this time—He sent His beloved, only Son, Who had been with Him from everlasting. And He entered by the ear of the pure Virgin ; and dwelt in her for nine months ; and He is the fulness of heaven and of earth. And after nine months He was born of Mary the daughter of David, [He,] the Word which became flesh. And He did not destroy her virginity ; and He was seen among men, the Word of God, like a humble man, except without sin. And when thirty years were fulfilled, He took to Himself chosen disciples ; and they followed Him when He was wandering in the desert

f. 99 b with them ; for He turned the water into wine in Cana, one of the cities of Galilee ; and from five loaves He satisfied five thousand men, besides women and children. And there was something over from them, and it fell. And He opened the eyes of the blind : and healed the dumb and the speechless. And He brought to life the daughter of Jairus, ruler of the synagogue, after her death ; and she is till now alive with her father ; and if thou dost wish to see her, go beside them. And He brought to life the son of the widow in the city of Nain, when they were going to bury him. And He raised Lazarus after he had stayed in the grave four days. And I have more of these things, if thou dost wish to hear and to trust, O Secundus ! But as for the nation of the Jews, they rejected Him, and delivered Him up to Pilate the Pontius, and stripped off His clothes, and put a crown of thorns on His head. And when they had crucified Him, the sun was darkened, and its light was extinguished from the third hour till the ninth hour. And the veil of the temple was rent, and the rocks which were upon the mouths of the sepulchres were shaken, and a number of the dead came forth from them, proclaiming with their voices, saying : ' This is the Light of the Creator.' And they went and bore witness to Him while He was upon the Cross. And a man took Him, whose name was Joseph, and swathed Him in raiment of linen, and put him in the grave. And He rose

f. 100 a after three days, and we saw Him, and talked with Him, and ate bread with Him. And we felt Him with our hands[1] ; and we believed in Him, that it was He Who was with us, the Word which became flesh. And He ascended to heaven, and sat on the right hand of the Father ; and He gave Him authority to give good things unto those who trust Him. And He said unto us : ' Go ye and baptize the people, in the name of the Father and the

cf. Mark xvi. 15, 16. Son and the Holy Ghost. And he who is baptized and believeth shall live, and he who is not baptized and believeth [not] shall be condemned.' And I beseech thee now, O Secundus ! by my knowledge of thee, and by thy freedom, for I have seen thee and proved thee in these days ; and have found

[1] Cf. John xx. 27.

thee according to what is necessary; for thou lovest the strangers and the poor. Hearken unto my speech, and count it not falsehood. And if thou desirest, go with us to the land of Galilee, that I may shew thee him who was dead, really alive; and blind men [who] really see; and lepers [who] are really cleansed; and if thou hast believed in Him, and hast not seen Him, thou art greater than he who hath seen Him and communed with Him."

But Secundus, the owner of the bath, was sitting looking at him, confounded at the words which he had heard from him. And he said unto him: "How wonderful is what thou hast seen in Him! If this man be not as thou sayest, and hath not descended from heaven and hath not been born of a virgin woman, we must needs call Him a God because of these His deeds; for He raised the dead, and made the water wine. And in truth He is f. 100 b God in opposition to this Artemis, who did not cure my son. And for more than sixty years I have made offerings to her, and my son is blind, and seeth not yet. And I wish thee to keep this secret, until thy Lord shall desire to shew it. For thou art a foreigner, and I fear that if any one hear of thee that thou dost not worship Artemis, they will burn thee with fire. But nevertheless henceforth I believe, and I trust firmly in thy Lord. And I desire from thee, that this bath should suffice for thee and for me; and that thou shouldest take care of the revenue, and superintend the expenditure."

John said unto him: "It is not meet for me to eat anything, if I do not work." And he reckoned with him every morning; and he and his household wondered how the revenue of the bath increased since John had directed it. And Secundus came to John, and listened to him. Then he baptized him and his household, and prayed; and God healed his blind son. And he abode with him for twenty-five days. And in the first hour of that day the son of the lord of the city sent to him, that he should make the bath ready for him. And his name was Menelaus; and the name of his father Tyrannus. And this was troublesome to John. Then he did what he was commanded to do, and prepared the bath for him. And Menelaus came and went into the bath; and brought with him a fallen woman; and he took her into the bath-house and prostituted her in it. And when John knew that they had come out of the bath, he said unto the young man: "See that thou come not hither [again] because thou f. 101 a hast degraded thy person which was created in the likeness of God, and hast taken a fallen woman in with thee......"

Then the young man drew nigh unto him, and lifted his hand, and struck John. And John said unto him: "Verily I say unto thee: If thou return another time to the bath thou shalt not go out hence." And after two days had passed, he sent two of his slaves, saying, " Prepare the bath for the son of the lord of the city. And he prepared the bath. And an hour later that young man came, and with him the same fallen woman. And John was beside the stokers. And when he returned, they said unto him : " Behold ! the son of the lord of the city hath gone into the bath, and that woman with him." And when John the Pure heard that the fallen woman was with him, he wept, and this grieved him. And he sat down until they both came out with their clothes on. And when he saw the young man, he said unto him : " I say unto thee, may Jesus the Christ smite thee ! He whom the Jews crucified, and He died and rose on the third day, and He is the Word of God ; and He ascended to heaven, and sat down on the right hand of the Father. He is able to slay thee on the spot." And straight-way at the word of John, the angel of the Lord smote him, and he died in the very place. And John sat beside him, the young man being thrown

f. 101 b down in the place opposite to him. And when the people saw his face, they knew him, and some of them went to his father, and told him about the death of his son at the door of the bath-house. And Tyrannus sprang up in haste, and rent his garments, and sprinkled dust on his head, and went running to the bath-house, all who knew the story accompanying him. And when he saw his son dead, and John sitting, they attacked him ; and they put a chain on his neck, and bound his hands and feet fast with cords. And Tyrannus commanded that his clothes should be stripped off, that he might see him naked. And when they had taken away the ragged coat and the rough hose, and the worn mantle in which he was wrapped, they came on a cross on his neck. And Tyrannus commanded them to take the cross from him. And when they drew nigh to him to take it from him, fire came out from the four limbs of that cross, and burnt their hands. And the multitude cried out with a loud voice, saying : " This man is a wizard, take care of him till we ask his friends about him." And the magistrate commanded them to drag him by his feet to the interior of the prison ; and that the dead man should be buried. But as for the magistrate, he threw himself on the face of his son. And John had said unto them : " That youth is not dead ; and if he were dead, I would raise him up." And while they were dragging him, Secundus the owner of the bath-house being opposite to him, weeping, for he imagined that John would

f. 102 a be killed—and Tyrannus thought that he was weeping because of his son —John said unto Secundus : " Do not grieve nor be terrified, for the Holy Ghost is pleased to make known his cause."

And the saint said unto the father of that young man : " Command the people to be silent." And he did it. .Then John cried out in a loud voice,

and said : "I say unto thee, O Menelaus, the young man ! In the name of
the Lord Jesus the Christ, Whom the Jews crucified in Jerusalem ; and He
died, and was buried, and He rose on the third day ; and He ascended into
heaven and sat on the right hand of the Father, I say unto thee, Rise up
from thy place." And at the word of John, Menelaus the young man
arose and did obeisance at the feet of John. And when he saw him with
a chain on his neck, and his hands tied behind his back with cords, the
youth sprang towards him, and embraced him. And he loosed him and
quieted the people, and began to relate from the beginning, and the affair
of the harlot, and his taking her into the bath-house, and how John
prevented them from doing it ; and they did not obey him : and the people
said : "And what did he do unto thee to make thee die ?" And he said
unto them : "John, this man, spake thus unto me : 'May Jesus the Christ
smite thee ! He Whom the Jews crucified in Jerusalem ; and He died and
was buried ; and He rose in three days ; and He ascended into Heaven,
and sat on the right hand of the Father.' And straightway the angel smote
me, and took my soul, and I saw what I cannot describe with a tongue, f. 102 b
unless Saint John allows me." Then they besought John that he would
command him to speak. And John said unto him : "Speak." And he said :
"I saw angels without number, and they had wings ; they covered their
faces with some of their wings, that they might not see the Creator. And
with some they covered their feet ; and with some they flew and said : ' Holy,
Holy, Holy ' is the mighty Lord, with Whose praise heaven and earth is
full. And I saw twelve men in one place ; and in another place seventy
men, and they were gazing up into heaven. And I saw the right hand
of a man coming out from among the angels like unto fire, [and]
commanding them to go out and baptize the people in the name of the
Father and the Son and the Holy Ghost, and whoso believeth shall live
for ever. And whilst I was above, I trembled with fear, [and] I said unto
those seventy apostles, 'Who is that ? And they said unto me : 'That
is the Son of God, Whom the Jews crucified in Jerusalem, and all that
thou hast seen—He is its king ; for He is the Power and Wisdom of God.
And He it was Who sent Him into the world, that He might draw men
unto His Father.' And I saw twelve disciples ; and I saw this John with
them, and he was clothed in shining glorious raiment, and he stood among f. 103 a
the foremost of them, clinging to an old man. And the twelve were
looking at him lovingly. And his eyes were gazing up to heaven, and he
was weeping. And the old man drew nigh to him and said unto him :
'Why weepest thou, O my son ?' And he returned him an answer,

saying, 'Because of the......of the city of Ephesus.' And I asked what was the name of the old man. And they said unto me: 'This is Simon Cephas.' And I saw also fingers which made a sign to him with a voice saying unto him: 'All which thou hast asked of Me I have accepted it from thee; and I have answered thee about it.' And while I was terrified I knew that it was he whom I had wished to slay, because he had reproved me for fornication. Then I heard his voice; and I came down to him; and lo! I am standing beside you; and I entreat him to bring me near to the truth. And ye are they who have seen this wonder. And do ye return from your error and put away the idols from you; and come that we may be his disciples, and our souls may be saved; and we will trust and believe in the Father and the Son and the Holy Ghost henceforth and always and for ever and ever. Amen."

And all the citizens believed except the money-changers and the scribes of Artemis. And they said: "This man is of the race of Artemis our mistress." But John was crying out, saying: "I am a man like you, f. 103 b a mortal; but my Master, Jesus the Christ, is the Son of God; Who came down and dwelt in the virgin for nine months; and she gave Him birth, and He did not destroy her virginity; and He went about in this world like a man, yet without sin; and He was like God His Father. And the Jews crucified Him upon the tree; and He died and was buried, and rose again on the third day. And He ascended into heaven and sat on the right Hand of the Father. And He it is Who hath chosen me."

And when the Governor heard these words, he fell prone on his face with the rulers of the city. And they besought him that he would baptize them. And they said unto him: "All thy words are true." And there were people with Artemis their goddess; and they said: "But is this more worthy to be worshipped than Jesus the Crucified?" And on that day 36,706 souls of them believed in the Lord.

But the priests of Artemis and those who were with them set candles before Artemis and worshipped her. And the Governor thought of sending people to them to kill them. And John said unto them: "Do not kill them; the Christ may make them turn towards the truth, even after a long time." And at nightfall the unbelievers resolved that they would burn the city with fire, and say, "Artemis is angry and hath burnt the city."

And John said unto the believers: "Go about in the city, and whomsoever ye meet of the people, say unto them: 'There are two places for f. 104 a prayer in the city, one to the devils in the house of Artemis; and the other to Jesus the Christ; whithersoever ye wish to go, go.'" And John commanded them to give [him] a place of baptism, and that it should be twelve cubits broad by twelve [long], and its depth two cubits and a half. And he commanded; and they filled it with scented oil.

And John, the noble man, worshipped upon the ground, and looked towards heaven and said: "Holy be the Father and the Son and the Holy Ghost, for ever and ever. Amen." And all the people said: "Amen." And then he made the sign of the cross over the oil, and cried out with a loud voice: "Praise be unto the Father and the Son and the Holy Ghost. Amen." And on the spot the oil boiled up and blazed like fire, but was not burnt. And two angels stretched out their wings above the fire, crying out: "Holy, Holy, Holy is the mighty Lord." And when the people saw this wonder, they feared, and worshipped towards the east. And when the oil was consecrated, he approached the water, and said: "In the name of the Father and the Son and the Holy Ghost, to all eternity." And the people said: "Amen." And the angels came and stood above the water, and said: "Holy, Holy, Holy is the Father and the Son and the Holy Ghost." And John said unto the people: "Arise by permission of God." And they arose, and lifted up their hands towards heaven, and said: "We believe and we confess the Father and the Son and the Holy Ghost." And the Governor drew near and stripped off his clothes, and John signed him with the oil. Then he went down into the water, and the f. 104 b Apostle laid his hand upon his head and said: "In the name of the Father." And they said: "Amen." And he said the second time: "In the name of the Son." And they said: "Amen." And he said: "In the name of the Holy Ghost." And they said: "Amen." And he baptized them: and the number of those whom he baptized on that day was thirty-nine thousand and five souls.

And after some days John the Pure determined to go forth from amongst them; and the Governor besought him to remain with them, and not to forsake them. And he said unto him: "O my brethren! I desire that ye would shew me the place of those erring ones." And they went to the temple of Artemis; and thought of slaying her priests. But John dissuaded them from this; and said unto them: "Make me here a hut." And they determined to build him a grand edifice. And he forbade them. And the priests of Artemis said one to the other: "Come, let us offer a sacrifice to Artemis; that we may know what hath made her angry with us; and how she hath allowed the city to become two factions." And they did this. They drew near to Artemis and heard a rumbling noise from within her, and a whispered speaking. And the devils said unto them: "This little hut will destroy the great house of Artemis. And do not resist much, because he who is in the hut, if he should call on his Lord, we fear that He will destroy us and drown us, as He drowned our companions when they were in f. 105 a the swine. We desire that we should not be conquered. And if He conquer us, his Lord hath conquered our master before us." And the priests said: "And who is the master of this man?" And they said: "He is the Son of God, Who came down from Heaven, and was made flesh; and our master thought concerning Him that He was a man; and knew not that He was God, and that He would rise after death and would ascend to heaven. And He is still wroth with us."

And when the priests heard these words from the devils of Artemis, they were terrified and amazed. And the people said unto them: "Whence is your perplexity? Tell us what Artemis our mistress said. The priests answered, saying: "Artemis said that this hut would uproot this temple; and she commanded us to fear the man who is in the hut."

And the multitude said: "Artemis is to be rejected, she in whom there is no good. If she hath no force, no power, no strength ⌜against⌝ this man, who is but a slave and a servant, how much more will his master be stronger and more mighty!" And they smote upon their faces and their breasts and said: "Woe unto us! and to our negligence, and to our destruction, and the loss of our souls!"

And the priests said unto them: "Do what ye wish; but as for us, we will serve Him who can make alive or dead."

Then they went off to John the Pure; and besought him, and did obeisance, that he might seek forgiveness for them, and might baptize them.

And the crowd tied cords round Artemis, and dragged her through the f. 105 b city, and said unto her: "O our Lady! rise now and save thyself from those who are dragging thee. By my life! thou didst not come down from heaven; and thou hast no honour! But rather the artizans made thee and the devils created thee." Then they broke her to pieces, and went to the holy John—and the Governor was with them—and they besought him that he would seek forgiveness for them and baptize them. And when the unclean Philip heard of the deed of the people of Ephesus, he sent to John and brought him out into the desert; and he sent to the lord of the city and imprisoned him, and took everything which belonged to him, and made promises to the citizens with all wickedness.

And when three days were past, at midnight, when Caesar was asleep, lo!

there appeared unto him a man who came unto him clothed in white, shining with light. And he said unto him: "Open thine eyes." Then the angel lifted up a sword which he had; and pointed it at his body, and said unto him: "Send back the man whom thou hast made to go out of the city to his place. And if thou do it not, I will smite thee in thy heart with this sword." And straightway his tongue became dumb, and continued howling like a dog. And he commanded them to bring him parchment, and he wrote to the people of his house, and they came in unto him. And he wrote to them, saying: "If ye are able, let not John sleep until ye shall have brought him to Ephesus, along with every one of the Ephesians who hath been imprisoned with him for his sake, and on his account."

And they went unto John; and they met with him standing and praying towards the east. And they said unto him: "The Emperor hath f. 106 a commanded us to bring thee unto Ephesus." And he went with them until he arrived. Then the Holy Ghost commanded Matthew to write the Gospel; then Mark followed in his footsteps; and after him Luke. And Peter and Paul came to John in Ephesus; and gave him [the salutation of] peace. And he rejoiced in them with a great joy. And they said unto him: "Matthew, and Mark, and Luke have written Gospels; and thou must needs write one too. And the day when Peter and Paul came into Ephesus was a Monday. And they abode with him five days; and they besought him to write the Gospel. And John said unto them: "Let the will of God be done." And when it was the night of the First Day, at the time when our Lord Jesus the Christ rose from the grave, John was left alone, and he sat down and wrote the Gospel. Then he came out and delivered it to Peter and to Paul.

And when the sun had risen, they went out with it to the temple of prayer; and read it before the people of the town. Then they prayed and made the offering, and remained with John for thirty days. And after these things they went forth to Jerusalem to James; and returned to Antioch.

And John the Pure sat in that hut winter and summer, until a hundred and twenty years had gone over him. Then his Lord hid him in that place as He hid Moses in the mountain of Moâb. And whoso trusteth and believeth in the Father, and the Son, and the Holy Ghost, and in the f. 106 b miracles which the Apostles, the disciples of our Lord the Christ, did, shall receive pardon from God, and prayer from good men; and shall inherit the kingdom of our Lord Jesus the Christ, to whom be praise and glory for ever and ever.

THE DEATH OF THE APOSTLE JOHN.

This is the story of the Repose of John the Apostle, the Author of the Gospel. And his death took place on the twenty-sixth day of Ailûl[1].

The blessed John was sitting with the brethren the disciples, on the Sabbath-day, rejoicing in the Lord. And when they rose on the morning of the First Day, they assembled, [and] he said unto them: "O my brethren, servants of my Lord the Christ to whom good fortune hath come with me in the kingdom of heaven. Ye have known how much the Lord hath given me of power and of wonders and of gifts of healing, and learning, and doctrine, and excellent service. And be ye strong; and if they deny the signs which have been done before you; know ye the guidance and the secret which the Lord hath made for the sake of the life of man. And the Lord seeketh that from you. And beware lest ye grieve Him, and do not make our God angry, the Merciful, the Holy, the Pure from all stain; the Near to every prodigal, the Everlasting; the God of truth, in Whom is no falsehood; Who receiveth no reward. And He is more exalted than all mankind, Jesus the Christ the Son of God; He rejoiceth in all the good that ye do. And walk ye in purity, and chastity, and ye must needs partake with Him in

f. 107 a sufferings. For He rejoiceth in us when we are humble, and delighteth in us when we walk in His ways. And these are my words to you in this hour, O my brethren! for I am going to my Lord; and I shall pay the debt which our father Adam hath bequeathed to us. Why should we multiply [words] to you? Ye have the grace of our Lord and the earnest of His mercy. Ye have joy in His presence; [a joy] that is from Him[self] for ever. And He will forgive you what is past of your ignorance. And if ye return to your first works, after that ye have known Him, He will not forgive you your debts that are past."

And when he had spoken these words, he prayed and said: "This crown is the work of Thy hands, O Jesus the Christ! Thou art He Who hast presented to Thyself this fragrant flower whose scent will perish. Thou art the beauty Who hast sown the fruit of these words. Thou art the Compassionate One, the Maker of good things. Thou art He who dost not appear too exalted for the sinner. Thou art the Lover

---

[1] *i.e.* September.

of mankind. Thou art He Who shalt deliver the just. Thou art the
Everlasting before the ages. Thou art the Encompasser of all; and King
of all; Jesus the Christ, the Son of God. Cover, O Lord! in Thy mercy,
those who lean upon Thee. Thou knowest the wickedness of our Enemy
and his iniquity. Help Thy servants, O Lord! with Thy mercy. For
with what praise, or with what offering, shall men approach to Thine
adoration, O Jesus the Christ, with Thy Father and Thy Holy Spirit? to
the glory of Thy name, O Lord! Who wast sent from the Father. We praise
Thy name, O Lord, that thou wast called the Son. We praise Thee in f. 107 b
the path of life. We praise Thy name, because of the resurrection which
Thou hast shewn to us by Thy resurrection. We praise Thy·ways; we
praise the seed of Thy word; we praise Thee with our trust. Thou art the
Treasure of life. Thou art the Plough and the Net wherein Thou hast caught
us. We praise Thy greatness. Thou art the Garland which for our sakes
hath been called the Son of Man. Thou art He Who hast given us light,
and joy, and freedom and love. Thou art He who didst inspire us to flee
unto Thee from being rebels. Thou art our Lord, and the Spring of the life
which dieth not; the Fountain which faileth not; the Foundation of all
creation. Thou art the God Who hast made all things for the sake of man.
We call unto Thee, for we know that Thy coming, which is unseen
in this world, is only to the pure, those to whom Thy Godhead is
manifest, notwithstanding Thy body. Look, O Lord! upon those who
believe in Thee; and bless this offering, and us for its sake. For Thine be
the praise with the Father and the Holy Ghost. Amen."

And he prayed for us all together; that we might be meet for
the Lord's mercy, and worthy of the holy offering. And after these
things he drew nigh and said: "Give me good fortune and a share in
it, O Lord! May the peace of the Lord be with you, O my beloved ones!"
And he said unto Byrrhus: "Take another person with thee, and a basket,
and an axe, and follow me." And Byrrhus did as the Lord's servant,
John, had said unto him. And he went out and continued till he had
reached the grave of a man belonging to our brethren. And he said
unto the brethren: "Dig, O my children." And they dug, as he had f. 108 a
commanded them. And he said unto them: "Make the hole deep." And
they dug while he spake to them the word of the Lord, and exhorted
them, and strengthened them in the commandments of the Lord. And
when they had finished digging, he took the garments which were upon
him, and threw them into the grave, and lifted up his hands to heaven, and
began to pray and to say: "Thou, O Lord! Who didst choose us to be

L. A.   Y

Apostles from Thyself to believers; and didst send us into the world:
Thou art He who alone didst manifest Thyself in the Law and the
Prophets.   I beseech Thee that thou wouldest guide Thy servants the
believers in Thy mercy.   Thou art He who didst become incarnate,
because Thou didst love perishing souls.   And those who were brutes, by
Thy coming and Thy miracles Thou didst make them chaste lambs.   And
Thou didst save sinners, and didst rescue them whom the devil had
overcome: and Thou didst write a law for them when they took refuge
with Thee.   Thou art He who didst give them Thy hand, and didst raise
them up and deliver them from Gehenna and its works.   Thou art He
Who didst make them to know Thee with certainty; our Lord and our God
Jesus the Christ! the God and the Law of those who believe in Thee.
Receive now the soul of Thy servant John, whom Thou didst make an
evangelist.   And didst keep me[1] from human defilement, and didst appear
unto me when I wished to marry in my youth.   And didst say unto
me, 'I want thee, O John!'   And when I sinned, Thou didst wear me out
with sickness; and didst prevent me three times.   And in the third hour
of the day Thou didst appear to me on the sea, and didst say, 'O John,
if I had not taken Thee to Me, I would have allowed thee to marry.'
Thou, O Lord! art He Who didst make me blind for two years, and didst
make me call on Thee weeping.   And in the third year Thou didst open
my eyes and my heart, and I obtained my outward sight, and Thou
didst put a veil over my eyes after Thou hadst healed my heart from
beholding the face of a woman.   Thou art He Who hast kept my love to
Thyself in purity.   Thou art He Who hast made my paths unto Thyself
easy, and hast inspired me with faith in Thyself without any distraction,
by the certainty of [my] knowledge of Thee.   Thou art He Who wilt
recompense every one according to his work.   Thou art He Who didst
make my soul value Thee more than all.   And in this hour, O my Lord
Jesus the Christ! I have finished the service with which Thou hast
entrusted me.   Make me meet for Thy kingdom and for everlasting
life.   Put far away from me the fire and the outer darkness; and quench
the fire of hell.   Make good angels follow me; that they may keep away
the spirits of the devils from me, and confound all their powers; and
destroy all who hearken unto them.   And make the way unto Thyself easy
for me; without stain and without sin.   And reward me with what Thou
hast promised to those who love Thee; those who live in purity and make
supplication unto Thee."

f. 108 b

[1] MS. "him."

Then he made the sign [of the cross] on his body, and said : " Thou art with me, O Lord Jesus the Christ! for ever." And he went down into the grave, and laid himself in it; and said : " The mercy of our Lord be with you, O my brethren! for ever, Amen." And he yielded up his spirit on f. 109 a the spot in peace. And the brethren departed. And when it was the morrow, the brethren came unto him. And they found him not in the grave. And [when] they arrived at this ground, it sent forth a sweet scent. Then they remembered the word of the Lord which He said unto Peter about him : " If I will that this man tarry until I come, what is John xxi. 22 that to thee?" And they returned in strong faith, and praised God for the miracle which had happened ; and they glorified Him ; and sang Hallelujah to Him for ever and ever. Amen.

In the name of the Father and the Son and the Holy Ghost, One God.

This day, O my brethren! and my beloved, is the day of the spiritual feast. In it John the fisherman, the beloved of our Lord Jesus the Christ, the Saviour, hath assembled us from all places and countries to this blessed feast. This is the disciple whom our Lord loveth. John, who threw the net and caught the Gospel ; he threw the rod and caught the word of God. John, who was not like the sailors ; and was the wisest of the wise. For whose sake ye are assembled to-day to listen to this encomium. He was a preacher about God; speaking about divine things in the knowledge of our Lord Jesus the Christ, whilst he bequeathed [it] to us from the pulpit of a father.

But who can venture to narrate the virtues of this saint? For if ye hearken to my words, [words] of a poor creature, I will teach you the truth with certainty. For I went from this land and I saw with my eyes, and f. 109 b I heard with my ears from the fathers, as saith the holy Gospel: " What we 1 John i. 3 have heard and seen, declare we unto you." I desire to inform you, O my beloved! concerning the death of this Apostle John ; if it be rightly termed death.

The saint told his disciples to dig a grave for him. And while they were digging, he prayed for them, and stretched out his body in the grave ; and yielded up his spirit to his Creator. And on the morrow his disciples went to the grave, and found nothing in it. And the Pure One was lifted up to his Beloved, the Christ, like Moses. For God said unto Moses, " Go up to the mountain, for there thou shalt die." And after his cf. Deut. xxxii. 49, death the children of Israel sought for his body ; and they found it not. 50

And the disciples of Saint John built a fine church over his grave. And after a little while, Constantine the blessed Emperor, in whom was the fear of God, desired to take a portion of the bones of the saint to the city which he had built. And he sent people, and commanded them to dig up the place where he had been buried, and to take something of his bones for him. And when the messengers came to the grave, they dug, and remained for many days, seeking, and found nothing.

And the saint of God, John, appeared unto the king and said unto him : "Be not unhappy, O lover of God! about the quest for me in the ground, because of thy love and thy good disposition. For I am with my Lord the Christ, Who hath given thee the kingdom. He it is Who hath taken up my body to Himself; and hath received it. I have beheld the force of the Lord's words which He said unto Peter : 'If I will that he tarry until I come, what is that to thee?'" And until this our day there is in that place a light more abundant and brighter than the stars in heaven. And it springeth from the grave of the saint, a pool which healeth all sicknesses and all evil spirits. And as the water of the sea never faileth, in like manner neither doth this pool. And if a man should desire to narrate the wonders and the signs which have been made manifest in that place upon all the palsied and the sick, he could not do it. And the Apostle left this after his death; if it can be called death. And the Prophet David the Just hath said : "Great and precious with the Lord is the death of the righteous." And now who is able to relate his wonders in their order? But let me tell you one of the miracles which he did; that so from it you may know his goodness. There was a temple in Ephesus to Artemis close to the city. And the votaries of the images honoured it with the greatest of honour, more than to all their idols. And the people were wont to go to it from every place because of that feast, [in number] like sand. And when the blessed John saw the multitude of people he went in amongst them in their procession and looked at them. And he sought him out a high place, and climbed up and stood upon it. And he cried out with his voice, saying : "O men of Ephesus! why do ye go astray and think that Artemis is a god? Why do ye provoke God against you, and worship idols which repel nothing from themselves? And now hear my voice. Choose ye one of two courses. Either pray ye to your image; and beseech it, and let it kill me alone; or else I will pray to my God, and He will kill you all together."

And they were terrified at this word, with a great terror; and they fell

f. 110 a

John xxi. 22

Ps. cxvi. 15

f. 110 b

prone upon their faces, trembling; because most of the people knew his confidence in his God, and the power of his word from the miracles which he had done. And they thanked him and said unto him: " O John, O good servant of God! have mercy upon our souls, and destroy us not." And when Saint John saw their repentance and their turning unto God, Who desireth not the death of a sinner, but rather that he should return unto Him and repent, he commanded them to go to a distance from the temple. And he lifted up his hands to heaven, and prayed for them; and ceased not to hold up his hands to heaven. And the temple fell down until there remained not one stone upon the other; like as Moses lifted up his hands ^{cf. Exod.} to heaven, and was victorious over the Amalekites, so did this Apostle until ^{xvii. 11} he had destroyed their impure god, who was unable to suffice [in] anything for himself. And when they saw the miracle which the saint had done, they all cried together and said: " Great is the God of John, Who ^{f. 111 a} hath done a wonder like this, for the profit of souls." And rebellion departed from the city from that day forth until now. And they established a new festival to God on that day until this our day. And who is able to relate or to report what took place on that day, the miracles which God wrought by the hands of Saint John?

And when the temple of Artemis fell down, the brother of the priest who had served the temple was killed. And his brother took him up with firm faith, and brought him to Saint John. And they were crying out all together, saying: " O servant of God! thou hast freed us from error. And thou art he who hast made us lift up our eyes unto heaven. And thou art he who hast guided us and delivered us from rebellion, and henceforth we shall never again worship stones. Thou art he who didst bring this vast multitude nigh unto God, and didst save their souls from an evil death." And the priest wept and said unto him: " All these people are going away to their homes rejoicing; and I am left alone to mourn; but I would like to go and rejoice like them in thy God." And when Saint John saw the beauty of his faith and his love, he prayed for him in that place, and the dead man lived.

Behold and wonder! What God is like unto our God, Who accepteth the repentance of sinners? and bringeth the dead to life by the prayer of His Apostle; as He accepted the prayer of the robber on the cross, and made him to dwell in Paradise. Thus John also, this renowned man, he ^{f. 111 b} who saw the mighty Father, and the Son, and the Holy Spirit, preached to the people about Him, and they turned from error. This[1] is also

¹ MS. "Thus."

Saint John, the preacher, who received heavenly grace ; and purified and sanctified the creatures. Thus John the renowned, who was a mediator for the grace of the Father and the Son and the Holy Ghost, the mighty Lord, received also the spiritual Mysteries. He it was who said : " In the beginning was the Word ; and the Word was with God ; and God was the Word." This was John who spake a word greater than the word of Moses the Prophet. Moses preached to the people and said : "God created the heaven and the earth." But John the Evangelist said : " In the beginning was the Word ; and the Word was with God ; and God was the Word." To Whom be glory and honour and majesty for ever and ever. Amen.

John i. 1

Gen. i. 1

John i. 1

THE STORY OF PETER AND PAUL.

In the name of the Father, and the Son, and the Holy Ghost, One God. f. 1 a
*This is the story of Peter and Paul, two disciples of our Lord Jesus the
Christ, for the commemoration of worship and praise.*

When the two disciples had entered the city of Rome, and when Paul
had believed in our Lord Jesus the Christ, and the miracle which they
had done for the daughter of the Emperor, amongst many miracles, may
her prayer be with us! Amen.

Saint Paul had opposed the holy church of God, and had persecuted
the Nazarenes until the Lord the Christ appeared unto him, when he was
journeying to the city of Damascus, that he might destroy the community
of the Nazarenes who believed in the Christ.

And he believed, and was baptized by Hanânia the Apostle. And the f. 1 b
Lord said unto Paul: "Go to the city of Rome; and I will send Peter
with thee; and he shall tell thee how thou shouldest fight the Devil."

Then the Lord commanded the Archangel Gabriel to go with the
Apostles upon a shining cloud. And the Apostles came to our Lord, and
worshipped Him. And the Lord said unto them: "Peace be upon you,
O my brethren!" Then all the Apostles rejoiced [when they saw
Paul] with our Lord. For at first he had opposed [the truth]. And
the Lord said unto Peter: "Go with thy brother, and shew him how
he should fight the Devil in Rome."

And Peter said unto the Lord: "Whither dost thou wish me to go?" f. 2 a

The Lord said: "Whither the clouds go with you, there fight ye the
foe. And be not terrified; but be strong, for I will put him beneath your
feet. Go in My name, and doubt not, and I am with you until the end."

Then the Lord commanded a cloud; and it carried the Apostles in the
air; and let them down in the midst of the palace of the Emperor in the
city of Rome before Bar'amûs, the infidel heathen Emperor. And he was
sitting upon the seat of his throne; and the chamberlains were standing
round him, on his right hand and on his left. And when the Emperor saw
the Apostles coming down from the clouds, he was terrified, and his colour
changed. And the chamberlains hastened to beat the Apostles. And the
Emperor cried and said: "Lift off your hands from these men; and do
not beat them; for the similitude of an angel doth appear in them."

Then he said unto the Apostles: "How were ye so stupid as to come
f. 2 b in here without my command? And if my only daughter had done this,
I would have taken her head off with the sword. And if I had not seen
the likeness of angels in you, I would have promptly destroyed you.
But tell me your tale, and whence ye have come, and whose friends
ye are."

And Peter said unto Paul: "O my brother! wilt thou speak first, or
shall I speak?."

And Paul said: "Speak, O my brother! for thou art he whom He
hath made head over the congregation."

And Peter signed himself with the sign of the cross; and he answered
the Emperor and said unto him: "I am from the city of Saida of
Galilee; and this is my brother Paul from Tarsus. And our coming is from
the land of life. And we are slaves of the Christ the Lord God, King of
kings, Who hath made heaven and earth and the seas, and whatsoever
f. 3 a moveth therein. He formed men in His own image and likeness; He
Who was born of Mary the pure and chaste Virgin; Who made the water
wine; and satisfied many people in the wilderness with five loaves;
[He] Who healed the lepers, and cured the sick, and opened the eyes
of the blind, and made the deaf to hear, and the dumb to speak, and cast
out devils, and made the crooked straight, and the dead live. And
the nation of the Jews hated Him and delivered Him to an earthly
sentence of death. And He went up on the cross. And he suffered that
for our sakes, and because of our sins. And he was lifted up on the wood
of the cross: and the sun was darkened at His pain; and the creatures
were perplexed; and He descended to hell; and death was terrified
at Him; and hid itself because of Him. And the dead arose from the
f. 3 b graves. And they returned the greetings of the people. And He arose
on the third day, and appeared to His Apostles; and told them the divine
secrets; and sent them to preach about His kingdom. And He must needs
come at last, in great power and glory with His pure angels. The heavens
shall be changed by His word and shall be folded up like a scroll by His
command. And the trumpet shall sound in the height; and every one
shall rise from his place, and all flesh shall spring up from its dust. And
He shall sit on His throne to judge the quick and the dead. Then the sons
of Adam shall rise from their graves, naked before him, without covering.
And He shall separate the good from the bad, and every one shall [receive?]
at that time what he hath gathered. And He shall be perfected in His
servants the righteous. And He shall judge the sinners, and reveal their

secrets. And in the power of this God we have come hither this day to f. 4 a
chase away the Devil. And Paganism shall cease from the city of Rome."

And the Emperor answered and said unto the Apostles: "If your
speech be true, ye have spoken much; but I wish to prove that, and to
know it and to understand the power of your God. Behold! I have an
only daughter, and a bird from heaven hath come down upon her, and
hath plucked out her right eye. And I brought the doctors, and the wise
men, and the philosophers in my dominions, that they might cure her; and
they could do nothing for it. And I sent unto the rest of the kings; and
I spent much money to find a man who could restore her eye; and I did
not succeed: and I desire to bring her before you; and I shall see if your
God, of Whom ye have spoken, will heal her."

Then Peter was inspired by the Holy Ghost, and he said unto the
Emperor: "Bring thy daughter, and thou shalt see the power of the Lord,
which is never destroyed. And come now with thy daughter Lûhîth." f. 4 b

The Emperor answered and said unto Peter: "Lo! I see that thou
knowest the name of my daughter."

And Peter laughed and said unto the Emperor: "Yea, and Dôrôtheus
the father of thy father. And if thou wilt believe in the Christ, thou shalt
see greater things than these."

Then the Emperor was astonished; and said unto the Apostles: "Truly
God dwelleth within you, when ye know the names of people, ye being
foreigners. And ye know the name of my daughter Lûhîth, and the name
of my grandfather."

Then the Emperor commanded his daughter to be brought; and she
came and her mother with her. And when the Apostles saw the girl, they
were grieved at what Satan had done to her. And Peter said unto the
Emperor: "I would fain have thee tell us how thou hast sinned; and in f. 5 a
what way the bird plucked out the eye of thy daughter."

And the Emperor said unto Peter: "How many doctors and wise men
have stood before me! and this is a thing about which they have never
asked me. And I have not heard it from them. And unless ye know
certainly that ye will cure her, shut your mouths, and go out from my
presence."

And the Emperor said this, only from shame before his wife, and
before the company who were with him, lest he should [have to] confess
his sin.

And Paul said unto Peter: "Come, let us pray before our Lord; that
He may give us patience and victory in this contest."

And Peter said unto Paul: "Yea, my father Paul! do not think that I am better than thee; know that I denied the Christ, the Saviour, three times in one night; and I swore and affirmed with a curse that I knew

f. 5 b Him not; so that the devil who spoke at that time will not rest in me. My Lord received me and forgave what I had sinned because of my tears, and of His mercy on me."

And Paul said also unto Peter: "And thou, O brother Peter! know that I was an enemy to the Christ, and a persecutor of all who worship Him; and I was not worthy to be called His Apostle because of my opposition to the Church of God, and in His goodness and mercy He hath made me meet to be called His Apostle and His disciple; that the rest of the sinners may become like me, and may be saved eternally. And now do thou pray, O my father Peter! and I with thee; and if thou art worthy, let us call the bird which took out the eye of the Emperor's daughter, and it will come, and will tell the Emperor about his sins and his shame."

f. 6 a And Peter cried with a loud voice and said: " O thou bird! which went to the daughter of the Emperor Bar'amûs, the heathen Emperor of Rome, in the name of my Lord Jesus the Christ, the God of all creation, appear instantly and tell the heathen Emperor what he did to his daughter, which he doth not desire to confess, and tell him of his sins; that God may forgive him."

And straightway the bird appeared, and all who were present saw it; and it spread out its wings in the air, and stopped between the sky and the earth, saying, "Who are Peter and Paul the servants of the Christ?"

And Paul wept and said: "If we are worthy of this name, we are the servants of the Christ. But speak, O thou bird! and fear not; and rebuke the Emperor for his sin and make him ashamed." Then the bird answered:

f. 6 b "Hearken, O chosen ones of God! and behold the folly; and I will speak before you. When it was the birthday of the heathen Emperor, he made a great feast; and he drank and was drunken, and he saw an exceedingly beautiful girl, and sought to sleep with her, and she did not consent to this; and when he insisted on it, and she did not submit to him, he was enraged at her, and shut her up in the stable of the cattle, and commanded that no bread and no water should be given to her. And whoso should give her anything to eat or to drink, his head should be taken off with the sword. And the girl remained in great distress for twelve days; and after that the daughter of the Emperor remembered her in her heart, and said: 'Woe is me! that this girl, whom my father hath

shut up in his folly and stupidity, should die from hunger and thirst; woe f. 7 a
is me! and I can have no consolation from her.'

"And the Emperor's daughter drew nigh and reached her bread and
water from the window, and I, the bird, was standing; and something
came into my mind, and I know not what I did. Then I went down
near to the daughter of the Emperor, and I plucked out her right eye; and
I flew away, going to the desert, and as I was going my right eye became
blind, and I fell beneath a tree for thirteen days; and I tasted nothing.
And now I have come against my will to tell you what I had done, and f. 7 b
what the Emperor had done. And I am persecuted by the Heavenly
King, your God, Who is the Christ."

Then Peter said unto the Emperor: "Tell us now—whose mouth hath
shut the mouths of these two, or thy mouth?"

Then the Emperor wept in their presence, and said: "I have no
courage[1] to speak to you, for this bird hath made me ashamed; and that
is by the power of your God."

Then the Empress rose, and brought her daughter Lûhîth before the
Apostles; and said, "I entreat you, O my lords! to have compassion on me,
and to cure this my daughter; the only girl whom thine handmaiden hath."

Then Peter laid his hand on the eye of the Emperor's daughter and
said: "In the name of my Lord Jesus the Christ, the Light of the world, f. 8 a
become like thy fellow." And straightway [the eye of the damsel became
like its fellow.] ....

And the people assembled, and the Emperor went up, and the f. 8 b
company of the magistrates, and the Empress, and her daughter, and

---

[1] Literally "face."

the rest of the people, to see what the Apostles would do. Then Peter and Paul arose and stood in the midst of the people. And the multitude of the people of Rome cried, saying: "Shew us to-day the power of your God, that we may see and that our faith may be assured and confirmed."

Then Paul said unto them: "O people of Rome! hearken unto my words. Whoso is sick, or ailing, or dumb, or insane, or blind, or lame, or dead, even if he be asleep and buried, let them bring him here; and he will receive him whole in the name of the Lord Jesus the Christ."

f. 9 a Then a multitude of the people of Rome went and collected the rest of the sick people, and left them in the midst of the theatre, and began to cry, saying: "Cure our sick people for us, O Apostle of the Christ! that we may see and give glory and honour to your God."

Then Peter beckoned to them to be silent from shouting. And when they were silent, he made the sign of the honoured cross on himself, and he was filled with the Holy Spirit, and he preached in the Roman language.

And he said: "O people of Rome! how long will your hearts be blind? and will ye have no knowledge, and be strangers to the faith in God? And ye hasten to the idols which are carried about by the hands of their maker, and ye forsake the mighty, the great God, in whose hands are your souls. Forsake now the wicked, heathen unbelief; and return to the............the Lord, the Christ, Who alone is the Everlasting God of f. 9 b truth; and there is no God beside Him. Who hath made the heaven and the earth by His wisdom, and hath gathered the waters in the seas, and He Is. xl. 12 set bounds to the water, that it may not change. Who hath measured the earth with His span, and weighed the dust in His hand, and it is He Ps. cxxxvi. Who hath weighed the mountains in scales, and the hills in a balance, and 8, 9 hath made the sun as ruler of the day, and the moon as ruler of the night. Ps. civ. 4 Who maketh His angels of wind, and His ministers of flaming fire; He Heb. i. 7 to Whom the spiritual hosts give glory, the seraphim and the cherubim, shining with the light of His beauty; Who sitteth on a throne of flame, and a river of fire floweth before Him; a thousand thousand and myriad myriads Ps. civ. 32 praise His name, Who numbereth the stars, and giveth them names, Who f. 10 a looketh upon the earth, and it trembleth at Him; and chideth the mountains, and they smoke. Who rideth upon the cherubim; and flieth upon the wings of the winds. It is He who created Adam. This was the Son of the Highest, sent for the sake of mercy. This is the Lamb of God, Who taketh away the sins of the world, He in Whom the Father is well pleased. He is the manna which came down from heaven; and was kept in

a golden pot, which was Mary the Virgin.   He is the Bread of the Angels, Ex. xvi. 23
Who in His grace purifieth whosoever eateth thereof.   This is the Fountain
of Life: whoso drinketh of it shall not thirst.   This is the Slayer of death,
and the Destroyer of sin.   This is the Light of the world, and they who
believe in Him are illuminated.   This is the Lord of the conflict; the f. 10 b
Giver of Crowns to the combatants in His obedience.   He is the Good
Tree; by Whom spiritual beings are nourished.   He is the Ladder, which
leadeth up to the height; and by Him they bring the offerings up to the
Lord's presence.   He is the Door of God; and by Him the just enter.
He is the Hope of the pious, on Whom those who lean shall not be
ashamed: and come unto Him, O sons of Rome! and lean upon Him, and
your faces shall not be ashamed, and the rich shall become poor and shall
hunger; and the poor shall be satisfied and shall have abundance.   And
if ye seek the Lord He will not hide His good things from you."

And when Peter had said these words and more, the people of Rome
cried out and said: "O Apostles of the Christ! cure our sick people for us."
And Peter said unto Paul: "Fill a cup for me with water, and put it before
me."

Then Paul brought him a cup of water and put it before him.   And f. 11 a
Peter signed over it the sign of the cross, and said: "In the name of
my Lord Jesus the Christ, the Healer of all pains, Who hath made this
water to spring [from the ground] and become drink; and Who hath
healed divers diseases and pains."

And he gave it to Paul and said unto him: "Go, O my brother! and
sprinkle it upon all the sick; and they will straightway be healed in the
name of our Lord, Who hath sent us, Jesus the Christ."

And Paul took the cup of water and sprinkled it upon all the sick
people; and immediately they were healed.   And they arose and gave
much praise to God.   And with this sprinkling which was made on all the
people, that water which was in the cup did not fail; but it remained as it
was, full.

Then all the people of Rome cried out and said with one voice: f. 11 b
"Truly this man is the great God, Who is the God of Peter and Paul;
Who hath shewn us this wonder to-day.   And we have not known this
God; but He in His mercy hath sent us a Saviour."   And they drew near
to the Apostles [and] worshipped them, and fell prostrate before them;
and went with them with glory and praise to the king's palace.

And then Peter said: "O sons of Rome! we are men like unto you;
and the praise is not ours, but the praise and the glory are due to our

Lord and our Saviour Jesus the Christ, Who in His compassion and the abundance of His mercy hath sent us unto you."

Then the Apostles abode in Rome for six months, and made disciples
f. 12 a of many in the right faith. And they went out thence and went to the city of Philippi; as the Lord shewed unto them. And when the Apostles entered the city of Philippi, they did not keep silent nor did they cease from healing in the name of the Christ by night and by day: and the Lord strengthened them and confirmed their affirmations by the signs and the wonders which they did.

And when the Enemy saw and knew what the Apostles did, he summoned his chiefs and his friends and said: "What shall I do with these disciples of the Son of Mary; for they have vanquished us, and have spoilt all our works and our power? But come with us, let us work deceit: perhaps we may be able to spoil what they have put right."

f. 12 b   Then Satan altered his form and changed his colour, and became like a Hindoo man; and put on the garments of a king; and set a crown upon his head. And he summoned an Afrît, and made him his horse, and rode upon him. And he summoned four of his chiefs and made them resemble Roman men carrying staves, and walking before him like princes. And he came to the palace of the Emperor in Rome and said unto the door-keepers: "Go ye in and say unto Bar'amus the Emperor, that 'thy brother the King of India standeth at the door, desiring an entrance unto thee.'"

And the doorkeepers went in and told the Emperor. And he allowed him to enter. And the four entered with him who were his chiefs. And
f. 13 a when the Emperor of Rome saw him, he rose to welcome him, and shook hands with him and made him sit along with him on the throne of his kingdom.

Then the King of India began to weep and to sob, and [so did] those who were with him. And Bar'amûs said: "Wherefore, O my brother! dost thou weep and sob? and wherefore art thou sad? though this is the time for bringing in the table? But tell me thy tale after the meal, and what hath happened unto thee; and I will use [my] power, and will make thee attain thy desire."

The King of India replied and said unto him : "I am, as thou seest me, in contempt and humiliation and sore affliction. I was a king like unto thee, and I [ruled] over Scindia and India. And I had many armies, and strong soldiers in the country of Greece[1] and of Nubia; and I had

[1] Er-Rûm.

governors and captains to the East of the land and to the West, and in f. 13 b
Egypt and Syria, and Irâq and the land of Palestine, and in the lands
of the Hilâlians[1] and the Armenians; and [in] the land of Teman
and the Arabs; and the land of the Berbers. And there was not a
nation in the world, nor a tongue, nor a tribe, who did not submit to
me and to my rule. Honour and quiet were in my dominions; until
two men came to me, wizards, magicians; the name of the one was Peter,
and of the other Paul. And they came down upon me from a cloud, and
stood before me in the midst of my palace; and I was sitting upon the
throne of my kingdom ; and my chamberlains standing on my right and on
my left. And when I saw them, I was terrified, and I changed my colour.
And the chamberlains sprang upon them, to strike them, and I did not f. 14 a
allow them, for I saw the likeness of angels in them. And I asked them
about their story, and whence they were. And the elder of them answered
and said unto me: 'I am Peter of Beth Saida of Galilee. And this is my
brother Paul; and he is from Tarsus; and our journey is from the land of
life ; and we are the slaves of Jesus the Christ the Lord, the God, the King of
kings, Who hath created the heavens and the earth, and the seas, and whatsoever moveth therein. Who hath created men in His own image and
likeness. And He was born of Mary the Virgin. And He made wine out
of water; and from five loaves He satisfied a multitude; and He healed the
lepers; and cured the sick; and opened the eyes of the blind ; and made
the deaf hear and the dumb speak; and He cast out devils; and gave life
to the dead ; and wrought miracles.' And they spake with many words
in my presence ; and they led my viziers astray and my chamberlains, and f. 14 b
my friends. And they all rejected me, and drew their weapons, and
hurled them in my face. And they said : 'Take thine arms away from us,
for we have no need of them, for we have found a heavenly God
better than thee, and He is the King of Peter and Paul, the Ruler of the
whole world.' And none remained to me of these chamberlains and
captains save these four Greeks, and they have come with me; and these
are they whom thine eye beholdeth. And now, O my brother! I am anxious
that thy kingdom should not fail like me, and I have come from a far
country to tell thee and to warn thee, that they may not come unto thee
and lead astray thy friends with their sorcery, and deny thee and leave
thee quite alone, powerless, and without soldiers ; and thou come to an end,
and the kings of the earth overcome thee."

Then the Emperor arose from his throne, and crossed his hands, and f. 15 a

[1] p. 3, El-Halâliim.

bowed to him, doing obeisance.   And he said: "I thank thee, O my brother, the beloved of my soul! because thou hast taken pity on me, and hast come from afar to tell me of this matter.   Truly I say unto thee, that they have come to me in this form which thou hast described, as they came unto thee, and thus have they come unto me.   And the report of them had reached me; and they have gone to the city of Philippi, to lead them astray with their sorcery, as they have led thee and me astray; unless I send letters in pursuit of them that they may come with them, their arms being bound together, and chains about their necks. And I will flay off their skins and will make them wine bottles.   And I will burn them with fire as thy spirit desireth."

Then Bar'amûs the Emperor summoned one of his captains; and com-
f. 15 b manded him to take a thousand soldiers with arms, and go to the city of Philippi, and bring Peter and Paul, being dragged with chains on their necks.   And he swore and said: "By the life of my daughter Lûhîth! if thou doest this, I will exalt thy dwelling."

And the captain went out from the Emperor's presence, and he took soldiers with him, and they went to the city of Philippi, and besieged it on every side.   And the people of Philippi saw the Romans drawing near to them, clothed in armour, and besieging the city.   And they feared exceedingly.   And they closed the gates and climbed to the top of the wall. And they said unto the captain: "Why hast thou come to us with these soldiers? we being servants of the Emperor.   And he hath sent the Romans to lay our city waste."

The captain answered and said: "The Emperor hath not sent to lay your city waste: but we are come to take Peter and Paul, the arch-wizards.   And deliver ye them up to us, and we will turn away from you."

f. 16 a   Then the people of Philippi answered and said unto them : "But there are no wizards in our city; nevertheless we have two men who are just and wise.   They heal souls and bodies.   And now grant us a respite, that we may tell them.   And if they like to go with you, we will deliver them up to you.   And if they do not wish this, then we and their God, the Christ the Heavenly King, we will fight for them with thee, and with thy foolish Emperor who hath sent thee."

And when the Apostles heard that they had been called wizards they thanked God greatly and said: "Thanks be unto Thee, O Jesus the Christ; for Whose holy name's sake we are this day worthy to be called wizards."

And they opened the gate of the city and went out unto them.   And the captain commanded that fetters and chains should be hung on their necks. And when the people of Philippi saw the Apostles with iron upon their necks, they began to weep. And Peter said unto them: "Weep not, O brethren! but be patient, and ye shall behold the power of the Christ, f. 16 b our God; and what shall happen to these people and their foolish Emperor who hath sent them." And the captain and the Romans who were with them rode upon their horses. And Peter said unto the captain: "If thou wilt, do thou dismount from thy horse that thou mayest pray; and whatsoever the Christ commandeth us, we will do."

And the captain said unto him in anger: "O wicked sorcerers! the anger of Bar'amûs[1] burneth like fire, and thou standest by thy sorcery." Then they and the citizens turned to the east and stood in prayer. And Peter prayed, saying: "O Sender of His servants to every country! Who dost help His slave in every place to fight in every conflict, come at this time to our succour who call on Thee, and put Bar'amûs[1] the Emperor to shame, who hath denied Thee after [his] faith; that the believing citizens of Philippi may be assured that thou art the Everlast- f. 17 a ing God of truth." And from that hour the angel of the Lord came down from heaven, and went in amongst the horses and cut them; and they overset each other and made their riders fall upon the ground. And the horses trampled upon them with their feet, and dragged them with their mouths with a great dragging. And all the horses neighed with one voice; and they all prayed and did obeisance before the Apostles. And they also did obeisance before God, and stretched out their hands towards heaven like the Apostles of the Christ. And the people of Philippi cried, saying: "We thank Thee, O God of Peter and Paul! because we see the beasts giving glory to Thee with their voices." Then that [captain] drew near, weeping and crying; and the Roman soldiers who were with him said: "Have mercy upon us, O Peter and Paul! Apostles of the Christ."

And Peter said unto them: "What do ye desire that we should do unto you?"

They said: "We desire of you that ye would entreat your God that f. 17 b He would make us servants like you."

And Peter said unto them: "In the raiment which ye now wear ye cannot serve our King; but if ye desire to contend with us in this conflict hearken unto our words. Our King is the Christ, and [in] His service are weapons. And our power is life; and our raiment is a spiritual garment which we wear from baptism; and the helmets which are upon our heads

[1] MS. "Barghamûs."

are the blessing of the priesthood. And the spurs which are upon our feet are the confirmation of the Gospel, wherewith we trample upon the serpents and the scorpions, and all the powers of the enemy. And our cuirasses are the true faith, with which we receive all the darts of the enemy. And our swords are the word of our Lord Jesus the Christ, with which we cut through all the wiles of the cursed Iblîs: And our horses are the clouds which carry us in the air in the name of our God. And our spear is the cross of our Lord Jesus the Christ, and His pure, life-giving blood.

f. 18 a   "And now, O brethren! arise, go unto the Emperor who hath sent you, and renounce him openly; and throw down your arms before him, and say unto him: 'Take thine arms from us, for we have found a heavenly King; and He is greater than thou; and He is the King of Peter and Paul.' And know this for a surety, that the Emperor will be wroth with you, and will cast you into prison; but fear ye him not; for Jesus the Christ, the Heavenly King in Whom ye believe, will speedily deliver you from him."

Then the Apostles arose, and blessed them in the name of our Lord Jesus the Christ, and sent them to Rome. And they went in unto Bar amûs the Emperor, and he said unto them: "Where are the men, the wizards, to whom I sent you?"

And they said unto him: "O thou Emperor! the good, the just men, for whom people are thankful, dost thou call them wizards? And wilt f. 18 b thou recompense thus the people who have healed thy daughter gratis, who for thirteen years had her eye plucked out?" And then they pulled off their arms, and threw them down before him, and said unto him: "Take thine arms from us; we have no need of them; for we have found a heavenly King better than thou; and He is the King of Peter and Paul; Whose kingdom shall never fail." Then the Emperor waxed wroth, and rose from the throne; and began to smite the face of that captain with his hand, saying unto him: "Truly I will burn thee alive in the fire, that I may see if the God of Peter and Paul will save thee from my hand."

Then they answered and said: "The God of Peter and Paul is able in His compassion to quench thy fire and thy wrath."

And the Emperor commanded that they should be thrown into prison. f. 19 a And while they were going towards the prison they were giving glory to God, for Whose sake they were to be shut up.

Then the King of India said unto Bar'amûs, "Did not I say unto thee that they would lead thy friends astray by their sorcery and their speech?"

And the Emperor of Rome said: "Truly, by the gods and the life of mighty Rome all that thou hast said unto me is true."

And the Emperor summoned another captain, and said unto him : "Take with thee four thousand horsemen, and go to the city of Philippi, and let it be sacked; and destroy its inhabitants with the sword; and spare neither old nor young; for they have been led astray by the power of their sorcery; and are resisting our will."

And the captain went out from the presence of the Emperor; and he commanded the soldiers and gave them a sign to blow[1] the second trumpet, [and] to mount and go with him.

Then the Holy Ghost appeared unto the Apostles as they were in f. 19 b Philippi, and told them what the King of India had spoken about with the Emperor of Rome; and what the Enemy had plotted against them. And Peter answered and said : "O my brother Paul ! arise, let us pray before our Lord Jesus the Christ, that He would save us from their wiles during this night. O my brother ! Patroclus hath arranged to come in search of us from the city of Rome : and four thousand armed men are with him ; and they say that they will allow the city to be sacked and burnt, and will destroy its inhabitants with the sword for our sake. But, O brother ! arise and let us pray before our Lord and our Saviour Jesus the Christ; that He may do by His power as thou desirest."

And at the time when the Romans arose and journeyed towards f. 20 a them, straightway a cloud descended and carried the Apostles, and let them down in the midst of the palace of the Emperor Barʿamûs[2]. And he was sitting upon the throne of his kingdom, meditating about the first captain and his companions, how he should destroy them. And when the Emperor saw the Apostles standing before him, he cried against them, saying : "O Peter and Paul ! ye wizards who lead astray the souls of the people of the world."

Peter said unto him : "We are no wizards, but we are come to drive the devil away from thee, who hath always deceived thee by his sorcery."

Then the Emperor summoned the [chamberlains] of the palace who were at its door, and said unto them : "Go to.........and send to......... that he may not go to the city of Philippi." f. 20 b

And when it was the morrow, the Emperor commanded, and the trumpet was blown in all the city ; that the people might be assembled to see the burning of Peter and Paul, the wizards. And the Emperor commanded that two idols should be brought, and that they [the Apostles] should be brought into the midst of the city. And he commanded that two helmets of iron should be placed in the fire, and put upon their heads. And they

---

[1] MS. "beat."   [2] MS. "Barghamûs."

did this unto them; and he began to smear fat below them and to say: "Now let the Christ come and save you from my hands, and quench this fire from you."

And his words pained Peter greatly. And Paul spoke to him in Hebrew and said: "Pray, O my father Peter! before the Christ, and entreat Him to save us from this torment; for I am in great tribulation because of it; and my soul draweth nigh unto death." But Peter was

f. 21 a untouched by the pain of that torture, because he had had much experience and temptations. And Peter answered and said unto Paul: "Be patient, O my brother! for a little while; for [it is written[1]] The just shall be justified by patience, that he may receive [a great reward[1]]."

Then Peter prayed, and said: "O our Lord Jesus the Christ! come to our help at this time, and save us from this tribulation and from Bar'amûs[2] the unbeliever; and may he be put to shame with his teacher, the King of India; and may the captain and his believing friends come out of prison; and may they behold Thy glory and Thine honour; and be confirmed in Thy faith."

And the prayer of the Apostles was heard immediately; and the angel of the Lord descended from heaven, and brought Peter and Paul down from the prison; and set them upon the ground; and took the helmets off from their heads, and made them like dust, and the Apostles were not in the least hurt.

f. 22 a "long-suffering. But send and take out the captain and all his friends whom thou hast imprisoned in thy delusion."

Then the Emperor answered and said: "Whom shall I send, for we are suspended?"

Peter said: "If thou desire it, send thy daughter Lûhîth."

And the Emperor wept and said: "Lûhîth, take pity on me! and have compassion on thy father; for he is fallen, and is become a wonder in the world."

cf. Gen.
iv. 10   And his daughter said: "If I take pity on thee: and have compassion on thee, yet the blood of that maiden whom thou didst imprison in

---

[1] Photograph of MS. indistinct.   [2] MS. "Barghamûs."

thy folly crieth from the ground before God. And it is He Who hath sent thee the chastisement."

And he said unto her: "I entreat thee, O my daughter! go and deliver the prisoners, lest they come and beseech the Heavenly King about me."

Then Lûhîth went and brought them out of the prison. And when f. 22 b the Apostles came near, they found the Emperor and the rest of his friends hanging. And when the Emperor saw them, he said unto them: "Have mercy on me, O happy apostles of the Christ!"

Then they said: "Praise be unto God at all times! Who hath humiliated thy kingdom; and hath brought down thy boasting; and hath delivered us from thy hand, by which we were oppressed."

Then Bar'amûs the Emperor answered and said, with all who were suspended with him: "Let the King of India have no good remembrance for ever! he who hath deluded us and led us astray after our right belief. And he it is who hath delivered us over to this dreadful torment. And we entreat God that no honour may remain to him and no dominion for ever."

Then the Emperor wept bitter tears and said: "O Peter and Paul, servants of the merciful Christ! entreat about me, O beloved of the f. 23 a merciful Christ! that we may be released from this dreadful torment, and do ye receive me with your hands."

Then Peter was inspired by the Holy Ghost, and said unto the Emperor: "By the life of the name of the Lord the Christ! in Whose hands I remain by night and by day, thou shalt not come down from here, and there shall be no joy to thee nor rest in thy soul, until thou believe with thy mouth and write with thy hand; and thou shalt be suspended in thy place; for there is no power nor authority in the heavens or the earth save Jesus the Christ." And then the Emperor wept from the severity of the torture and said: "Bring me an ink-horn and paper[1]. Truly I will write, that perchance I may be saved from this torment and tribulation."

And the captain rose and brought him an ink-horn and paper; and said unto him: "Why dost thou not believe in the Christ, when thou art f. 23 b standing suspended upon the ground, vanquished?"

Then he took the pen in his hand and wrote thus: "I say that I believe and am assured, I, Bar'amûs, Emperor of Rome, and I have been, I and my company, and the people of my city Rome, suspended, vanquished, that there is no other God either in heaven or in earth, except Jesus the Christ, the King of Peter and Paul. And henceforth and for ever I will

---

[1] *i.e.* papyrus.

believe; and no one shall blaspheme the name of the Christ, the Nazarene.
And whosoever shall deny Him shall not continue upon the face of the
earth, but shall be cast into the depths of the sea; he and all his house.
For there is no God like unto Him, who saveth His worshippers and His
friends from misfortune and from fire."

Then the Apostles lifted up their hands to heaven, and said: "O our
f. 24 a Lord Jesus the Christ! the good God, Who wilt not requite any one
according to his works; do thou, O Lord! forgive Bar'amûs[1] the Emperor,
and his friends who are suspended with him; because it is the King of
India who hath led them astray."

And straightway the angel of the Lord descended, [and] loosed them,
and brought them down to the ground. And the Apostles remained for
three years and six months; and they founded a great Catholic church;
and in it they appointed four-and-twenty bishops, and forty presbyters,
and seventy-two deacons, and a hundred and twelve sub-deacons and
they made a canon and a law for them; and commandments suitable
to the service of the Lord the Christ.

And they departed thence on a journey. And Satan, when he saw
that he was vanquished and conquered by the Apostles, summoned his
f. 24 b potentates and said unto them: "What shall I do with the disciples of the
Son of Mary, for they have vanquished us, and have frustrated us, and
have spoiled all our devices?"

Then Satan changed his form and became like a naked Hindoo man;
and he sought after the Apostles for a distance of three miles; and he
kept crying out in a feeble voice along their track, saying: "O Peter and
Paul! disciples of the Lord Jesus the merciful Christ, take pity on me, and
be good to me, lest I die for your sakes."

And Paul turned, and beheld him naked, and he was far away on their
track. And he said unto Peter: "Take pity, O my brother! verily we will
see why this man runs seeking us."

And they waited for him; and he stood before them. And he was
naked and inflamed like fire. And he was unable to speak from the
eagerness of his diligence. And Paul said unto him: "Why dost thou run
f. 25 a in our track? Dost thou not think that we will prove ourselves more right
than Bar'amûs[1] in any way? By the living name of the Lord Jesus
the Christ! we possess nothing in this world save the clothes we have on,
wherewith we cover our bodies, nothing else. And if thou desirest it, we
will give thee something of what we have on. And I shall do it."

---

[1] MS. "Barghamûs."

And the Enemy replied to the Apostles and said: "I entreat you, O my lords! by the mighty power which hath brought us low, have compassion on me. I will go away from you; for a burning fire serveth you."

And Peter said: "Swear unto us, that in the place whither thou goest, thou wilt not pursue us, nor disturb us, nor spoil what we are doing."

And the Enemy swore and said: "Nay, and by the fire of hell, prepared for me and for all my friends, the place where thou and thy friends shall be my foot shall never tread it." And the Apostles let him go.

And when he was a little way off from them, he changed his shape, f. 25 b and became a black bull; and hastened to butt Paul. And Paul was terrified at him; and began to embrace Peter. And he said: "O my father! save me from this devil frightful in shape."

And Peter said: "Be not dismayed, O my brother! by the power of our Lord Jesus the Christ, do thou pull a horn, and I a horn, and we will drag him down."

And they each of them began to pull a [different] way. And then the cursed one cried out and said to the Apostles, "By the truth of Jesus the Saviour, let me go. I will go quite away from you; for your power is great with your God."

Peter said unto Satan: "May the Christ put thee to shame! and all thy[1] potentates."

And the cursed one said unto Peter: "Thou didst deny the Christ three times in one night, [and say] that thou knewest Him not. But as for me, what shall I do? for if I have fought with one of you about f. 26 a anything, and have overcome him, he goes and weeps in the presence of the Christ; and sobs and is forgiven."

And Paul said unto the Enemy: "Blessed be the Christ! Who hath put thee to shame! and hath confounded thy face; and hath put thee trampled beneath our feet; and in His name we have vanquished thee."

Satan said unto Paul: "Be afraid, O bald pate! and meanest of all men! Thou thinkest that thou hast overcome me by thy strength; if the mercy of God had not saved thee from me, I would have destroyed thee by means of the sin whereto thou wast harnessed for the rest of thy life."

Then Paul wept and sobbed before the Lord, till he said unto him, "By

---

[1] MS. "your."

the mercy of the Lord thou wast saved from me, from the yoke of the sin wherein thou wast harnessed."

Then they let Satan go. And Peter said unto him: "Thou dost swear and dost lie, that thou wilt not oppose us."

f. 26 b   The Enemy replied, laughing: "Give praise and glory to the Lord, Who giveth this power unto His servants who believe in His name; and who do His pleasure."

And to our Lord be glory and majesty, and worship and honour henceforth, and always, and for evermore. Amen.

The tales of the Holy Apostles are completed with the help of God— praise be unto Him!—in Ailûl....

And praise be to God continually. And on us be His mercy! Amen

THE MARTYRDOM OF PETER AND PAUL.

From Cod. Sin. Arab. 405.

In the name of the Father, and the Son, and the Holy Ghost, the One God, [*on*] *the twenty-ninth of this month, the martyrdom of the two great Apostles, Peter and Paul, the chiefs of the Apostles, was related.*

When Paul had returned from Spain to Rome, a company of the Jews approached him, saying: "Take heed that thou support our faith in which thou wast born; it is not right that thou shouldest be a Hebrew, and [born] of Hebrews, [and] shouldest say that thou art a teacher of the Gentiles, and shouldest support the uncircumcised. And thou art thyself circumcised, and thou makest void the faith of the circumcised. When thou shalt see Peter, do thou contend against his teaching; for he hath abolished all keeping of our law, and hath closed the Sabbaths, and the times of the first days of the months, and the legal holidays."

And Paul answered and said unto them: "But I am a true Jew; and by this ye may prove me, that until now I have observed the Sabbath, and have attended to the true circumcision. For on the Sabbath day God rested from all His works; and ours are the Fathers and the Patriarchs, and the Torah. And what King is it Whom Peter doth proclaim among the Gentiles? But if one amongst us desire to introduce teaching: tell him without any disturbance or hatred, or trouble, that we will look at his teaching, and consider it, and I will reprove him in the presence of you all. And if his doctrine be true, and is confirmed by the testimony of the books of the Hebrews, I command [that] it is fitting ye should submit to him and obey him [in peace]."

And when they had said this, and things like it, unto Paul, they went and said unto Peter: "Paul the Hebrew hath come from Spain, and doth invite thee to come unto him. For they who have accompanied him say that no one of those who desire to talk with him can do so after he hath appeared before Cæsar."

p. 2

And when Peter heard [this] he rejoiced with a great joy. And he arose straightway and went to him. And when each of them saw the other, they wept for gladness; and they embraced, and each of them poured out many tears upon the other. And Paul related to Peter the story of his deeds: and how he arrived with many toils in the boat; and Paul[1] related to Peter also what difficulties he had endured from Simon Magus.

And when the evening came, Peter went away to his dwelling. And when it was morning, at the dawn of day, Peter approached and found a multitude of Jews before the door of Paul's dwelling. And there was a great tumult amongst the Jews between the Christians and the heathen. But those of the Jews who believed said: "We are the chosen race, the royal priesthood, the friends of Abraham, and Isaac and Jacob, and all the prophets to whom God confided [His] secrets; and He shewed them His secrets and His great wonders. But ye who are of the Gentiles, there is nothing great in your descent, but ye have become infatuated with sculptured idols, dirty and contemptible." And when those of the Jews who believed had said this and other things like it, those of the Gentiles who believed replied to them, saying: "Whenever we heard the truth we at once followed the Christ, who verily is Himself the Truth, and we forsook our error; but ye have known the miracles of the fathers; and ye had the teachings of the Torah and the prophets; and ye crossed the sea with dusty feet; and ye beheld your enemies marching proudly into the depths. And a beacon of light appeared unto you by night, and the cloud overshadowed you by day. And manna from heaven was given unto you; and water overflowed unto you from a rock, and ye believed not. But after these things ye made yourselves an idol; and ye set it up; and ye worshipped a graven thing; and we saw nothing of the wonders; p. 3 and we believed in the true God, Whom ye forsook when ye had rebelled against Him."

While they were disputing about these things and others like them, the Apostle Paul said: "Let there not be any more of these contentions and controversies between you, but, O my brethren! hope for this, for God
Gen. xii. 3 hath fulfilled His promises, about which He sware unto Abraham our father,
2 Chron. xix. 7 that in thy seed all the nations should be blessed, for there is no acceptance
Gal. ii. 6 of persons with God; for whoso hath sinned, having a law, by the judgment
Acts x. 34
Rom. ii. 11 of their law they shall be judged: but all those who have sinned, having no law, shall perish without the law. And we, O my brethren! let us take heed that we thank God; for He in His mercy hath chosen us a holy nation for Himself, so that it is meet that we should glory in Him; if ye be at first either Jews or Greeks, ye are all of you one in the faith in His name."

---

[1] The Latin and Greek texts have more correctly "Peter related to Paul"; see Lipsius, *Acta Apostolorum*, p. 123.

And when Paul had said this discourse, those who were Jews and those who were Gentiles were appeased. And after the same manner Peter taught them, saying: "God promised to the Patriarch David, saying: 'Of the fruit of thy body I will place upon thy throne,' this [man] the Word of God. And He sent His Son. And He was made flesh from his seed concerning Whom David himself testified, saying: 'Thou art my Son, this day have I begotten Thee.' And the Father Himself beareth witness from Heaven, saying: 'This is my beloved Son, in Whom I delight, hear ye Him.' And He it was Whom the high priest and the chiefs of the nation crucified from the impulse of hatred: and for the salvation of the world He freely allowed all this to come on Him. And by Him God hath opened an entrance to all, to the children of Abraham and Isaac and Jacob, and to every nation of the earth by faith. Their confession and their confirmation in Him will be to them life and salvation by His name, because what God hath promised to Abraham He hath fulfilled. And therefore David the prophet saith concerning Him, 'The Lord hath sworn, and will not repent: Thou art the priest for ever, after the order of Melchisedek.' For the Saviour became a priest that He might offer unto God the whole fruitful sacrifice—the sacrifice of His body and His blood for all the world."

And when Peter and Paul said this and things like it, they all held their peace; and listened to their teaching from themselves. And they preached the word of God to all the believers. And every day there were thanksgivings (= Eucharists?) of those who believed in our Lord Jesus the Christ, a multitude which could not be numbered. And when the chiefs of all the Jews and the priests of the Greeks perceived that by their preaching all the people of Rome had believed, save a few, in our Lord Jesus the Christ, they began to raise a tumult against them and a murmuring amongst the nation; and praised Simon Magus before a multitude of those who followed the two Apostles. And they strove to lay the matter before the famous Emperor Nero. And they spake falsely against the Apostles of the Lord; and in a multitude of the people which could not be numbered who had turned unto the Lord by the preaching of Peter, it happened that Livia, the wife of Nero, and the wife of his Vizier Agrippa, whose name was Agrippina, believed. And they believed in such a way that they withdrew from cohabitation with their husbands. And through the preaching of Paul many despised the army and cleaved unto God, so that even some people of the Emperor's palace devoted themselves to them, and became Christians; and did not wish to return again to the army,

Margin notes:
cf. Ps. cxxxii. 11

Ps. ii. 7
Matt. xvii 5

p. 4
Ps. cx. 4
Heb. vii. 21

nor to the palace. And from this the rogue found his opportunity and roused a tumult among the nation and made it murmur. And moved with envy, he excited them to say wicked libels against Peter, calling him a wizard and a deceiver. And those who were amazed at his miracles p. 5 believed in him. For he made a brazen serpent [move] of itself, and images of stone laugh and move of their own accord, and he made himself, on being summoned, suddenly appear in the air before them. But Peter was healing the sick with a word, and making the blind see ; and when he prayed, by his command the demons fled and the dead were raised. And he said unto the people that they should flee from the deceit of the seducer Simon, but they also bare witness to him, so that they might not be deluded into serving the rogue.

And thus it happened because all the pious people had rejected Simon Magus and were asserting that there was no good in him. But those who adhered to Simon told lies against Peter and gave false witness, that he was bewitching all the followers of Simon Magus, until the report reached Nero Cæsar. And he commanded that Simon Magus should be brought into his presence. And when he entered, he stood before him. And he began suddenly to change his shape, so that he had become one time instantly a boy and shortly afterwards an old man ; and another time a youth, for he had altered in face and in stature to divers forms, growing very tall and making himself a servant of the devil.

And when Nero saw him he was so astounded that he himself thought him the Son of God. But the Apostle Peter said : "This man is a liar and a wizard and a bad man, a good-for-nothing and a rebel, and in everything an opponent of the will of God. And nothing remained but that his crimes and iniquities should be made manifest by the command of God, and should become clear to every one." And when he went in unto Nero the Emperor, he said : "Hearken, O thou good Emperor! I am the Son of God ; who came down from heaven. And until now Peter hath claimed for himself that he is an Apostle hypocritically in my likeness ; but now the evil of him and of Paul is doubled ; and they are teaching by these things p. 6 and believing firmly the opinions that are against me. I mean the preaching in which they persist. And therefore if thou dost not command them all to be destroyed, it is evident that thy dominions cannot be firmly established."

Then Nero enquired anxiously [about it] and straightway commanded that they should be promptly brought to him. And on the next day Simon Magus went in unto Nero, and Peter and Paul, the Apostles of the Lord

And Simon said: "These two are the disciples of the Nazarene. And it is not very good that He is of the Jewish nation."

And Nero said, "And what is the meaning of a Nazarene?"

And Simon said: "There is a city in the country of the Jews, which hath always been much opposed to us; it is called Nazareth." And he said: "And the Teacher of these two came from it."

And Nero said: "God careth for every man and loveth him: and thou, why dost thou persecute these two?"

And Simon said: "These two men seek to turn all the race of the Jews, that they may not believe in me."

And Nero said unto Peter: "Why do your race oppose and hate each other?"

Then Peter said unto Simon: "Thou hast power with a multitude by thy tricks; but against me thou canst do nothing. And a multitude of those who are deceived by thee, God seeketh to turn them from their error by me, and thou hast fought and art not able to overcome me; and I am astonished at how thou hast changed into every colour in the presence of the Emperor, and hast magnified thyself. And thou dost think that by thy magic craft thou canst conquer the disciples of the Christ."

And Nero said: "And who is the Christ?"

And Peter said: "He Whom Simon Magus doth vainly boast himself to be; he is a very wicked man, and his works are deceitful; and he doth claim that it is he himself. And if thou wilt investigate, O good Emperor! what things were done by the Jews in the affair of the Christ and the report of it, cause the writings to be brought which arrived from Pontius p. 7 Pilate who sent them to Claudius; and then we shall know everything."

And Nero commanded that the writings should be brought, and should be read before him. And there was in them after this manner: "From Pontius Pilate unto Claudius greeting. It happened that there was in my days an occurrence which I will report unto thee clearly. The Jews, because of their envy of each other and their resistance, have been punished with severe judgments; for their fathers told them about what it had been decreed should happen, that their God would send unto them His Holy One from heaven, Who would be rightly called their King; and He promised that He would send Him on the earth from a virgin. He when He came down during my reign over Judæa, the God of the Hebrews, I saw Him give light to the eyes of the blind; and cleanse the lepers; heal the palsied; and drive away the devils from the people; and raise the dead; and rebuke the winds, walking with dusty feet upon the waves of the sea;

and He did many miracles; and a multitude of the Jewish nation said that He was the Son of God. And the chief priests were moved with envy against Him. And they laid hold of Him, and delivered Him up to me; and spake falsely against Him of divers things, and said that He was a wizard and did acts contrary to the Law. And I believed that their sayings were true; and I delivered Him unto them, having scourged Him according to their judgment. And they crucified Him. And when he had been buried they placed guards over him. And the guards were from my army. And He rose on the third day. And therefore the wickedness of the Jews was kindled to such a degree that they gave silver to the soldiers, saying:

Matt.
xxviii. 13
'Say ye that His disciples came by night and stole His body.' But they took the silver; but they were not able to hide the fact; and they bare
p. 8 witness that He had risen; for they saw Him standing. This I make thee observe, lest some one should speak falsely; and they should believe in the false sayings of the Jews."

And when the letter had been read, Nero said: "O Peter! tell me, have all these things been so done?"

And Peter answered: "O Emperor! the matter is thus; I pray thee to be assured of it. But this Simon is full of lies and deceit. Nevertheless in the Christ is the consummation of all victory because of the Deity and for the sake of the Manhood which He took, and because of this is the incomprehensible glory which makes the people worthy of Him through His being man. And this Simon consists of two elements, man and devil; and as a man he seeketh to impede men."

And Simon replied: "I am verily astonished, O thou good Emperor! how thou dost imagine this thing. [This is] a man without good breeding, an extremely poor fisherman, with no power of speech, nor of family connection. But that I may not endure this enemy further I will now command my angels that they may avenge me by their coming."

And Peter said: "I fear not these thy angels: will they not rather fear me, by the power of our Lord Jesus the Christ, and the trust in Him, against Whom thou thyself hast spoken falsely?"

And Nero said: "But dost thou not fear Simon, who confirms his divinity by his deeds and by feats?"

And Peter said: "He will shew thee the divinity, who searcheth the hidden things of the heart. Let him tell me now, what I am thinking of, and what I am doing. And the thought which I am thinking, before he lieth about it, I will reveal it to thine ears; so that he dare not speak falsehood, and distort what I have thought about."

And Nero said: "Come near to me, and tell me what thou hast thought of."

And Peter said: "Command that a barley loaf be brought, and given [to me] secretly." And when he had commanded it to be brought, and be given secretly to Peter, Peter said: "Let Simon tell me what I have thought of; or what hath been said; or what hath happened." p. 9

And Nero said: "Dost thou wish me to believe that Simon doth not know this, who hath raised the dead, and when his head[1] was struck [off] rose himself after three days? And whatsoever I have told him to do he hath done."

Peter said: "But he will not do anything with me."

And Nero said: "Hath he not done all this in my presence? and he commanded his angels to come to him, and they hastened to come to him."

And Peter said: "As he hath done the great thing, why doth he not do a small thing, and tell me what I have thought of? and what I have done?"

And Nero said: "What sayest thou, O Simon? but as for me, I have verified nothing of your affair."

And Simon said: "Let Peter say what I purpose."

And Peter said: "What Simon hath thought, I shall make it known by my doing what he hath thought."

And Simon said: "Know this, O good Emperor! that no one knoweth the thoughts of men, except God alone; and Peter is therefore a liar."

And Peter said: "O thou who sayest of thyself, that thou art the Son of God! tell me what I have thought about, and what I have just now done in secret. If thou art able to do this, let us know it clearly." For Peter had blessed the barley-bread which he had taken and had broken it, and had touched it with fingers of his right hand and his left hand.

Then Simon, being angry because he could not tell the secret of the Apostle which he had not uttered, growled, saying, "Let dogs come forth and devour him before Cæsar." [And] suddenly great dogs sprang upon Peter. And lo! Peter stretched out his hand in prayer, and proffered the bread which he had blessed. When the dogs saw this they shewed [their] tongues no more. p. 10

Then Peter said unto Nero, "Behold! I have shewn thee that I knew what Simon Magus was thinking of, not in words only, but by deeds; for he hath no angels to let loose against me; for he hath brought dogs against me, to shew of himself that he hath no divine angels, but doggish ones."

---

[1] Literally "neck," *passim.*

Then Nero said unto Simon: "What is it, O Simon! I think that we are put to flight?"

And Simon said: "Thus hath he done these things unto me in Judæa and in all Palestine and in Cæsarea; and he hath withstood me many times and hath made this known, because he is opposed to these things. And he hath made this known that he might drive me away; because no one can know the thoughts of men, except God alone."

And Peter said unto Simon[1]: "Thou dost imagine of thyself that thou art God indeed: and why dost thou not disclose the thoughts of every man?"

Then Nero turned to Paul and said: "Thou, O Paul! why dost thou not say something?"

And Paul answered and said: "O Cæsar! be sure of this, knowing that if thou dost grant a delay to this wizard to do such wicked deeds, a great evil will grow in thy country, and thy dominion be split because of his resistance."

And Nero said unto Simon, "What dost thou say?"

And Simon said: "If I did not shew myself publicly to be as God, no one would bring me the worship which is due to me."

And Nero said: "And why dost thou linger now, and dost not shew thyself to be a God; that these twain may be punished?"

And Simon said: "Command that a high tower be built for me, of wood, and I will climb it, and will summon my angels; and will command p. 11 them to lift me up in the sight of every one to my Father, who is in heaven. And if these two cannot do this, they will be reproved, because they are men without good breeding."

And when Nero heard [this], he said unto Peter: "Hast thou heard, O Peter! what Simon hath said about this affair? It will be shewn who hath the power, this man, or thy God."

And Peter said: "O thou mighty Emperor! if thou wilt, I shall make thee observe this man, that he is possessed by a demon."

And Nero said: "Why do ye make delay with your perplexing talk? to-morrow your cause will be tried all together."

And Simon said: "But believe, O thou good Emperor! that I am of great dignity, because I died and rose again." For Simon the rebel, amongst his [other] bad deeds, had said unto Nero, "Command my head to be struck off in a dark place; and leave me there slain; and if I rise

---

[1] MS. "And Simon said unto Peter."

not on the third day, know that I was a wizard. And if I rise, know that I am the Son of God."

And when this had happened by the command of Nero, he contrived this trick by his magic art that in the darkness the head of a ram was struck off. And it appeared as if it were Simon until it was beheaded. And when the head of the ram was struck off in the darkness, the swordsman took the head and found that it was the head of a ram. But he did not dare to say this to the Emperor, lest he should scourge him, seeing that he had commanded him to do this in secret. And when one hour had passed the Emperor desired to know the certainty of this. And when he saw the head he wondered. And from that time Simon said that he had himself risen after three days; because after the head had been shewn to the Emperor he lifted the limbs also by sorcery, that is, the corpse. But the blood remained there; and on the third day he shewed himself to Nero the Emperor and said: "Command that my blood which was shed be wiped away: for I the slain one am whole, as I said that on the third day I would rise."

And when Nero said: "To-morrow your affair will be proved," he p. 12 turned to Paul and said unto him: "Thou, O Paul! why dost thou say nothing? or who taught thee? or who was thy master? or how hast thou taught in the cities? or what things have happened through thy teaching? And I think that thou hast no wisdom, and that thou canst not accomplish any miracle."

And Paul replied: "Dost thou wish me to converse with a wicked man, a wizard, who hath given himself over unto death, who will go quickly to destruction and ruin? or is it meet that I should talk to a man who answereth as what he is not, and mocketh people with his magic craft, and draweth them down to destruction? And if thou choose to hear his sayings, and help him, thou wilt ruin thyself and thy dominion, for he is a very bad man. And like as the Egyptian magicians Iannes and Iambres led Pharaoh and his army astray, until they were drowned in the sea, so doth this man by teaching the deceit of his father persuade people, and thus he deceiveth any simple people to the trial of thy dominion. And I, when I see the words of the cunning one overflowing in this man, renew the groanings of my heart with the Holy Spirit, beseeching that he may be able to know what he is; as I think that he wishes to be exalted to the heavens, and will sink down to an equal distance in the depths of hell, where there is weeping and gnashing of teeth. But as for what Matt. viii. 12

L. A.   C C concerneth the teaching of my Master, about which thou hast asked me—none can comprehend it, save the pure in heart who keep firmly to the faith; for I have taught the precepts of faith and love and peace: round about from Jerusalem even unto Illyricum I have fulfilled the word of peace; for I have taught that the people should give honour to one another; and I have taught that the strong and the rich should not be high-minded, and

p. 13 should not trust in mean riches; but should place their trust in God. And I have taught them to be content with simple food and clothing. I have taught the poor to rejoice in their poverty. I have taught fathers to teach their children good manners in the fear of God: and the children to be submissive to their parents in the saving preaching. And I have taught those who possessed authority to pay tribute. I have taught women to love their husbands, and to reverence them as lords; and the men to preserve faithfulness to the women. And I have taught masters to be considerate to their slaves with mildness; and slaves to serve the masters faithfully. And I have taught all believers to serve the One God, the

Gal. i. 11, Almighty, the Invisible, the Incomprehensible. This is my teaching; and
12 it is not of men, nor is it by man; but it was given to me by Jesus the Christ, Who spake to me from heaven."

And Nero said: "Thou, O Peter, what sayest thou?" and he replied, saying, "All that Paul hath spoken is true; for of old he persecuted the faith in the Christ. And a voice called to him from heaven, and taught him the truth; because he was not an enemy from hatred of our faith, but was in error; because many false Christs arise, like this Simon; and false apostles and false prophets, who appear with glorious signs and forms eager to make void the truth. And this man was obliged to destroy their cause; and put an end to their opinions; he who from his infancy had done no other thing than search into the secrets of the divine Law, by which he had become a disciple and a defender of the truth, and an assailant of falsehood. And as his persecution did not come from hatred, but from zeal for the Law, the Truth Himself [said unto him, 'I am the very Truth which thou art fighting against; cease to persecute Me[1]'].

p. 14 "And when he knew him thus he neglected what he was contending about and began to support this Way, which is the Christ's, which he had persecuted."

And Simon said: "O thou good Emperor! look at these two men how

---

[1] My photograph is here deficient; but the Latin version has: dicens ei! Ego sum veritas quam defendis: cessa me persequi.

they have conspired against me. I am the truth; and these two are conspiring against my religion."

And Peter said: "There is nothing whatever of truth in thee; but thou speakest all thy words in falsehood."

And Nero said: "O Paul! what sayest thou?"

Paul said: "I affirm that all the words which I have heard from Peter are my words, for we are of one mind; and have one Lord, Jesus the Christ."

And Simon said: "O thou good Emperor! dost thou imagine that I can speak with these two, who have conspired against me?"

And he turned to the Apostles of the Christ and said unto them: "Hearken, O Peter and Paul! if I am not able to do anything to you here, come ye to where it will be right for me to judge you."

And Paul said: "O thou good Emperor! see with what threats he would frighten us."

And Peter said: "Why is it not meet that we should laugh at thee, O vain man! cursed by the demons, who imagineth that he is able to act of his own accord?"

And Simon said: "I spare you until I can shew my power."

And Paul said: "See that thou go out hence acquitted."

And Peter said: "Except thou dost behold, O Simon, the power of our Lord Jesus the Christ, thou wilt not believe that thou art not a Christ."

And Simon said: "O thou glorious Emperor, do not believe these two, for these circumcised people are rogues."

And Paul said: "Before we knew the truth, we circumcised the body; and when the truth had been manifested we were circumcised with the circumcision of the heart, and are circumcised." p. 15

And Peter said: "If circumcision, O Simon, be bad, why hast thou been circumcised?"

And Nero said: "And, Simon, hast thou then been circumcised?"

And Peter said: "He could not deceive souls otherwise, except by his claiming to be a Jew, and appearing to teach the law of God."

And Nero said: "O Simon! I see that thou art persecuting these two with a hatred which encompasseth thee. And as I perceive that this is because of a great jealousy betwixt thee and their Christ, so I fear that thou wilt be vanquished by them, and wilt be involved in great misfortunes."

And Simon said: "Thou art mistaken, O thou Emperor!"

And Nero said: "In what am I mistaken? only I say what I see in thee: that I see thee a persistent enemy to Peter and Paul, and to their Master."

And Simon said : " The Christ did not become a teacher to Paul."

And Paul said : "Yea, by revealing Himself to me He trained me and taught me.   But do thou tell us about the question which I asked of thee, why wast thou circumcised ? "

And Simon said : " Why do ye both ask me about that ? "

And Paul said : " We have asked thee this question, hast thou an excuse to bring forward about what we have asked thee ? "

And Nero said : " Why art thou afraid, perplexed about answering it ? "

And Simon said : " Hearken, O thou Emperor ! at the time when circumcision was commanded to us by God, I received it, and therefore I was circumcised."

And Paul said : " Hast thou heard, O thou good Emperor ! what Simon hath said ; if circumcision be good, why hast thou betrayed the circumcised people, and forced them to be slain in imprisonment ? "

And Nero said : " I am not sure that I hear any true wisdom from either of you."

And Peter and Paul said : " If thou hast investigated our cause, whether it be true or evil, let not the cause be delayed, in order that what is necessary may be finished, what our Master hath promised to us."

p. 16   And Nero said : " And if I do not choose this ? "

And Peter said : " Not what thou wilt, but what He Who hath promised us willeth, shall happen."

And Simon said : " O thou glorious Emperor ! these two men are using the opportunity quickly of thy good-will and requirement."

And Nero said : " It is thou who hast silenced me with thy perplexities as to how I should look at it."

And Simon said : " How many beautiful things and wonders hast thou seen from me ! and I am amazed at how thou dost doubt."

And Nero said : " I neither doubt, nor do I praise anything of thine ; but what I ask you, answer me concerning it."

And Simon said : " Henceforth I shall answer thee nothing."

And Nero said : " Because thou art a liar, therefore thou sayest this.   But if I am not able to do anything to thee, the God Who is able will do to thee what thou dost merit."

And Simon said : " I shall answer thee nothing at all."

And Nero said : " And henceforth I shall count thee as nothing, for as I have found out that thou art a liar in everything, I desire not much speech.   Ye three have made manifest of yourselves that your opinion is of no account and there is no [need to] talk about it.   And ye have made me doubtful about all your confused sayings, so that I cannot believe in the cause of one of you."

And Peter said: "But we preach one God, the Father of the Christ, the Saviour, with the Holy Ghost, the One God, the Creator of all, Maker of Heaven and earth and the sea, and all the creatures that are in them, He Who is the true King, to Whose kingdom there is no end."

And Nero said: "Who is the Lord, the King?"

And Paul said: "He is the Saviour of all nations."

And Simon said: "I am he whom ye seek."

And Peter and Paul said: "There is nothing good in thee, O Simon Magus! the [man] filled with bitterness."

And Simon said: "Hearken, O Nero Cæsar! that thou mayest know p. 17 that these two men are liars, and I am the apostle from the heavens; that I may verily go to the heavens to-morrow, and may make those who believe in me blessed. And I will shew my anger on these two who do not believe in me and deny me."

And Peter and Paul said: "God hath called us for His glory; but thou art the called of the deceiver, hastening to torment."

And Simon said: "O Nero Cæsar! hearken unto me, and put far from thee these two whisperers; that when I shall have departed to heaven to my father I may be a forgiver unto thee; and have compassion on thee."

And Nero said: "And wherewith shall we prove this, that thou wilt go to heaven?"

And Simon said: "Command that a lofty tower be built of wood, so that when I mount on it, my angels may meet me and find me in the air; for they are not able to come to me on the earth among sinners."

And Nero said: "I would fain know, if thou wilt fulfil what thou sayest."

And then Nero commanded that a great high tower should be made in the place which is known as the Campus Martius, and that all plebeians of the city and all dignitaries should assemble to see the spectacle. And on the next day when the crowd were assembled, Nero commanded Peter and Paul to be brought; and he said unto them, "Now the truth will appear."

And Peter and Paul said: "We shall expose this thing; but our Lord Jesus the Christ, the Son of God, against Whom this man hath spoken falsely, He Himself will expose his hypocrisy."

And Paul turned unto Peter and said unto him: "I shall bow my knees unto God in supplication ; but as for thee, do thou pray, because thou art the chief; thou wast chosen first by the Lord, and appointed a shepherd." And when Paul bowed on his knees Peter prayed.

p. 18 Then he lifted up his eyes to Simon, saying : " Thou hast finished what thou hast begun ; for the time is come for the exposure of thy affair ; and He is calling us. Behold ! I see the Christ Who is calling me and Paul."

And Nero said : " And whither will ye go away from me without my consent ? "

And Peter answered : " To heaven, our Lord calleth us."

And Nero said : " And who is your Lord ? "

And Peter answered : " Jesus the Christ, Whom, behold ! I see calling us to Himself."

And Nero said : " And do ye affirm that ye are going to heaven ? "

And Peter answered: " To where the God Who is calling us shall please."

And Simon said : " O thou Emperor ! thou shalt know for certain at my departure to heaven that these two men are deceivers ; and at that time I shall send my angels unto thee, and I shall make thee come unto me."

And Nero answered : " Do henceforth what thou sayest."

And then Simon climbed in the presence of all the spectators into the tower, his head crowned with laurel-leaves. And he stretched out his hands and began to fly.

And when Nero saw him flying, he said unto Peter : " This Simon is the true man, and thou and Paul are deceivers."

And Peter answered: " At this time thou shalt know that we are true disciples of the Christ ; and this man shall be known that he is not a Christ, but a magician, and a cheat, and a malefactor."

And Nero said : " And do ye two still oppose him, though ye see him going into heaven ? "

Then Peter looked at Paul and said : " O Paul ! look and see."

And Paul raised his eyes[1], and his tears overflowed, when he saw Simon flying. And he said, " O Peter ! why dost thou linger in finishing what thou art hesitating about ? and lo ! our Lord Jesus the Christ is calling us."

And when Nero heard them, he mocked them scornfully, and said : " These two are frantic when they see themselves conquered."

And Peter said : " Thou shalt see now that we are not frantic, and we do not groan."

p. 19 And Paul turned and said unto Peter : " Finish what thou art hesitating about."

---

[1] Literally " gaze."

And Peter looked at [the] spectacle, and said: "I adjure you, O angels of Satan! who are bearing him in the air in order to deceive the hearts of those who do not believe in God the Creator of all things and in Jesus the Christ, Whom He raised from the dead on the third day— do not bear him up again from this hour, but let him go."

And straightway at that moment he was let go; and he fell on the place called the Sacra Via, which means the road to the temple; and he was split into four pieces and died the worst of deaths.

Then Nero commanded concerning Peter and Paul that they should be bound and chained in iron; and that the body of Simon should be kept carefully for three days, thinking that he would rise after three days.

And Peter replied: "He will not rise at all; for he has really died and perished in everlasting torments."

And Nero answered him: "And who hath commanded thee to do a terrible thing like this?"

And Peter replied: "His blasphemy and his calumny against my Lord Jesus the Christ have led him to this destruction."

And Nero said: "Shall I not destroy you with a bad destruction?"

And Peter said: "This is not from thee to purpose our destruction; but what our Master hath promised us must needs be accomplished."

And thereupon Nero called for Agrippa, his Vizier Admiral[1], and said unto him: "Two men are to be condemned with a severe sentence; they must needs die. And I therefore command that great iron stones be fastened on them and that they perish in the sea."

And Agrippa the Vizier answered: "O thou glorious Emperor! this which thou hast decided is not suitable; for Paul has made his cause manifest that he is more innocent than Peter."

And Nero said: "And with what kind of torture shall we destroy them?"

And Agrippa answered and said: "As it has occurred to my mind, a just sentence would be that Paul's head should be struck off; and Peter should be hung upon the cross, because he hath been the cause of a murder." p. 20

And Nero said: "Thou hast judged a proper judgment."

Then the two Apostles, Peter and Paul, were driven from the presence of Nero. And as for Paul, his head was struck off on the Via Ostiensis. And as for Peter, when he drew near to the cross, he said: "Our Lord Jesus the Christ, because He came down from heaven to earth, was lifted up on the cross upright. But as for me, who am deemed worthy to be called from

---

[1] Probably ναύαρχος, but the Arabic text is here very corrupt.

earth to heaven, it is meet that the head of my cross should be fixed on the earth, to make easy the journey of my feet to heaven; and because I am not worthy to be crucified like my Lord."

Then they reversed his cross, and nailed his feet upwards. And a numerous crowd were assembled, reviling Cæsar, insulting [him] and resisting because of the killing [of Peter]. And Peter forbade them, saying: " Do not shew your dislike to him : for he is the servant of Satan his father. But I must needs fulfil the command of my Lord, for a few days ago the brethren asked me about the tumult which had been caused against me by Agrippa, that I should go forth from the city. And the Lord Jesus the Christ met me, my Lord : and when I had worshipped Him, I said, 'Whither goest Thou, O Lord?' And He answered, saying unto me: 'I go to be crucified in Rome.' And I said unto Him : 'O Lord! hast Thou not been crucified once?' And the Lord answered and said : 'I saw thee fleeing from death ; and I desired to be crucified instead of thee.' And I said: 'O Lord! I will go and will fulfil Thy commandment.' And He said unto me, ' Fear not, for I am with thee.' And therefore, O my children! do not stand in my way[1]; for my feet shall go at once on the heavenly path. And grieve not, but rejoice in me: for to-day I shall receive the fruit of my toils."

p. 21   And when he had uttered these things he said: " O Thou Lord Jesus the Christ! I thank Thee, O Thou Good Shepherd! that the sheep which Thou hast confided to me sympathize with me. And I beseech Thee that Thou wouldest give them a good portion with me in Thy kingdom."

And when he had said this, he gave up his spirit to the Lord. And straightway there appeared noble men, their appearance being that of foreigners, saying one to the other: "We have come from Jerusalem on account of the two most holy disciples, the chief ones." And with them was a man whose name was Marcellus, the Lystrian[2], who had believed by the preaching of Peter, and had forsaken Simon, and he carried his body secretly, and they laid it down by the terebinth tree near the Naumachia, in a place which is called Vâtîcânôn. But as for the men who said that they had come from Jerusalem, they said to the people: " Rejoice and be glad, for ye have been deemed worthy to have the two great Teachers with you. And know that this Nero after not many days will disappear, and his kingdom shall be given to another."

And after these things an assembly of the people stood up against him

---

[1] Literally "impede my way."   [2] Latin "inlustri viro."

tumultuously: and when he knew it, he ran off to desert places; and his soul was driven away by hunger and thirst; and his body became a prey to wild beasts.

And devout people from the districts of the East determined that they would snatch away the bodies of the saints. And immediately there was a great earthquake in the city. And when they knew the cause, the people of the city assembled and took them away; and the men fled. Then the Romans took them and put them in a place three miles distant from the city; and kept them there for a year and seven months until the two temples were built, which they prepared in order to place them [there]. And after these things a crowd of people assembled and transported them with doxologies and hymns to p. 22 the two temples which had been built for them. And the most holy, noble Apostles Peter and Paul accomplished their testimony on the twenty-ninth day of the month Hazîrân, in Jesus the Christ our Lord, to Whom be glory and majesty to the end of the ages. Amen.

THE MARTYRDOM OF PETER.

In the name of the Father and the Son and the Holy Ghost,
the One God.

And this is a second story about the martyrdom of Peter, the chief of the Apostles, and his wonderful works in Rome, when the angel summoned him to it. May his prayers encompass us! Amen.

I desire to tell you this story also which is about the chief of the Apostles, Peter, the first of all the Apostles, as the Lord called him and said unto him: "Thou, Peter, chief of My disciples, the great city of Rome hath need of thee; for there are many people in it whom Satan hath led astray. Haste thee to go unto them, that thou mayest turn them from error and sins." And so it was that Peter, when he had heard that saying, began to weep before his Lord, and speak unto Him thus: "Thou knowest, O Lord! that I am very weak from old age, and poor, and I have no strength, and no power except in Thee, and I cannot walk, and Thou hast not commanded me, O Lord! and Thou hast not permitted me to possess anything of the rubbish of this fleeting world, neither gold, nor silver, nor clothing, nor beast of burden, nor staff that I can lean on, not to speak of other things. And behold! I see that Thou dost wish to send me into foreign countries, far distant, and to be reached by a hard road. And I beseech Thee, O my God! that Thou wouldest put me to death

p. 23 on this spot wherein Thy resurrection took place."

And the Christ said unto him: "Fear not to go thither, for thou art upon earth, and I am in heaven, and I will be sufficient for thee. And the king shall do obeisance unto thee; and the mighty men shall offer tribute to thy hands; and Rome shall acknowledge thee, and shall forsake her false gods fabricated and worshipped instead of the Creator for five thousand and five hundred years, because they have forgotten Me, and have not known Me. And in truth I am He Who provideth them with all good things and fine things. And I make My sun to rise upon them; and their mouths are full of blasphemy against Me."

And Peter answered Him, saying: "O Lord! have compassion upon me, and look at my weakness with the eye of Thy divine pity. Tell me how I shall be able to go to Rome, and to preach about Thy name in it; and it is a city of mighty men; and their clothing is of gold, and pearls, and bracelets, and fine raiment. And there are in it, as Thou knowest, haughty people, and stupid people who boast, and their proud children. And not one of the prophets hath ever entered it. And not a man in it extolleth Thy name. And this is a great command, difficult of purpose, far away to strive for; and I am poor and weak amongst mankind. And I shall go and shall die like a fool. For they, whenever they shall hear Thy name from my mouth, will kill me without mercy or pity. And my life will go for nought."

And the Lord said unto him: "And where is My divine strength, and My essential power? And where is My might, with which I have given unto thee the keys of heaven, and the keys of earth, and of the height? And go now, and fear not, and if thou shouldest see people who dispute with thee, shew them My miracles and My wonders. And if they do not hearken unto thy teaching, and do not accept thy preaching in My name, and do not believe thy sayings, tell the earth to swallow them up; and it shall obey thee by the authority of My Deity, and the might of My power, which I have given thee. And be not anxious about an argument where- p. 24 with to contend, nor the answer which thou shalt make to them; for My Holy Spirit shall speak on thy lips and thy tongue immediately in everything that thou shalt wish; and everything that thou shalt ask Me and shalt entreat of Me shall be quickly given to thee in the presence of the nobles. And go now and tell whomsoever thou wilt of the dead to arise by the strength of My Deity. And likewise do thou sprinkle the eyes of the blind that they may see; and they will obey thee. And wheresoever thy voice shall fall thence shall issue My mercy."

Then the Lord called to the sea, and it answered Him. And the Lord said unto Peter, "Arise now, and walk upon the sea, in like manner as thou dost walk upon the land. And walk above the water, as thou dost walk above the dust." And Peter did this at the command of his Lord. And he walked above the sea until he came to Rome. And he sat at the gate of the city, and he saw a crowd of people; and they were worshipping before the impure images and the idols of the unclean demons; and the devils harangued them from inside of them. And when Peter saw this action he trembled violently. Then he turned back toward the shore of the sea, terrified. And when he was with his three friends amongst the disciples, who were Thomas, and Andrew, and John, Peter said unto them: "Peace be upon you, O my brethren!"

And they returned his greeting in like manner.

And he said unto them: "Pray for me, for I am going out from among you, in the appearance of a dying man; and I am journeying on the road which the Lord hath told me of."

And they said unto him: "Go, O disciple of the Lord and saint of God! His Spirit is with thee, and He will not lose thee, and thou shalt not go away from us; for He is our Lord and our Master."

And Peter went until he came to the city of Rome. And he sat outside the gate above a dunghill; and he had ragged clothes on him; and he cast dust upon his head, and began to weep. And the gatekeeper had a leprous daughter, and she looked at him, sitting weeping, and the dust upon his head. And she went to her father the gatekeeper, and said unto him: "O father! there is a feeble, poor old man here, in ragged clothes, and he is weeping and scattering dust on his head. And, father! I have seen a number of poor people, but anything like the poverty of this man I have never witnessed. And if thou dost approve, O father! I will go unto him and bring him to thy house, and I will give him food and drink; and I shall be blessed by his prayer. I will do this by thy command."

And he said unto her: "Go, O my daughter! to that poor old man, and take him into my dwelling: and do thou take his prayer. As for me, I do not need his prayer."

And the girl, the daughter of that gatekeeper, came unto Peter, who was sitting, weeping. And she said unto him: "Rise, O father! and do not weep, for thou hast attained thy desire."

And Peter arose, and went with her into her house. And she set for him a chair of silver, and he sat upon it. And he sought water from her; and she brought him a vessel with some water in it; and she covered her hands with her sleeves. And he said unto her: "O my daughter! as for thy house, thou hast received me in it, and hast made me to sit on a silver chair; and hast given me to drink from a cup of water. And why dost thou cover up thy hands from me? tell me."

And she said unto him: "I will tell thee, O father! As for me, my father hath married me to one of the nobles of Rome. And it was upon the night in which I went to the house of my husband, this disease came upon me to this extremity. And I have been since that time as thou dost see, a leper."

Then she uncovered her hands to him, and shewed him them. And she said unto him: "Because of this I have covered my hands from thee."

And Peter hearkened, and took that vessel, in which was the rest of the water: and he bowed and prayed over it with a true conscience, acceptable, spiritual, nothing material being mingled with it. Then he held the vessel out to her, and said: "Wash thyself with this water."

p. 26

And she did it; and straightway she was cleansed and healed from that disease, and she became like the snow, as if sickness had never touched her. And when she saw that, she was terribly frightened. Then she went away, going to the gatekeeper, her father. And she said: "O father! why dost thou sit here? Arise and look at me, that thou mayest see this wonder."

And she uncovered her arms for him and her face, and shewed him how the leprosy had ceased; and her body was pure from it, like silver, and she was cleansed. And he wondered greatly at it. And he said unto her: "What is this thing, O my daughter? and what was the manner of it? tell me."

And she said unto him in a shrill voice: "Truly I say unto thee, O father! that the God of truth hath entered our dwelling to-day."

And her father went with her to Peter. And he said unto him: "O thou old man! cure the rest of my daughter's body from this leprosy. And ask of me what thou dost choose of gold or silver, that I may give it thee."

And Peter said unto him: "I will heal the rest of thy daughter's body from this leprosy; but I have no need of thy gold nor thy silver. Yet I desire from thee that thou wouldest serve our Lord the Christ; and leave these impure images, which thou hast hitherto worshipped."

And the gatekeeper said unto him: "Thou hast this from me, that I will do as thou wouldest have me when thou hast cured her."

Then he was baptized. And he [Peter] set up a baptismal font at once. And he took the girl, and dipped her in that hour, and cleansed her as if nothing of it had ever been in her. And when her father saw this, he believed in the Christ, and forsook the images with the demons whom he had worshipped. And Peter abode with them for a day and a night. Then he desired to enter the city. And the believing gate- p. 27 keeper came in and looked at him, and said unto him: "Whither dost thou desire to go? Know that thou canst not enter the city of Rome, and [amongst] its people; for they have a festival; and if they see thee in these rags, I fear for thee concerning them that they will kill thee."

And Peter said unto the gatekeeper: "I must needs enter; for my Lord hath sent me as upon this day. And I cannot rebel against the commandment of my Lord."

Then Peter went until he entered the city. And he heard the people crying and saying: "Whomsoever we find not finely dressed in brocade and purple and gold embroidery with many jewels, and going towards the shrine of the honoured gods, it is lawful to kill him."

And the people looked at Peter, and he was clothed in rags. And they said unto him: "O thou foolish old man! where dost thou wish [to go] in these rags which are upon thee? for if the Emperor of Rome see thee he will kill thee. Go and put on gold and purple, and come to the shrine of the gods."

And Peter said unto the kings, and the soldiers, and the crowds: "This is the raiment of my Lord Who gave it to me; and there is no God but He." And they forbade it to him with the worst of refusals. And they were wroth with him with a great wrath. Then they wished to stone him with stones for his saying that the Christ was his Lord. And when Peter saw a thing like this, he went to a towering place where their gods were. And he turned towards the Lord with a true conscience, acceptable and spiritual in that place.

Then the Emperor of Rome came out, and with him were many kings and crowds, and soldiers innumerable. And with him were a hundred girls whom they had bedecked; and (the people) wished them to be p. 28 sacrificed; and made vows to the gods and the demons. And when Peter saw this, he lifted up his eyes to heaven, and said: "O my Lord and my God! I have no patience after what I see. O Lord! grant Thy strength which is needed in this hour."

And He responded to the supplication of Peter, and sent a great cloud and a strong wind also, and all these images fell and were broken. And when the Emperor saw that, he said unto the girls: "Go in peace; for my empire hath vanished by reason of this hut which is upon this high place." For fire had come out upon the crowds from the neighbourhood of the eminence upon which Peter was.

And at that moment a messenger from the Emperor's house approached him, and said unto him: "O Emperor of Rome! what causeth thee to linger when thy beloved son is dead?"

Then the Emperor commanded the rest of the kings, and the soldiers, and the crowds to follow him; and there were many thousands, who could not be numbered; and they followed him until he reached his dwelling. And his wife came out, and said unto him: "Thy son and thy beloved one is dead. Come, let us weep for our only child."

And then this girl came who had been a leper, and she went in to the

Emperor and said unto him: "What causeth thee to weep, O thou Emperor! for thy son? and there is a very old man in the country, feeble and poor, wearing ragged clothes; and if thou wert to send to him, he would raise thee up thy son alive this day."

And the Emperor said unto her: "O my daughter! speak not thus ; if thou dost affirm that the dead rise, and the blind see, and the stones speak; and that my only one may rise. Put away these sayings from thee, and come, weep with us for our child, thou . and all thy companions."

And she said unto him: "O Emperor of Rome! dost thou know me?"

And he said unto her: "Yea, thou art well known as the leprous p. 29 daughter of that gatekeeper."

And she said unto him: "I am not leprous." Then she uncovered to him her face and her arms.

And the Emperor said unto her: "What is this? and how did thy cure happen?"

And she said unto him: "Truly I say unto thee, O thou Emperor! that there is a feeble, poor old man in Rome; and he it is of whom I reminded thee; and he it is who will raise up thy son to thee this day."

And the Emperor sent unto the kings, and the soldiers, and they said unto them: "Seek for this old man with diligence and desire. And if ye find him in the city, bring him to us in his rags."

And when they waxed earnest in seeking him they found him; and they set him before the Emperor. And the Emperor said unto him: "O thou old man! behold, I say unto thee! that if thou dost raise up my dead child alive this day, my empire and all that pertaineth to it shall be thine."

And Peter said unto him: "I raise up thy son to thee, but I desire not thine empire. Only I desire from thee that thou worship my Lord, the Creator of heaven and of earth. He is Jesus the Christ, beside Whom there is no God; and that thou forsake these images and demons whom thou dost serve."

And the Emperor said unto him: "I will do that, O Peter!"

And Peter said unto him: "Send unto the kings, and the tribes, and the soldiers from the rest of thy dominion, those of them who are within, and those of them who are without. Then collect them and bear this thy dead son upon a couch; and come unto the place of thy gods whom thou dost worship."

Then he sent those who assembled all the people of his dominion and his empire to him, those domestic and distant[1].

---

[1] Perhaps " Cisalpin and Transalpine."

And he caused his son to be borne upon a couch, and he came with it to the place of his gods whom he had worshipped.

p. 30   Then Peter stood facing the east, by the side of the couch on which the dead man was; and he made supplication to his Lord with a true conscience, spiritual [and] acceptable. And our Lord heard his supplication, and raised up his dead one to him. Then he came down from the couch and approached Peter until he worshipped him. And he said unto him: "Peace be upon thee, O thou whose supplication the Lord hath heard! and hath given me back my spirit after my death, and [after] its departure from my body."

Then the lad drew near to his father and said unto him: "Woe unto thee, O father! in what sins and what darkness we have been! Woe unto thee, O father! for the angels were conversing with this blessed old man."

And in that place God commanded Peter, and he arose and set up the font where the images of their gods had stood. And he baptized the son of the Emperor, and his father, and cleansed them, and the rest of the army and the kings. And when Peter saw that he could not baptize the people all together, he took some of that water and sprinkled [it] upon them. And on whomsoever a particle or a drop of that water fell he was baptized. And whosoever believed in God was cleansed. And all who were present of peoples and tribes worshipped His Son, to Whom be majesty and power at all times and always. Amen. *May God forgive him who readeth and hearkeneth; and have mercy upon the poor copyist.*

THE MARTYRDOM OF PAUL.

This is the Martyrdom of the Blessed Paul, disciple of Jesus, which he finished in the city of Rome, on the twenty-ninth day of Hazîrân. May his prayers preserve us! Amen.

The blessed disciples, Luke who was from Barûâ, and Titus who was from Dalmatia, were waiting in Rome for the arrival of Paul. And when he came to them, and beheld them, and they beheld him, they all rejoiced exceedingly at this. And Paul hired a dwelling outside of the town, and abode in it with the brethren ; and he preached in the name of the Lord ; and taught every one who came unto him, and his words were reported in the city of Rome; and many people followed him, believing in the Christ, when they saw the wonders which God wrought by his hands. He healed those who were stricken with divers diseases in the name of the Lord Jesus the Christ and by the sign of the honoured cross. And many of the household of the Emperor Nero followed him ; and there was great joy in the city. And a boy whose name was Patricius, the butler at the Emperor's table, was present at the place where Paul was teaching during the night to hear his doctrine ; and he was unable to approach him because of the multitude of the crowd who were round about him. And he climbed to a high place and leant over it[1], and he was overcome with sleep ; and he fell from the top of that high place and died. And the news came to the Emperor Nero that Patricius was dead. And he mourned for him with a great grief, for he had been very fond of him.

And when Paul knew by the Spirit what had happened, he said unto the brethren and to those about him : " Satan, the enemy, desireth to tempt us. Go forth to the outside of the gate ; ye will find a dead boy lying down : carry him and bring him to me." And they went out and found the dead man as he had said: and they came in with him to Paul the Blessed Disciple.

And when the multitude beheld him and knew that it was Patricius, they were greatly perturbed, because they knew that he enjoyed great favour with the Emperor. And Paul said unto them : "O ye brethren! be not shaken and fear ye not ; in this hour your faith will be manifest. Rise, let us make supplication unto the Lord Jesus the Christ, that He

Cod. Vat.
694
f. 12 a

f. 12 b

---

[1] Literally " projected."

L. A.   E E

may have compassion upon us; and may give life unto this dead man, lest we all die."

f. 13 a And Paul straightway fell prostrate on the ground and besought the Lord with continual supplication and lifted up his head. Thereupon the dead man arose whole, with no pain whatever about him.

And Paul sent him to the palace of Nero the Emperor his master. And Nero was in the bath at the time when he heard of the death of Patricius, and after he had come out he went to his house and found that Patricius had already arranged the table as was his wont. And all his retainers came out to him telling the news of Patricius being alive, and that he was at the table as usual. And when the Emperor Nero looked at Patricius, he said unto him: "Art thou alive? and who is it that hath restored thee to life after thy death?"

And Patricius' heart was filled with the grace of the Holy Spirit; and he said unto his master: "The Lord Jesus the Christ, the Eternal King, Who is thy Lord and thy God; He it is Who hath brought me to life."

Nero the Emperor said unto him: "Is that He Who thou dost think shall reign for ever; and He Who shall abolish all the kingdoms and the
f. 13 b kings and those who rule them, which are beneath the heavens?" [And Patricius said:][1] "He shall abolish them; and He alone shall endure for ever. And there is none beside Him, and no king shall conquer His dominion!"

And Nero struck him on the hands and said unto him: "And thou, Patricius, dost thou believe in that?"

And Patricius answered him: "Yea, O my lord! I believe in Him, for it was He Who made me alive from the dead."

And whilst he was saying this, there drew nigh unto the Emperor four noblemen, servants of the Empire, whom he loved, and preferred to all people who were in the palace, those who were never absent from his presence at any time. And these were their names: Farnsâs, Festus, Farstus, Kanmastus. They replied unto the Emperor, saying: "Know, O thou Emperor! that from this hour we have enlisted in the palace of the Heavenly, the Eternal King, Jesus the Christ, the Son of the Living God." And this frightened the Emperor Nero, and he commanded that they should be tortured with a cruel torture, and afterwards be cast into prison. And the Emperor went in the fierceness
f. 14 a of [his] anger and hatred against every one who believed in the Eternal Christ. And he commanded in this manner, saying: "Whosoever shall be

---

[1] These words seem to have been dropped from the Arabic text. They are found in the Latin one.

found to have enlisted in the palace of the King, Jesus the Christ, shall be slain."

And when all the men of the soldiery heard what the Emperor had commanded them, they dispersed themselves all over the city, and arrested every one who believed in the Lord Jesus the Christ, and brought them before him in chains. And there was a great crowd of prisoners hustling each other, gazing at Paul and listening to his words, and to all that passed between him and the Emperor. And when the Emperor beheld him in chains, he said unto him : " O thou man who dost belong to the Eternal, the Mighty King ! behold thou hast been delivered unto me in chains. Tell me what hath brought thee [to do] this deed upon which thou hast ventured, to come into my city, and to collect soldiers from my kingdom for thy King ? "

Saint Paul replied to him in the presence of them all: " O thou Emperor ! it is not from thy kingdom [alone] that we collect soldiers for my King, but from all the world. Thus hath our Lord commanded us that we should f. 14 b not shut a door before any man ; and it would be incumbent on thee also to enlist in His palace. Because this kingdom and this glory will not save thee unless thou fall down and worship this King, and beg Him to grant thee salvation ; because He will come to judge the world and give life to all who believe in Him. But those who do not believe in Him, and the sinners will He judge, and will deliver them over to everlasting punishment." And Nero the Emperor did not believe in what Paul said unto him, and commanded that whosoever believed should be burnt alive with fire, Paul being present in chains, and commanded concerning Paul that his head[1] should be struck [off] as the law of the Romans enjoins. And he delivered Paul to the chamberlains that they might take off his head. And their names were Ligos and Justus. And they bore him out from the presence of the Emperor.

And Paul began to speak unto them in words[2] .   .   .   .   .

.   .   .   .   the help of God, and to all who followed f. 15 a him. Because many people had gathered themselves together unto him, wishing to behold his martyrdom. And in the city of Rome there was a great power of the Devil assisting in the slaughter of those who believed in Jesus the Christ. And an innumerable multitude of them were slain. And the people of Rome, the chief men of the city, assembled at the palace of the Emperor and cried out to the king, saying : " O thou Emperor !

---

[1] Literally "neck."   [2] Lacuna

thou wilt slay these men; and they are Romans. Why dost thou weaken the empire of Rome and her armies?" Then he commanded that the sword should be lifted up; and that they should not seek for the Christ in order that he might examine them.

And after this commandment the man who had smitten Paul brought him into the presence of the Emperor, in order that he might also hear his words about the people of Rome. And his amazement increased at the number of the multitude who had responded to the preaching of Paul.

Paul answered and said unto the Emperor, "This life of mine, which f. 15 b belongeth to my King, is not a life which hath a certain length, but is an eternal life which hath no end. And thou hast commanded that my head should be taken off, and yet I appear unto thee, and I am alive, that thou mayest know the truth of my words; that I live to my King, Jesus the Christ, Who will judge the quick and the dead; and will recompense every one according to his works, whether it be good or evil."

And when Nero heard this from the speech of Paul, he made a sign in anger to the chamberlain that he should be speedily slain. And when Festus and Ligos the chamberlains heard, they bore him out to take off his head [and] they said unto Paul: "Where is your King, He in Whom ye believe and Whom ye will not reject, but will be patient in all this torture because of Him?"

Paul answered them: "O ye men! over whom error reigneth, and want of the knowledge of God, turn ye and repent, that ye may be saved from the wrath which is to come upon the unbelievers. It is not as ye imagine: that we collect soldiers like yourselves for an earthly king, but that we enlist [them] for the palace of the Heavenly King, Who because of the f. 16 a sins of the world is coming to judge the earth. And to whosoever believeth in Him He will give life eternal."

And when the chamberlains heard [a saying] like this, they did obeisance unto him, saying: "Make us meet to be the subjects of this King and we will set thee free so that thou mayest go whithersoever thou wilt."

Paul said unto them: "I am no coward, and I fear not your torture, that I should flee from God; but I am the slave of my master Jesus the Christ, the Living King. For if I knew that this death were an eternal death, I should do what ye say. But I shall live with my King for ever. And I am obedient to Him, and I shall go to Him, and with Him I shall return when He cometh in the glory of His Father." The chamberlains said unto him: "How canst thou, after thy neck hath been struck, be

in the second life?" And whilst they were speaking, the Emperor sent
two messengers to learn if Paul's neck had been struck or no. And when
they saw him in life, Paul said unto them: "Believe in the Living God Who   f. 16 b
will make alive from the dead whosoever believeth in Him, and will give
them life for ever."

They answered him, saying: "Behold, thou shalt die, and if we see
thee rise from the dead, we will believe." And they returned to the
Emperor.

But Ligos and Festus continued to enquire of Paul, saying unto
him: "Teach us the path of life and salvation."

Paul said unto them: "Go ye early to-morrow to the grave in which
my body shall be left; ye shall find two men standing praying; they are
Titus and Luke; it is they who will give you the token of salvation; and
will present you to the Lord Jesus the Christ, the true God." And Paul
looked towards the east in the presence of all who had come to behold his
martyrdom, and he lifted up his hands and prayed for a long while in the
Hebrew language.

And when he had finished his prayer, he spoke again to all the
multitude who were present about faith in God, until a great company
believed through the sweetness of his words, and the light which was in his   f. 17 a
face, and the grace which rested upon him.

And the two messengers returned to Nero the Emperor, and told
him that they had found Paul speaking to Ligos and Festus and
teaching them his faith. And the Emperor was very wroth, and sent
a brutal swordsman to strike off the head of Paul forthwith. And when
the swordsman came the saint stretched out his neck and was silent;
he did not speak, and stood for a long time with outstretched neck; and
the swordsman standing over against him with his sword drawn, and his
hands shaking, being powerless to bring it down upon him.

And at last the swordsman stood and struck the saint a blow which
made his head fall upon the ground; and milk and blood issued from his
holy body, until it left stains on the garments of the swordsman. And
the multitude were amazed, and glorified God, Who had given this power
and great gifts to His holy disciple. And the swordsman returned and
reported to the Emperor what had happened. And Nero wondered
at it, he and all the philosophers who were about him, and remained
perplexed.

And when it was the ninth hour of the day, Paul appeared unto them,   f. 17 b
and said unto the Emperor: "I am the captain who belongeth to Jesus

222   THE MARTYRDOM OF PAUL.

the Christ, I am he who came to thy city to take from it soldiers for my King.   Behold, I am alive, I have not died ; but as for thee, many evils shall come upon thee ; for thou hast shed much blood of innocent people. And after a few days all that I have said shall come upon thee."

And when Paul had said this, he departed from him.   And the Emperor Nero commanded that all who were in prison should be released, who believed in the Lord Jesus the Christ.   And Patricius, the page of the Emperor, and another whose name was Ligos, and Festus, of the Emperor's retainers, went early to the grave of Paul.   And when they drew nigh to it, they beheld two men standing and praying, and Paul standing in the midst of them in great glory.   And they were afraid, and trembled from fear of what they had beheld of his glory.   And as for Titus and Luke, they were afraid, and fled from their presence.   But the servants of the Emperor, who have been mentioned already, ran in pursuit of them, and

f. 18a rejoined them and said unto them : "We are not seeking you for death; but rather that ye may give us life eternal, as Paul said, he who hath just stood in the midst of you."   And when Titus and Luke heard words like these from them, they rejoiced greatly, and spake to them with words of exhortation; and made known to them the faith in our Lord Jesus the Christ, and gave them the token of the life everlasting.

The Martyrdom of Saint Paul was finished on the twenty-ninth of Hazîrân, in the peace of the Lord Jesus the Christ.   May his prayers preserve us and be with us henceforth and for ever and ever !   Amen.

PALIMPSEST FRAGMENTS OF THE ACTS OF JUDAS THOMAS.

...Judas. And the king said unto him, "What art dost thou know to practise?" Judas saith unto him, "I am a carpenter, the servant of a carpenter and an architect." He saith unto him, "What dost thou know to make?" Judas saith unto him, "In wood I know (how) to make yokes and ploughs, and rigging for barges and ferry-boats, and masts for ships; and in hewn stone, tombstones, monuments (ναούς), and palaces for kings." The king saith unto Judas, "I also want such an artificer." He saith unto him, "Wilt thou build me a palace?" Judas saith unto him, "I will build it and finish it, for I am come to work at building and carpentering." Sin. Syr.
30
f. 153 a
Wright
vol. II.
p. 159

And he took him and went outside the gate of the city, and was talking with him about his constructing of the palace and about its foundations, how they should be laid. And when he had reached the place where the king wished him to build a palace for him, he said unto Judas, "Here I wish you to build for me a palace." Judas saith unto him, "(Yea), for this is also a place which is suitable for it." Now it was of this sort...... it was a meadow, and there was plenty of water near it. The king saith unto him, "Begin to build here." Judas saith unto him, "Now I cannot build at this time." The king saith unto him, "And at what time wilt thou be able to build?" Judas saith unto him, "I will begin in Teshrī (Oct.—Nov.) and I will finish in Nīsan (April)." The king saith unto him, "All buildings are built in summer, and thou buildest in winter!" Judas saith unto him, "Thus (only) is it possible for the palace to be built." The king saith unto him, "Why not trace it out for me, that I may see, because after a long time I shall come hither?" And Judas came and took a cane, and began to measure; and he left doors towards the east for light; and windows towards the west for air; and (he made) the bake-house to the south; and the water-pipes for the service (of the house) to the north. The king saith unto him, "Verily thou art a good artificer, and art worthy to serve a king"; and he left a large sum of money, and departed from him. Wright
p. 160

f. 153 b

And he was sending silver and gold to him from time to time. And Judas was going about in the villages and cities, and was ministering to the poor, and was making the afflicted comfortable, and was saying, "What is the king's shall be given to the king, and many shall have rest." Wright
p. 161

Then the king despatched messengers to Judas, and sent a messenger to him (thus): " Send me (word) what thou hast done, and what I shall send (thee)."

f. 158 a
Wright
p. 171
l. 26
p. 172

" I (am he who) stirred up Caiaphas and Herod by false slander, which is mine. I am he who gave a bribe to Judas, that he might deliver up the Messiah to death. I am he to whom the power of Shēōl (was given[1]). I am he whom the Son of Mary hath seized by force and taken what was His from me. I am the kinsman of him who is to come from the east, to whom the power is given."

And when the snake had said these things, because (Judas) was seeking ....who were subject......" feared that thy end was come." He saith unto him, " In the name of Jesus. Who until now hath struggled with thee for the sake of His own people, that thou suck out the poison which thou hast cast into this youth ; and that he may rise (alive)." The snake said unto him, " My destruction is not yet come, as thou hast said. Why compellest thou me to take (back) what I have put into this (youth), for were even my father to suck out and take (back) what he hath cast into the creation, it would be his destruction." The Apostle saith unto him, " Shew, then, the nature of thy father." And the snake came, and put his mouth upon the wound of the youth, who had become like purple (and) became white, and the snake was swelling. And when he had drawn out the whole of the poison from the youth, he sprang upright and ran and......at the feet of the Apostle Judas, and fell down and worshipped him. Then the snake burst, and the place in which the poison of the snake fell, Judas commanded the king and his brother to fill up the place, and to lay foundations, and make in it houses—hostelries for strangers.

And the youth was sorrowful, and wept [and said with] his [many] tears [unto the Apostle ; " What] wrong have I done [unto thee, O man] in whom are [two] likenesses?" "And as thou wilt........to him according as I see. For I have said unto this [man]......that thou art His Apostle, and say unto thee: ' I have many things to shew through thee, and thou hast many works to accomplish for Me, for which thou shalt receive their reward ; and thou shalt give life unto many that they also may become on high and in the light, as sons of God. Do thou, therefore, bring to life this

Wright
p. 173

f. 158 b

Wright
p. 175
l. 6

---

[1] Probably ⟨ܡܘܬܒܐ⟩.

youth, who hath been smitten by his enemy, because thou at all times beholdest thy Lord.'   Yea......hither."

...the Apostle (had said these things), all the multitudes were looking to f. 161 a Wright p. 181 l. 10 see what answer he was about to give to the colt.   And when the Apostle had stood a long time wondering and looking up to heaven, he said unto the colt, "Who art thou? and what is thine errand, that by thy mouth great wonders are uttered, that are more excellent than many?"   The colt saith unto him: "I am of that stock that served Balaam the prophet, and (thy God) and thy Lord rode upon my kin; and I am sent unto thee to give thee rest,......and that that other portion might be added unto me, which I have got to-day in order to serve thee and which will be taken away from me when I have served thee."   Judas saith unto it, "He who hath sent thee, and hath given thee this gift now, is to be relied on to give it hereafter too in full to thee and to thy kindred; for I am too little and weak for this mystery."   And he would not ride upon it.

And the colt was begging of him and supplicating him that it might be Wright p. 182 blessed by his riding it: and he mounted and rode it.   And the people were going after and before the Apostle; and people were running to see what would happen to the colt.   And when they reached the gate of the f 161 b city he dismounted from it and said unto it, "Go, be preserved as thou hast been."   And in that hour the colt fell down and died.   And all who were there were sorry for it, and were saying to the Apostle: "We entreat of thee, bring it to life again."   The Apostle saith unto them: "It is not because I am unable to bring this colt to life, that I do not bring it to life, but that perhaps this is what would be a profit to it."   And he commanded those who were with him to dig a place and bury its body; and they did as he commanded them.

And the Apostle went into the city, the multitudes accompanying him; and he was thinking of going to the house of the family of the youth whom he had brought to life, because he had begged (it) much.   And suddenly a fair woman cried with a loud voice and said unto him: "Apostle of the new God, who art come to India! servant of the holy God, Who by thee is proclaimed both the Saviour of the souls of those who come unto Him, Wright p. 183 and the Healer of the bodies of those who are tortured by the enemy; (thou) art become the cause of life to the whole people; permit me and command me, that they may bring me before thee, and that I may tell thee

what hath befallen me, and perchance I may get hope from thee, and these
who are standing by may be greatly strengthened in the God who is proclaimed by thee." And she saith unto him: "I am not slightly tormented by
the enemy, lo, for the space of five years. For I was sitting in ease, and peace
was around me on all sides, and I had no concern about anything, because
I knew no care. And it happened one day, as I was coming out of the
bath, a man met me, who seemed to me as one troubled in his aspect; his
voice and his speech were very weak. And he said unto me: 'I and thou
shalt be in one love, and do thou have intercourse with me with the intercourse of a man and a woman.' And I said unto him: 'I did not yield myself
to my betrothed, because I cannot bear a man; and to thee, who wishest to
have intercourse with me as in adultery, how can I give myself to thee?'
And I said to my maiden who was with me: 'See the impudence of this
young man, who talks as far as licentiousness with me.' And she said unto
me: 'Who is the old man whom we saw talking with thee?' And when
I had gone home to my supper, although my heart made me afraid of him,
because he had appeared to me in two forms; and I went to sleep thinking
of him And in the night he came, and......on me, and had filthy intercourse with me and by day too I saw him and fled from him; but by night
he used to come (in the shape) of his race and torture me. And lo, up to
the present, as thou seest,......for five years he hath not left me alone. But
because I know and believe that both devils and spirits and demons are
subject to thee and dread thy prayer............ (O) evil that cannot be
repressed! O enemy who art never at rest! O envious one who art never
quiet! O [thou who hast many] shapes and appearest as thou wilt, but
thy black colour changeth not, because it is thy nature! O bitter tree,
the fruits of which are like unto it! O lying slanderer, who strivest with
those that are not thine! who standing upon its...and upon its head,
dares! O wickedness, that creepeth like a serpent,...at virtue!"......And
when the Apostle had said these things, the enemy (came and stood)
before him, no one...

f. 170 a

f. 170 b
Wright
p. 184

Wright
p. 185

f. 167 b
Wright
p. 205
l. 13

and we too, if we bear not the burden that beseemeth this name, shall
receive punishment; and it shall be to us for judgment and vengeance."
    And Judas prayed with them a long prayer, and committed them
to our Lord, and said: "Lord of all the worlds which await Him, Lord
and Father of the spirits which hope in Him! deliver from error Thy[1]

---

[1] MS. "His."

people, freeing (them) from corruption and from fear and slavery those who obey Thee[1] and come to Thy[2] place of refuge; be Thou with the flock of Xanthippus, and anoint his flock with the oil of life.................. and guard it from wolves and from robbers, that they may not snatch it out of his hand." (And he laid his hand[3]) upon them and said unto them, "The peace of Jesus be with you, and may He go with us also."

And the Apostle set out to go on the way; and all of them were accompanying him with weeping, and were adjuring him by his Lord (to be) mindful (of them) in his prayers and not to forget them. And when the Apostle had mounted he sat in the chariot, and all the brethren remained behind. The general came and said unto the driver : ......" Now I am praying that I may be worthy to sit beneath the feet of the Apostle of our Lord Jesus the Christ, and to be his driver on the road which many know, that He may be my guide on that road on which each one of us is going."

And when they had gone about a mile Judas begged of the general, and made him get up beside him, and persuaded the driver to sit on his place. And as they were going along the road, and Judas was accompanying the general he conversed. And the cattle became tired from the much driving wherewith he drove them, (and) they stood and would not stir. And the general was struck with great pity; and knew not what to do; and (he thought) of running on foot, and bringing other cattle wherever he could (get them), or horses, because his time was becoming short. And when the Apostle saw (this), he said unto him : "Be not afraid and be not agitated, only believe surely in Jesus the Christ, He about Whom I told thee, and thou shalt see great wonders." For Judas saw a herd of wild asses feeding some distance off the highway, and he said unto the general : "If thou believest in Jesus the Christ, the Son of God, go to that herd and say unto them : 'Judas the Apostle of Jesus the Christ, the Son of God, saith; Let four of you come, for I require them.'" And the general went fearing, because...

Wright p. 206

f. 167 a

Wright p. 207

build for themselves, nor to practise the art of hewing stones, which stone-cutters know as their craft : but we are commanded (to do) some-

f. 164 b Wright p. 219 l. 23 p. 220

---

[1] MS. "Him."   [2] MS. "His."
[3] These words have been dropped out of the MS.

thing; that we should not do anything against any one[1]; and that we should beware of adultery, the head of all evils: and from murder, by reason of which the curse came upon others[2]; and from theft......which brought Judas Iscariot unto hanging; and from gluttony, which brought the curse upon Adam[3]; and from covetousness, unto which man is subject, he doth not discern what he doeth; and from vain-glory, and from destroying slander; and from evil actions and from deeds of shame; and from intercourse with women and from unclean connexion, in which there is eternal condemnation; and this is the mother which still trembleth[1]; and it seizeth the uplifted by force, and casteth them down to the depth, and bringeth them under power; and they do not discern what they do, and their works become hidden from them. And conduct yourselves with holiness, for this is chosen before God more than all the virtues, and with temperance, for this is conversation with the living God, and it giveth eternal life; and......the death of the flesh. (And with humility) for this is weighed with everything, and is heavy, and out-weigheth them, and gaineth the crown; and with gentleness, and............

f. 164 a   the needy;.........(with) holiness......all good works; for he who is not sanctified, is unable to do anything good; for all the virtues are after this of holiness. And holiness is seen of God, and destroyeth evil. Holiness is pleasing to God; therefore it proceedeth from Him. For

Wright p. 221   holiness is the athlete who is not overcome. Holiness is the truth that is unshaken. Holiness is the foundation that falleth not. Holiness is worthy to belong to God. Holiness is that which pleaseth when it is found with many. Holiness destroyeth corruption. Holiness is the messenger of concord, which bringeth the tidings of peace. Temperance (belongeth) unto him who acquireth it[4]. Temperance careth for naught but how it may please its Lord. Temperance holdeth on by hope, awaiting deliverance. Temperance sitteth at all times in tranquillity, because it doth nothing that is odious. Temperance is a life of rest and joy to all who acquire it, and exalteth those who are nigh to it......

f. 157 b
Wright
p. 262
l. 4   never pass away." And when Karīsh had heard these things, he went (and) told them to King Mazdai. And King Mazdai said: "Let us fetch him

[1] The reading is here doubtful.
[2] Dr Wright's text has "upon Cain."
[3] Wright "which removed Esau from his birthright."
[4] A phrase must have been dropped here.

and destroy him." But Karīsh his friend said unto the king, "Have patience with him a little, and bring him out, and speak unto him, and frighten him; perhaps he will persuade Mygdonia to be with me as she was."

And King Mazdai sent and fetched Judas the Apostle of the Lord. And all the prisoners were grieved that Judas the Apostle had departed from them, and were seeking him and saying: "Even the pleasure which we had they have taken away from us." And Mazdai said unto Judas: "Why teachest thou a doctrine which gods and men abhor, and in which there is nothing pleasing?" Judas saith unto him: "What do I teach that is bad?" Mazdai saith unto him: "Thou sayest that men do not live unto God, unless they keep themselves pure to the God Whom thou preachest." Judas saith unto him: "Yea, verily, this I say, and I lie not (in) what I say. Pr'ythee, can thy servants stand before thee in mean garb, or when soiled or dirty? Thou, therefore, who art an earthly king and perishing f. 157 a with the earth—thou requirest things fair and clean of thy servants. As for my King, how do ye say .... concern, and should be free Wright p. 263 from the heavy burden of sons and of daughters, and chiefly from the care l. 2 of wealth and from the trouble (and vanity) of riches? For thou hast willed that those who serve thee and obey thee should conduct themselves by thy actions; and if one of them transgresseth thy commandments, he receiveth chastisement from thee. How much more doth it behove us, who believe in the name of this God of mine, to serve our Lord in purity and in holiness and in temperance and in chastity and in ".........." If thou wishest to do aught unto me, delay not; for, if she hath really received what she hath heard, iron will not hurt her, nor fire, nor any other thing that [is worse] than this......

"I (will supply) it to thee without labour. Why dost thou do mischief f. 162 b to me, when thou canst not escape from my hands? For know that, if thou Wright p. 264 dost not persuade her, I will destroy thee, and I will not leave her in life. l. 17 And finally I will take myself out of the world. And if, as thou sayest, there be life and death, and condemnation and acquittal, and there be judgment and recompense there, I will stand with thee in judgment; and if thy God, Who teacheth thee, be just, and taketh vengeance justly, I shall be recompensed, as I have done thee no wrong, but thou hast afflicted me, and I have not sinned against thee, but thou hast sinned against me. But even here I can take vengeance upon thee, and do unto thee all that thou Wright p. 265

hast done unto me.   Hearken unto me, therefore, and come with me to my house, and speak unto Mygdonia, and persuade her to be with me as she was before she saw thy face."

And Judas went with him laughing, and said unto him: "Believe ye in me, that if men loved God as they love men, their fellows, all that they asked He would give them, and there would be nothing which would resist them."   And when he had said this, he went to the house of Karīsh, (and) found Mygdonia sitting, and Narqia standing before her; and her hands were placed on her cheeks, and she was saying to her nurse, "Would

f. 141 a that the days passed swiftly over me, my mother, and that all the hours were one, that I might go forth from the world to go and see that Beautiful (One) of Whom I have heard tell, that Living (One) and Giver of life to those who believe in Him, where there is (no) night nor day, and where there is neither light nor darkness, and there is neither good nor bad, and there is neither rich nor poor, nor slave nor freeman, nor any who are high and uplifted over those who are humble."

And whilst she was saying these things, Judas came in; and......before him; and she sprung upright and prostrated herself to him.   Karīsh saith unto him: "See, she feareth thee and loveth thee, and whatever thou sayest to her she will gratify thee (therein)."   Judas saith unto her: "My daughter Mygdonia, consent unto what thy brother Karīsh saith unto thee."

Wright
p. 266 Mygdonia saith unto him: "Thou art unable to name the deed to me, and how canst thou persuade me to do it.   For I have heard thee say: 'This life is a loan, and this rest which thou hast heard......and these possessions abide not.'   And again thou didst say: 'Whosoever hateth this life shall go and receive life everlasting; and whosoever hateth this light of day and of night, shall go and receive the light in which there is no night.'   And

f. 141 b again thou didst say: 'Whosoever forsaketh these earthly possessions shall go and find possessions that abide for ever.'   And now other things, because thou art afraid, thou hast spoken to me.   Who is there that doeth a thing and exulteth in it, and turning round[1] renounceth it?   And who is there that buildeth a tower, and overturneth and rooteth it up from its foundations?   Who is there that diggeth a well in a parched place, and throweth in stones and filleth it up?   And who findeth a treasure, and doth not make use of it?"   And when Karīsh, the kinsman of King Mazdai, heard these things, he said: "I am not like to you, and I will not be in haste to destroy you; but thee I will bind, because I have power over thee; and I will not let thee go and talk with him, for this (man)

---

[1] Dr Wright's conjecture of ܘܗܦܟ for ܘܗܦܟܗ is not justified by this text.

is a wizard. And if thou yieldest (good and well); and if not, I know what I will do."

And Judas went out from the house of Karīsh, and went to the house of Sîfûr the general, and was dwelling there. And Ṣîfûr said unto Judas, "Prepare for thyself an apartment, and be teaching in it"; and he did as he said unto him. And Ṣîfûr the general said unto him: "I and my wife and my daughter will henceforth live purely; in one mind and in one love; and we beg of thee that we may receive the sign from thy hands, and may become true servants to Him, and may be reckoned among the number of His flock and His sheep." Judas saith: "I am meditating what to say and am afraid; and I know that I am not able to utter what I know." Wright p. 267

f. 150 a

And he began to speak of baptism, and said: "This is the baptism of the remission of sins; this is the bringer forth of new men; this is the restorer of understandings, and the mingler......to men......participation... and the establisher of the new man in the Trinity, and becometh a participation in the remission of sins. Mayest thou have remission, who dost loose the hidden power which is in the Christ!" And he spake, and they brought a large vat; and he baptized them in the name of the Father and the Son and the Holy Spirit.

And when they were baptized and had put on their clothes, he brought bread, and placed it on the table, and began to bless it[1], and said: "Living bread, which came down from heaven, the eaters of which die not! Bread, that fillest hungry souls with thy blessing!...promised......and shalt be for the remission of sins, that those who eat thee may not die! We name the name of the Father over thee; the name of the hidden,......that is hidden from all." And he said unto Ṭerṭia......"In Thy name, Jesus, may the power and...of the blessing and the thanksgiving come and abide upon this bread; that all the souls which take of it may have their sins remitted unto them." Wright p. 268

f. 150 b

And he brake, and gave to Ṣîfûr and to his wife and to his daughter.

When King Mazdai had dismissed Judas he went to his house to sup. And he was telling his wife what had happened to Karīsh, the king's kinsman, and he said unto her: "See what hath befallen that afflicted (man). For thou knowest, my sister Ṭerṭia, that a man hath no one like his wife, on whom he relieth. Now it happened that she went to see the sorcerer of whom she had heard tell and of what he was doing, and he bewitched her, and hath parted her from her husband; and he knoweth not what to do; and I wished to destroy him. But do thou go, and Wright p. 269

---

[1] Literally "upon it."

advise him, that she may yield to her husband, and may not hearken to the vain words of that (man)."

And in the morning Ṭerṭia arose and went to the house of Karīsh, the kinsman of her king, and found Mygdonia sitting on the ground, with sackcloth and ashes cast upon her, and begging of her Lord that He would forgive her her former sins,...and that she might be delivered from the world speedily. And when Ṭerṭia came in to her, she said to Mygdonia: "My sister, and my beloved and close friend, what is this (folly) that hath taken possession of thee? And why art thou become like a mad woman? Be mindful of thyself, be mindful of thy family; and turn (thy thoughts) towards thy numerous kindred, and have pity on thy true husband Karīsh, and do nothing which doth not befit thy free birth."

f. 169 a

Mygdonia saith unto Ṭerṭia: "Thou hast not heard the tidings of the new life, and the voice of the preacher hath not fallen on thine ears; for thou hast not tasted the medicine of life, and art not freed from the troubles of corruption. Thou hast not seen the everlasting life, and lo, thou standest in the temporal life. Thou hast not become sensible of the true wedlock, and lo, thou art tortured by the wedlock of corruption. Thou art clothed with garments that decay, and lo, thou dost (not)[1] long for the garments of eternity. Thou art proud of thy beauty which is corruptible, and thou carest not about the hatefulness of thy soul. Thou art proud of a number of slaves, and thine own soul from slavery thou hast not set free. Thou art proud of the pomp of many (attendants) and thou art not delivered from the judgment of death."

Wright
p. 270

And when Ṭerṭia had heard these things from Mygdonia, she went to the house of...the general, that she might see the new Apostle who had come thither. And when she came in to him, he began to say unto her: "And what art thou come to see? A man, a stranger to every place, and despised and wretched above all men, and without possessions or wealth? But he hath a possession which kings and princes cannot take away from him, and which is incorruptible and cannot be plundered—Jesus the Christ, the Life-giver of all mankind, the Son of the Living God, Who giveth life to all those,......

f. 154 b
Wright
p. 271
l. 17

"And I went, (and) have heard of the new life and have seen the Apostle of the new God; and I believe that he is the Apostle of God, Who giveth

---

[1] The word "not" seems to have dropped out.

life to every one who believeth in Him and doeth His will. (It is my duty that I too should recompense) the kindness which thou hast done unto me; and I will give thee a good counsel, so that thou too shalt become a king and a prince in Heaven, if thou wilt be persuaded by me and do what I say unto thee. I beseech thee to fear the God Who hath come hither by means of this stranger, and to keep thyself pure unto God; because this royalty of thine will pass away, and this rest of thine will be changed into trouble. But come, go to that man and believe, and thou shalt live for ever."

And when Mazdai heard these things from Tertia his wife, he smote his face with his hands and rent his clothes, and said: " May he have no hope, who hath (cut off) my hope!.........his spirit......" And he went out sore troubled, and found his kinsman Karīsh in the street, and said unto him: " Why hast thou taken me as thy companion unto Shēōl? Why hast thou defrauded me, profiting thyself nought? Why hast thou killed me, not coming thyself to life? Why hast thou done a wickedness unto me, when thou wast not in equity? Why didst thou not let me destroy that wizard from me before he spoiled all my house?" And he was upbraiding Karīsh. Karīsh saith unto him: "What is this that hath happened unto thee?" Mazdai saith unto him: " He hath bewitched Tertia, and hath separated her from me."

And they two went to the house of Sîfûr the general, and found Judas sitting and teaching. And all the people sprang up and stood; but he did not stand up before them. And King Mazdai knew him who was sitting; and he seized the seat, and turned it over, and took it with his two hands, and beat him on the head and smote him. And he seized him and delivered him to his attendants, and said unto them, " Drag this (man) off, that I may sit and hear him publicly." And they were dragging Judas and going to the place where King Mazdai used to give judgment.

And when he came to the place he was standing whilst the attendants of Mazdai held him. And Vīzān, the son of King Mazdai, came and said to the attendants: " Give him to me, that I may talk with him until the king cometh "; and they gave him to him. And he took him within, to (the place) where the king used to sit. Vīzān saith unto him: "Thou knowest that I am the son of King Mazdai, and that I have liberty to speak to the king about all that I wish; and also that I say unto him (and) he letteth thee live, and say unto him, and he killeth thee. Say......"

f. 163 a
Wright
p. 275
l. 5
was enraged at him, and gave orders to heat plates of iron, and to make Judas stand upon them barefoot. And when they had made him sit down and he had drawn off his shoes¹ he was laughing and saying: "Far better is Thy wisdom, Jesus, than all the wisdom of all men. Do Thou take counsel, and let Thy loving-kindness make preparation against the anger of these (men)." And they brought the plates (glowing) like fire, and laid hold of Judas and made him go up on them; and suddenly much water rose out of the earth, and the plates were immersed; and the men let him go and fled.

And when the king saw the abundance of water he said unto Judas: "Ask of thy God, and He may deliver us from this death by the flood, that we may not die thus." And Judas prayed and said: "Lord, let this water be restrained and collected in one place. Distribute it to many places. (Thou) Who alone dost not......in order, giving many wondrous signs through Thy servant and Apostle Judas. (Thou) Who makest (me) long that I may again receive Thy splendour, give the reward to all the world². Healer of my soul in its nature that it may have no intercourse with the Devil, (Who) art the cause of my life at all times; do Thou make this flood cease, that it may not rear itself proudly and destroy; for there are some of those who are standing by who shall believe in Thee and live." And when he had prayed there was quiet; and little by little these waters were swallowed up and were not found, but that place became as if it had been dried up.

And when King Mazdai saw (this) he said: "Drag ye (him) off to prison (until) we can consider what we shall do (with him)." And Judas went to be imprisoned, and the whole people were coming after him; and Vīzān, the son of Mazdai, was coming at the right hand of Judas, and the general Ṣîfûr was at his left hand..............of many. And Judas began to say: "(Thou) deliverer of my soul from the slavery......I am glad and rejoice because I know that the times and the seasons, and the years, and the months, and the days, are at an end, and I shall come and receive Thee,.........I care. Lo, I shall give up hope, and shall receive truth. Lo, I shall escape from sorrow, and shall be without care and without sorrow and without distress, and shall dwell in rest for ever. Lo, I shall be set free from slavery, and shall go unto the liberty unto which I am called. Lo, I have served times and seasons, and I am raised above times and seasons. Lo, I shall receive my pay from a Paymaster,

¹ MS. "and he."
² Dr Wright's text has "labours."

Who doth not reckon, but giveth, because His wealth sufficeth for gifts. Lo, I shall take off, and I shall put on and not take off again. Lo, I shall sleep, and I shall rise and not sleep again. Lo, I shall die, and I shall live and not die again. I (shall be blessed). Lo, they shall rejoice and look on me, and I shall go and be united again with their joy, and flowers shall be placed in their garlands. Lo, I shall be made a king in Thy kingdom, for the hopes of it shall make me attain it. Put the wicked to shame, who thought to subdue me by their powers. Lo, the rebellious shall be destroyed before me, and I have become greater than they. Lo, I shall have the peace unto which the great shall be assembled."

And whilst Judas was saying these things, all those who were there were listening, for they were thinking that his departure from the world would be at that moment.

And Judas said: "Believe in Him Who healeth all pains, hidden and manifest, and the Giver of life to those souls which ask help of Him; this, the freeborn and King's son, Who became a slave and poor; this, the Healer Wright of His creation, and the sick because of His servants; this, the Purifier p. 278 of those who believe in Him, and the insulted by His slaves; this, Who f. 159 a setteth free His possessions from slavery and from corruption and from subjection and from loss, and is made subject to and insulted by His slaves; this, the Father (of nature?)[1] and Lord of the heights; and the Supreme Judge; this, Who (came) forth from the Father...Son...and became visible through the Virgin Mary; and was called the son of Joseph the carpenter; this, the littleness of Whose body our eyes have seen, and Whose majesty we have received by faith, and have seen it by works; this, Whose heavenly body we have felt with our hands; and Whose sad aspect we have seen with our eyes, and Whose Divine form on the mount we were not able to see by ourselves alone; this deceiver, Whom the rulers and the governors condemned to death; this True One Who deceiveth not, and the Payer of the tax and the head-money for Himself and for His disciples, this Whom when the terrible prince and the hosts who were with him saw, they were silent and were terrified. And he asked Him Who He was and what was said of Him; and he did not abide in the truth because no truth is found in him; this Who whilst He was lord over the world and over its pleasures and over its wealth and over its life, thrust them...from Him, and warned those who hear Him not to make use of these things." And when he had finished saying these things, he stood Wright up to pray and speak thus: "Our Father which art in Heaven, hallowed p. 279

---

[1] This word is uncertain. It may be ܟܝܐ "Pure."

f. 166 b   be Thy name; and Thy kingdom come; and Thy wishes be done in earth as in Heaven. Give us the constant bread of the day, and forgive us our debts, that we too, may forgive our debtors. Bring us not into temptation, but deliver us from the evil one. My Lord and my God, and my Hope and my Confidence, my Teacher and my Comforter, Thou didst teach me to pray thus. Lo, Thy prayer I am praying, and Thy will, lo, I am accomplishing. Be Thou with me to the end; Thou Who from my youth hast sown life in me, and hast guarded me from corruption; Thou Who hast brought me to the poverty of the world, and hast bidden me to Thy true wealth; Thou Who hast made me know that I am Thine, and I have not come near to a woman, that what is desired by Thee might not be found with stain. My mouth sufficeth not to praise Thee, nor my understanding to glorify Thy goodness which is upon me; Thou Who, when I was wishing to acquire and become rich, didst shew me in a vision that loss cometh to many from wealth and from possessions, and I believed Thy vision, and abode in the poverty of the world, until Thou, Who art the true wealth, didst manifest Thyself to me, and didst fill those who are worthy of Thee with Thy[1]

Wright p. 280

f. 166 a

wealth, and didst deliver them from need and from care and from avarice. Lo, then, I have accomplished Thy work and fulfilled Thy will. I have been poor and needy, a stranger and a slave, and despised and a prisoner, and hungry and thirsty, and naked and barefoot and weary for Thy sake. Let not my trust fail, nor my hope which is in Thee be put to shame. Let not my labours be in vain, and let not my toils be found useless. Let not my fastings and my urgent prayers...perish, and let not my works which are in Thee be changed. Let not the enemy snatch away Thy wheat-seed from Thy land, and let not his tares be found in it; for Thy land doth not receive his tares, and they cannot fall into the garners of Thy land."

And again he was saying: "I have planted Thy vine in the land; may it cast (its roots) to the depths, and lengthen its tendrils to heaven, and may its fruits be seen in the land; and may those who are worthy of Thee and whom Thou hast acquired, delight in them. Thy silver, which Thou gavest me, I have cast down upon Thy table; try it, and give it to me with its usury, as Thou hast promised me. With Thy talent I have gained ten; let them be added for me to what was mine, as Thou hast promised. To my debtors[2] I have remitted the talent; let it not be sought from my hands; and Thou hast remitted (it) to me. To the supper I have been bidden and

Wright p. 281

have come, and have excused myself from the field and from merchandise

---

[1] The word "true" is not in this text.   [2] MS. "beloved."

and from the plough; let me not be cast out from the wedding-feast and not eat of it. To the supper I have been bidden, for I have put on a white garment; may I be worthy of it, and may my hands and my feet not be bound, f. 146 b nor I be put out into outer darkness. My lamp is bright with His[1] light; while (I) keep it to its Lord until He leaveth the banqueting-room and I receive Him; may I not see it flickering because (it is failing)[2]. Let mine eyes receive Thee, and let my heart rejoice that I have fulfilled Thy will and accomplished Thy commandments. Let me be like to the sedulous[3] and God-fearing servant, who with prudent diligence neglecteth no(thing). I have wearied myself with watching the whole night to protect my house from robbers; it shall not be broken into. My loins are girded with truth, and my sandals are bound on my feet; their thongs may I not see loosened. I have put my hand to the ploughshare; I have not turned back; (my furrows) shall not be crooked. My fields are white and are already fit for reaping; may I receive my reward. May I receive a garment, for the one that weareth out is worn out, and the work that bringeth unto rest I have accomplished. I have kept my first watch with joy, and the second; in the third may I receive Thy Face, and worship before Thy holy beauty. I have pulled down my barns and destroyed them on earth; may I take of Thy treasure that faileth not. I have dried up the spring that was in me, that I may lie down; by Thy living spring I have rested. The bound, who is with me, whom Thou didst deliver unto me, I have slain; my soul is unbound in me by reason of its trust[4]. The internal I have made external, and the external internal; let Thy will be fulfilled in all my members. I have not turned back, and I have altogether f. 146 a stretched forward; let me not be a sign and a wonder; the dead I have brought to life, and the deficient I have filled up; let me receive the Crown of victory. Scorn have I received on earth; a recompense do Thou make me in heaven. The powers shall not perceive me, nor the rulers take counsel against me; the tax-gatherers shall not see me, nor the collectors of tribute oppress me. The low...shall not mock at me, and the wicked at the brave and the humble; nor shall the slave and the great exalted mean one dare to stand before me, because of Thy strength, O Jesus, which surroundeth me; they flee, they hide themselves from it, because they are not able to behold it. They are with every man; and suddenly do they fall because of the things that are heard by them. The portion of men, it

Wright p. 282

---

[1] Or "its."

[2] Perhaps ܪܡܫܚܐ. The word "oil" is not expressed in this text.

[3] Probably ܟܫܝܪܐ.

[4] I cannot see that any word has been omitted here. Cf. *Studia Sinaitica*, IX. p. 21.

Wright
p. 283

crieth out and discloseth. No one of them is forgotten, for it is the fragrance of their nature. Wicked men sprout as a tree whose fruit is bitterness; I will pass their place in silence, and let joy and peace support me, and I shall stand before (Thee?) alive, and let not the slanderer look upon me. Let his eyes be blinded by the light, which Thou hast made to dwell in me; and close his lying mouth, for he shall have naught against me."

And he began to say unto those who were with him in the prison: "Believe the Saviour, God, believe the Christ and the Helper of His

f. 145 b

servants; believe the Saviour[1] of those who toil in His service; in Him (in) Whom, lo, my soul rejoiceth, for the time is come that I may go and receive this fair One Whose beauty inciteth me to say concerning Him what He is, though I am unable to say (it). Thou art the Feeder and the Furnisher of my poverty and the Supplier of my need. Be Thou with me until I come and receive Thee." And the youth Vīzān was asking of him and saying unto him: "I beg of thee, (O) man, Apostle of the new God, permit me to go. I will entreat the keepers of the prisoners, and I will bring thee out, that thou mayest go with me to my house; and thou shalt give me the sign[2]; and I, too, shall become a servant to this God Whom thou preachest; because in these things I was walking before my father Mazdai constrained me and gave me Manashar (as) a wife.

Wright
p. 284

I am twenty-one years old to-day, and, lo, I have been for seven years united in marriage to a woman; for before I took a wife I knew no other woman, and by my father I was counted as good for naught. And I have not yet had son or daughter by the woman whom he gave unto me, and my wife also hath lived with me in chastity these many years. And to-day, if she were well, and had seen thee and had heard thy word, I should be

f. 145 a

(at rest) and she would receive everlasting life. But she is in great affliction, lo, for a time, through much disease. I will therefore entreat the keepers of the prisoners that thou mayest go with me, that thou mayest promise me to go with me, for I dwell in a house quite by myself."......

And when Judas, the Apostle of the Most High, heard these things, he said unto him: "My son, if thou believest, thou shalt see the wonders of God, how He giveth life unto His servants."

And whilst they were speaking, Ṭerṭia and Mygdonia and Narqia were standing at the door of the prison; and they gave three hundred and sixty-eight silver drachmas to the keepers of the prisoners, and they brought them in beside Judas. And (they saw[3]) Sîfûr the general and his

[1] Literally "Life-giver."
[2] i.e. baptism.
[3] These words are omitted in our text.

daughter, and Vīzān, and all the prisoners, sitting and listening to Judas. The three stood before him, and he said unto them: "Who permitted you to come to us? And who opened unto you the gate that was closed in your faces?" Ṭerṭia saith unto him: "Didst thou not open the door for us and say unto us: 'Come to the prison, that we may go and take our brethren who are there, and then our Lord will shew His glory in us? And when we came to the door thou didst disappear from us, and thou didst come and go into it without us, and didst hide thyself from us. And we heard the sound of the doors, and they were shut in our faces But we gave (money) to their keepers, and they let us in; and lo, we stand and beg of thee that thou wouldst do what we wish, that we might let thee escape until the wrath of King Mazdai cool towards thee." Judas saith unto Ṭerṭia: "Tell us first how ye were shut up." Ṭerṭia saith unto him: "Thou hast never quitted us, save for a moment, and dost thou not know how we were shut up? But (if) thou wishest to hear, hear. Mazdai sent and had me Ṭerṭia brought and said unto me: 'That conjuror hath not yet got power over thee, because I have heard[1] that he be- witcheth with water and with oil and with wine and with bread, and he hath not yet bewitched thee. But be persuaded by me, in what I say unto thee, that if thou dost not yield, I say unto thee that I will torture thee until I destroy thee; for I know that as yet with oil and bread (and wine) he hath not yet full power over thee.' And I said unto him: 'Whatever thou wilt, do. Over my body thou hast power; but I will not destroy my soul along with thee.' And when he had heard these things from me he shut me up beneath his dining-room in a dark place. And his kinsman Karīsh too brought Mygdonia and Narqia (and) shut them up beside me. And thou didst bring us out, and lo, we stand before thee. But give us the sign, and let the hope (of Mazdai) be cut off (from me)

Wright p. 285

f. 165 b

Wright p. 286

were in the way, Manashar his wife met them, coming to the prison. And she knew him and saith unto him: "My brother Vīzān?" He saith unto her: "Yea, and thou my sister Manashar?" She saith unto him: "Yea." He saith unto her: "Whither goest thou at this time alone? And how wast thou able to rise?" She saith unto him: "This youth laid his hand upon me, and I was healed. And I saw in my dream that I should go to

f. 152 b

Wright p. 287 l. 3

---

[1] Literally "it hath been heard by me."

the stranger, where he is imprisoned, that I might be healed." Vîzān saith unto her: "Who is the youth who was with thee?" And she saith unto him: "Dost thou not see him? For lo, he is holding my right hand and supporting me."

And whilst they were talking, Judas came, with Ṣîfûr and his wife and his daughter, to the house of Vîzān. And when Manashar, the wife of Vîzān saw him, she bowed down and worshipped him, and saith unto him: "Art thou come, my healer from sore disease? Thou art he whom I saw in the night, who didst deliver unto me this youth, that he might bring us unto thee in the prison; and thy kindness did not suffer thee (to permit) that I should come; but thou art come to me." And when she had said these things she turned backwards, and the youth was not (there). She saith unto Judas: "I am not able to walk alone, and the youth is not here whom thou didst deliver (unto me)." Judas saith unto her: "Jesus then will be a Supporter unto thee." And she was running beside them. And when they entered into the house of Ṣîfûr[1], the son of Mazdai the king, the time was night, and it was very light to them.

Wright
p. 288
f. 152 a

And Judas began to pray, and he spake thus: "Companion and Help of the feeble; and Hope and Confidence of the poor; Resort and Rest of the weary; Voice that came from on high; All-Majestic Who dwellest in the midst[2]; Resort and Haven of those that go forth to the regions of the Prince; Physician Who healeth of death the men who believe in Him; He was crucified for the sake of many; and for His sake, too, no man was crucified. And Thou didst descend into Shēōl. With mighty power Thou didst ascend. And when they saw[3] (it), the lords of death were not able to bear (it). Thou didst make them ascend[4] with glory, those who had sought refuge with Thee. And Thou didst tread for them the path to the height. And in Thy footsteps they all have travelled and believed. Thou didst bring them into Thy fold, and didst mingle them with the sheep. Son of mercy,...To us Thou wast sent from the Father, that we might praise Thee; Son, Who wast sent by the supreme and perfect Fatherhood, Lord of a possession that cannot be defiled; Hope...because (Thou art) rich, Whose creation is full of wealth. Poor (One) Who was needy and hungry for forty days; Satisfier of our thirsty souls with Thy bliss; be Thou, Lord, with Vîzān and with Ṭerṭia and with Manashar, and gather them into Thy number, and gather them into Thy fold, and be to them a guide (when they are) in the path of error. Be to them a guide in the place of sickness; be to them henceforth a strengthener in the weary place; sanctify

f. 168 a
Wright
p. 288

---

[1] This is evidently a mistake for Vîzān.

[2] 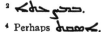.

[3] MS. "lived."

[4] Perhaps ܕܘܡܟ.

them in the unclean place; and cleanse them of corruption in the place of the enemy. Be a physician for their bodies, and give life to their souls; make them pure shrines and holy temples; and may Thy Holy Spirit dwell in them."

And when he had prayed, he said unto Mygdonia: "Strip thy sisters." And she stripped them, and put tunics ($\pi\epsilon\rho\iota\zeta\acute{\omega}\mu\alpha\tau\alpha$) on them, and brought them near to him. And Vīzān came near first. And Judas took...oil, and glorified (God), and said over it: "Fair Fruit, one of whose fruits shall not be cut off[1], for...a rest...of the word...strength...that men may put it on and conquer by means of their enemies and they went backwards and fell upon their faces; Let it abide upon this oil, over which we name Thy holy name." And he cast it upon the head of Vīzān, and then upon the heads of those (others), and said: "In Thy name, Jesus the Christ, let it be to those souls for the remission of offences and sins, and for the frustration of the enemy, and for the healing of souls." And he commanded Mygdonia to anoint them (with oil)[2] and he himself anointed Vīzān. And when he f. 168 b had anointed them, he made them go down to the water and said unto them: "In the name of the Father and the Son and the Holy Spirit; Wright in Thy name[3], Heavenly Word!" And when he had come up he brought p. 290 bread and a cup, and spake a blessing over it and said: "Thy holy Body, which was crucified for our sake, we eat, and Thy life-giving Blood, which was shed for our sake, we drink. Let Thy Body be to us for life, and Thy Blood for the remission of sins. For the sake of the gall which Thou didst drink for our sake let the bitterness of our enemy be taken away from us. And the vinegar which Thou didst drink for our sake...and for the spit which Thou didst receive for our sake, let us receive Thy perfect life. And since Thou didst receive the crown of thorns because of us, let us receive the crown that withereth not. And since Thou wast wrapped in a linen cloth because of us, let us be girt with Thy strength, which cannot be overcome. And since Thou wast buried in a new tomb, let us receive the new life which is in the Christ. And as Thou didst rise, and wast raised, let us be raised, and let us live, and stand before Thee in the judgment." And he also broke the Eucharist, and gave to Vīzān, and to Ṭerṭia, and to Manashar, and to Mygdonia, and to Ṣîfûr, and to the wife and to the daughter of Ṣîfûr, and said: "Let this Eucharist be to you for life and for joy and for the health and for the healing of your souls." And they said: "Amen"; and a voice was heard saying...

---

[1] Perhaps ⲡⲓⲁⲫⲥ.   [2] Perhaps ⲕⲩⲉⲥⲁ.

[3] It would not be possible to read "in thy blood" in the MS.

INDEX I.

SCRIPTURAL QUOTATIONS.

INDEX II.

REFERENCES TO SCRIPTURE WHICH ARE NOT DIRECT QUOTATIONS.

In the Deyr-es-Suriani MS.

GENESIS.

i. 1—25	... ...	f. 36 b
i. 27	... ...	ff. 45 b, 77 b, 119 b, 131 b
ii. 7	... ...	ff. 77 b, 140 b
ii. 10	... ...	f. 108 b
ii. 21, 22	... ...	f. 22 a
iii. 7	... ...	f. 108 b
iii. 15	... ...	f. 115 b
iii. 22	... ...	f. 112 a
v. 5	... ...	f. 45 b
viii. 7	... ...	f. 22 b
viii. 11	... ...	f. 22 b
xviii. 3	... ...	f. 32 a
xxviii. 12	... ...	f. 113 a
xxx. 27	... ...	f. 32 a

EXODUS.

vi. 8	... ...	f. 109 a
viii. 32	... ...	f. 60 b
xii. 3—11	... ...	f. 113 a
xiii. 21, 22	... ...	f. 109 a
xiv. 27—29	... ...	f. 109 a
xv. 13	... ...	f. 113 a
xvi. 14	... ...	f. 113 a.
xix. 19	... ...	f. 113 a
xxxiii. 9	... ...	f. 109 a
xxxiv. 6	... ...	f. 69 a
xxxiv. 30, 35	...	ff. 45 b, 76 a
xl. 38	... ...	f. 109 a

NUMBERS.

vi. 2—5	... ...	Vat. Arab. 694, f. 150
ix. 16	... ...	f. 109 a

GENESIS.

xi. 9	... ...	f. 113 a
xiv. 18	... ...	f. 69 a
xvi. 22	... ...	ff. 49 a, 50 a, 140 b
xvi. 31—33	...	ff. 40 a, 133 a
xxxii. 13	... ...	f. 109 a
xxxiv. 13	... ...	f. 108 a

DEUTERONOMY.

i. 33	... ...	f. 109 a
ii. 7	... ...	f. 109 a
vi. 7	... ...	f. 139 a
xxix. 5	... ...	f. 109 a

JOSHUA.

v. 6	... ...	f. 109 a
xiii. 7	... ...	f. 108 a
xiv. 3	... ...	f. 108 a

JUDGES.

xiii. 5	... ...	Vat. Arab. 694, f. 150 a

I SAMUEL.

i. 11	... ...	Vat. Arab. 694 f. 150 a
i. 27	... ...	Vat. Arab. 694, f. 149 b

I KINGS.

viii. 27	... ...	f. 69 b

II KINGS.

i. 10, 12	... ...	ff. 44 a, 138 b

II CHRONICLES.

ii. 6	... ...	f. 69 b
vi. 18	... ...	f. 69 a

MARK.

When ff. 41 b, 43 b, 49 b and 103 b of the Deyr-es-Suriani MS. are given in the above index, the Scripture quotations in them will be found in the Paris MSS., Fonds Arabe 75 and 81, which have supplied the deficiencies in my photographs.

In the Sinai MSS.

* Sinai Palimpsest.

INDEX III.

PROPER NAMES.

The numbers of pages enclosed in brackets are those belonging to the Suriani MS.
which have been supplied from the Paris MSS., Fonds Arabe 75 and 81.

Cambridge:
PRINTED BY J. AND C. F. CLAY,
AT THE UNIVERSITY PRESS.

For EU product safety concerns, contact us at Calle de José Abascal, 56–1°,
28003 Madrid, Spain or eugpsr@cambridge.org.